Joseph Jekyll, Algernon Bourke

Correspondence of Mr. Joseph Jekyll with His Sister-in-Law, Lady
Gertrude Sloane Stanley,

1818-1838. Preceded by some letters written to his father from France, 1775

Joseph Jekyll, Algernon Bourke

**Correspondence of Mr. Joseph Jekyll with His Sister-in-Law, Lady Gertrude Sloane Stanley, 1818-1838. Preceded by some letters written to his father from France, 1775**

ISBN/EAN: 9783337318789

Printed in Europe, USA, Canada, Australia, Japan

Cover: Foto ©ninafisch / pixelio.de

More available books at **www.hansebooks.com**

CORRESPONDENCE

OF

# MR. JOSEPH JEKYLL

WITH HIS SISTER-IN-LAW,

LADY GERTRUDE SLOANE STANLEY,

1818—1888.

*PRECEDED BY SOME LETTERS WRITTEN TO HIS
FATHER FROM FRANCE, 1775.*

EDITED, WITH A BRIEF MEMOIR, BY

THE HON. ALGERNON BOURKE.

LONDON:
JOHN MURRAY, ALBEMARLE STREET.
1894.

# CONTENTS.

## CHAPTER I.

JOSEPH JEKYLL TO HIS FATHER.

*En route* for France.—Brighton in 1775.—Dieppe.—Rouen to Paris.—French Fare.—Paris.—French Costume.—Sightseeing in Paris.—Orleans.—Life in France.—An Execution.—British Sportsman in France.—Orleans and its Neighbourhood.—Temperance of the French.—High Mass.—Mr. Martin.—Lord Galway and "Museum" Cox.—French Cookery.—The Source of the Loire.—The Comtesse de Béthune.—Arrival at Blois.—St. Gervais.—Taking the Veil.—A Wedding.—A Boar Hunt . . . . pp. 1-26

## CHAPTER II.

JOSEPH JEKYLL TO HIS FATHER (*continued*).

A Wedding Feast.—Blois.—Its History.—Poverty and Ignorance of the Peasantry —Amboise.—Madame du Barry.—The Duc de Choiseul.—Chante-loup.—Touraine.—Fêtes at Blois.—French Curiosity as to "M. Vilkes"—Chenonceau and Chartreux.—Celles.—Soin and Chambord.—The Cost of Food and Lodging.—M. la Vallière.—French Horses.—Feminine Fashions.—The French Stage.—The Vintage.—The Office of Hangman.—Defects of a French Education.—Madame de Pompadour.—The French Nobility.—*En route* for London.
. . . . . . . . . . pp. 27-65

## CHAPTER III.

MR. JEKYLL TO LADY GERTRUDE SLOANE STANLEY.

The Methusalems.—Ugo Foscolo.—Bishop Pelham's Lady.—Lord Erskine.—Sir R. Croft.—" Hat Vaughan."—Milman's

*Fazio.*—The Duchess of Devonshire.—Lord Ellenborough.—
*Tales of my Landlord.*—Mrs. Opie.—Sir Claude Hunter.—
Guests at Country Houses.—Lady Morgan.—Sir S. Romilly.
—The Dowager Empress of Russia and her Son at the Dance.
—Lord Byron's new Poem.—Rogers and John W. Ward.—
Lord Dudley.—Crabbe's Simplicity.—"Chic" Chester and
Nagle.—Chantrey and the Princess Borghese's Foot.—The
Opposition in 1819.—Mrs. Coutts.—The Regent's Ball to
Children.—"Mazeppa."—Lord Chancellor Erskine's Domestic Affairs.—The Travellers' Club.—Sir J. Mackintosh.—The
Persian Ambassador at Westminster School.—The Duke of
Richmond's Death.—"The Political House that Jack Built."
—*Don Juan.*—Mrs. Coutts' Dinner.—John Julius Angerstein.—James Bland Burgess.—*John Bull.*—An Estimate
of the Character of George III. and his Reign.—Rumours
of the Evidence against Queen Caroline.—Lord Alvanley
and the Duke of York.—*Ivanhoe.*—Queen Caroline and
Hunt the Radical.—The Methusalems.—The Cato Street
Conspirators.—The Merits of Beer and Whisky.—The
Duchess of York.—Lord and Lady Blessington.—The Queen's
Trial.—Bergami's Cross.—Story of Queen Caroline.—The
Solicitor-General Copley and Signor Ratti.—Signs of Weakness in the Queen's Defence.—Hatsell.—Forecast of the
Result of the Trial of the Queen.—Denman's Attack on the
Duke of Clarence.—Lord Alvanley.—The Queen at St.
Paul's.—Sir C. Bunbury.—Marlborough House.—Howard
and Gibbs and old Servants.—Harvey Aston.—Captain O.
Byrne's Account of the Duel.—George Harding and the
Bookseller.—Verses on Dr. Howley . . pp. 66-113

## CHAPTER IV.

MR. JEKYLL TO LADY GERTRUDE SLOANE STANLEY (*continued*).

The Coronation.—Queen Caroline at Brandenburg House.—Ladies
Hertford, Conyngham, and Jersey.—Lady Conyngham's Views
on the Government.—The King and his Love.—George IV.
on the Radical Movement.—Mrs. Heywood's Remark to
the Duke of Gloucester.—The Strolling Player and the Thin
Audience.—George Isted's Proposal.—The Sloanes become
Sloane Stanleys.—"The Pirate."—Opera.—Miss Tree and Mr.

Coutts.—The Ghost in *Hamlet* with a Cold in the Head.—Death of Mr. Coutts the Banker.—His Will.—Sir F. Burdett.—Lord and Lady Erskine's Matrimonial Differences.—Ministerial Changes.—Attack on Mrs. Coutts in *John Bull.*—" Werner."—Poet Sotheby and the Benchers of the Temple.—Canny Coutts and the Legacy Duty.—An Unpublished Caricature by Bunbury.—Fanny Kemble.—" Murder Maker to the Newspapers."—Scandal.—Newton the Painter.—Clara Fisher.—Wellington, Canning, and Lord Strangford.—Mr. Jekyll's Views on Public Schools.—Bowood.—Lord and Lady Lansdowne.—The Miseries of the Country.—Lord Dudley.—Literary Productions.—Lady Liverpool.—The Hertford Murder.—The Theatres in 1823.—Lord Grey and the Ghost.—Hospitality at Brighton.—Madame de Lieven    pp. 114-141

## CHAPTER V.

MR. JEKYLL TO LADY GERTRUDE SLOANE STANLEY (*continued*).

Life at Bowood.—Thomas Moore.—A Foreign Tour projected.—Poodle Byng and the King and Queen of the Sandwich Islands.—Lelyveld the Dutch Ambassador.—Lady Holland and Captain Medwin's "Conversations with Lord Byron at Pisa."—*Der Freischütz.*—The Public Taste for Hell and the Devil.—The Duchess of Rutland as a Rearer of Cattle.—French Reception of German and Italian Opera.—Scandal.—Change of Place a Disease of the Healthy.—The Italian's Epitaph.—The Confessor and Francis I.—Moore's "Life of Sheridan."—George Cholmondeley's Marriage.—Resurrection Men in France.—Hobgoblins.—Lady Holland at Paris.—Mrs. Coutts and the Duke of St. Albans.—Epigram on Greenwood.—Intrigues at Windsor.—Stewart Rose and Poet Rogers.—Criticisms on Moore's "Sheridan" by the *European Magazine.*—Ruin of Walter Scott.—Sir E. Antrobus' Death and Will.—The Ladies of Llangollen and Madame de Genlis.—*John Bull* and Rogers the Poet.—Dr. L'Afan at Cowes.—The Duke of York's Health.—Shields' Attack on the Duke in the *Morning Chronicle.*—Lord Lansdowne's Epitaph on Himself.—Latin Epigram by a Lady.
. . . . . . . . . . pp. 142-166

## CHAPTER VI.

MR. JEKYLL TO LADY GERTRUDE SLOANE STANLEY (*continued*).

Death of the Duke of York.—Cobbett and the Clubs.—Lord Morpeth's *Début*.—Lord Liverpool and his Administration.—Lord and Lady Wellesley.—The Lord-Lieutenant's Toilette.—The Zoological Gardens.—Mrs. Siddons.—Lord Guilford's Will.—George IV. and the Guards' Uniform.—Mistake of a French Author.—Don Miguel.—Political Changes.—Leigh Hunt and Lord Byron.—Lady Holland out of Office.—George IV. and Lord Ellenborough.—Allen's Consolation to Lady Holland.—Murder of de Loulé, by Miguel.—The Duke of Cumberland's Essay.—Society at Norman Court.—De Tilly's Memoirs.—The King's Illness.—The Duke of Wellington's Reticence.—Mr. Jekyll's Despair of Politics and Politicians.—Stories by Moore against Samuel Rogers.—Moore's Moral from Don Giovanni.—The Grand Duke Constantine.—Lady Holland at Brighton.—Scandal.—The Duchess of St. Albans' Menu.—Lady Goderich.—The Irishman's Account of his Birth.—Curious Story of two Eastern Travellers.—Ministerial Dissensions . . . . . . . pp. 167-191

## CHAPTER VII.

MR. JEKYLL TO LADY GERTRUDE SLOANE STANLEY (*continued*).

Pedro, Emperor of Brazil.—Some of the Advantages of Burking.—Sir G. Murray's Speech.—Captain Garth and his Affidavit.—The Stanleys and the Cockfighter at Valparaiso.—Mr. Palmer's Conversion on the Catholic Question.—Palmerston's Speech.—Prospects of the Catholic Bill.—The Duke of Wellington's Duel with Lord Winchilsea.—Anecdote of the Duke of Cambridge as a Boy.—Kew Gardens.—Cabinet Making.—Fanny Kemble's Success as Juliet.—New Uniform for the Guards.—L'Abbé Morellet's Scheme for the Arrangement of a Library.—The Irishwoman's Defence.—Molly Dacre, the Beauty of Carlisle.—Lord Stowell and Captain Morris, two of her Lovers.—The Circumstances of her Birth.—Lady Lyndhurst at Brighton.—Colman's "Random Records."—Society at Brighton.—Lord Glengall's Comedy.—Lord Petersham on Life in London.—Miss Tree in *Black-*

cyed Susan.—Mrs. Coutts.—Rogers on Fanny Kemble.—
Sir Sydney Smith's Account of his Escape from a French
Prison.—His remarkable Story of Napoleon at the Siege
of Acre.—"What's in a Name?" .  .  pp. 192-216

CHAPTER VIII.

MR. JEKYLL TO LADY GERTRUDE SLOANE STANLEY (*continued*).

Political Rumours.—Robert Alexander.—Lady Lyndhurst and the Duke of Cumberland.—Lord Albert Conyngham's Duel. —Sir Thomas Lawrence.—Scandal in London.—Foote and his Bass Viol Player.—Mrs. Parnther.—Moore's "Byron."—The Country Manager and the Snowstorm.—Politics.—Guardsmen in Tiger Skin Waistcoats.—Byron and Lady Surrey.—Proposed New Cemeteries.—The Earl of Chatham.—Unpopularity of the Duke of Cumberland.—Stapylton's Life of Canning.— Lord Ellenborough's Letter to Sir John Malcolm.—Woronzow the Russian Ambassador.—The King's Health.—Lady Jersey's Preparation for the Worst —Lady Conyngham and the King.—Madame du Barry's Memoirs.—Lord Wellesley and the Duke of Wellington.—Sellis, the Duke of Cumberland's valet.—Lord Wellesley's *jeux d'esprit*.—The King drooping.—His Death.—Attacks on his Character in the Press.—St. John Long, the Empiric.—The King's Will.—The *Gens d'arme* and the Passport.—Archdeacon Nares' Epitaph on Himself.—William IV. at the Funeral of George IV.— Theodore Hook.—Electioneering in 1830.—The French Mob under Fire.—Verses by Canning.—Politics.—Threatened Disturbance in the City.—The Duke of Cambridge and the King of Hanover as Boys.—Lord Burghersh's Opera.— O'Connell and Brooks's.—Buckingham Palace.—The Agricultural Troubles of 1830.—The Prince of Condé and French Opinion on his Death.—Curious Evidence of the organised Character of the Agricultural Disturbances.—Hook's "Maxwell."—The Soldier and the Innkeeper  .  pp. 217-262

CHAPTER IX.

MR. JEKYLL TO LADY GERTRUDE SLOANE STANLEY (*continued*).

Kindness of Lord Brougham and Lord Erskine.—O'Connell and Lord Anglesey.—The Rev. Robert Cholmondeley at Dettingen.—" Le Souverain va visiter le Roi."—Dr. Baillie and

his Lady Patient.—The Queen and the Ladies' Dresses.—
Lord Anglesey in Dublin.—Paradise's Translation.—An
English Lady's French Conversation.—Lady Blessington
and Comte D'Orsay.—The Duchess of St. Albans' Break-
fasts.— Theodore Hook's Improvisation. — Lady Sophia
Sidney.—A Dinner at Lady Blessington's.—The House of
Commons.—Leopold, King of the Belgians.—John Calcraft.
—The Coronation.—Lady Dudley Stuart.—Mr. William
Manning.—Epigram by James Smith.—Mr. Jekyll and the
Countess of Cork.—The New French Peers.—Madame de
Feuchères and the Prince of Condé.—Miss Sophia Dawes.—
Sir Robert Wilson.—Lord Dover as Author.—"Eugene
Aram."—Madame de Feuchères.—Cobbett.—Kean Drunk.—
The *Town.*—Jack Fuller.—The Duke of Devonshire.—Mrs.
Pitt and the Duchess of Gordon.—Charles Greenwood.—The
Duchess of St. Albans' Ball.—Lady Blessington's "Memoirs
of Byron."—Triumph of Reform.—Miss E. Law.—Conversa-
tion of the King and Queen.—Politics.—Homœopathy.—
Story of Diderot told by Mirabeau.—John Taylor.—Epigram
by James Smith.—Lord Alvanley's Plan for making a London
House interesting.—The Housemaid's Love Letter.—Edward
Jerningham.—Lady Jersey and King George IV.—Lady
Blessington and the Pamphleteer.—William the Fourth's
Dinner Parties.—G. S. Newton the Painter.—Politics.
. . . . . . . . . . . pp. 263-308

## CHAPTER X.

MR. JEKYLL TO LADY GERTRUDE SLOANE STANLEY (*continued*).

Byron's Verses on Rogers in *Fraser.*—The Duc de Brissac at
Versailles.—Lady Milbanke's Explanation of Lord Byron's
Marriage.—Smith's Epigram on Gully the Boxer.—Alderman
Hunter's French.—Parody of Pope by Smith.—Mr. Jekyll's
Opinion of "Notre Dame."—Burglary at Lady Blessington's.
—The Duchess of St. Albans and her First Husband.—A
Caricature by D'Orsay.—Politics.—The Blessington Memoirs
of Byron.—Captain Ross.—The learned Pig.—A Drawing by
Harry Bunbury.—Lady Holland in Office.—Lines by Lady
Blessington.—Morning Visitors.—G. S. Newton, R.A.—
Death of Lord Dudley.—Politics.—Lady Ellenborough.—The
Irishman at the Custom House Fire.—Samuel Prout and

Clarkson Stanfield.—Effect of Sydney Smith's Charity Sermon on the Countess of Cork.—Squibs by James Smith.—The Mayor of Oxford's Excuse for not saluting Charles II.— Lady Ellenborough in Bavaria.—Extinction of the Stowell Peerage.—Corporal Trim and the unfortunate King of Bohemia.—How Lady Ellenborough gained the *Entrée* of the Hungarian Court.—The French Actor and the Public.— Epigram on Mr. Jekyll and Hatchett.—Mr. Norton's Action against Lord Melbourne.—Contemporary Literature.— M. de Tartines and the Vagabond.—Lord Salisbury at the Opera.—Squibs by James Smith.—The Duke of Brunswick's Journey by Balloon . . . . . pp. 309-349

# MEMOIR.

THE family of Jekyll first became notable in the person of Sir Joseph Jekyll, Master of the Rolls in the reign of George II. A successful lawyer, and a man of staunch political convictions, he was one of the many contemporaries of Pope whose names are preserved in the poet's verses,—

. . . . . "Jekyll, or some odd old Whig,
Who never changed his principles or wig."

A brother of Sir Joseph, among other children left a son Edward, who entered the Royal Navy, rose as high as captain, and was the father of Joseph Jekyll, the author of these letters.

Joseph Jekyll was born in the year 1754. Of his childhood we know little or nothing, but that he had a sister, and was educated at Westminster. He matriculated at Christ Church at the age of eighteen in 1771, and took his degree of B.A. three years later.

A small collection of letters written by Joseph Jekyll to his father in 1775, and now in the possession of his daughter-in-law, Mrs. Edward Jekyll, of Godalming, has been very kindly placed at the disposal of the editor by that lady, and forms the first part of the present volume. These letters were written by young Jekyll during a year's residence in France after taking his degree, and they tell us all that is known of his early life.

We find that young Jekyll went abroad to acquire the French language, and that by the wish of his father he finally settled at Blois. His letters seem to show a youth of high spirit and much shrewd humour, and the impressions made on this young Englishman by the France of Louis XVI. are of interest. At first he saw little to admire in the French ladies. "As yet," says he, " I think I may safely say we have not seen half-a-dozen beauties"; but before his visit was over he considerably modified his opinions on this subject. He saw the unburied body of James II. in the chapel of the English Penitents, and at Orleans a burglar was broken on the wheel below his balcony window. He met an agreeable old chevalier who had been taken " by Mr. Keppel in the late war"; and we read that " Mr. Martin, a relation of the banker," was astonishing the country near Blois by his "chace of the fox, wolf, and boar."

One phase of French society of the period is admirably presented in an expression which young Jekyll quotes. Any young stranger who was unable or unwilling to join in the high play then prevalent was described in the phrase *le garçon est inutile*. He met the Duchesse du Barry, and was present at her toilette. A little mill with which that lady was accustomed to make her own butter at breakfast, says he, "pleased him mightily"; and by a curious chance he next day made the acquaintance of the Duc and Duchesse de Choiseul.

He presented himself with a companion at the Palace of Menars, built by Madame de Pompadour, and at that time occupied by her brother, the Marquis de Marigny, but was refused entrance by the Swiss Guards, some recent impertinencies by visitors having closed the rooms to the public. Jekyll, nothing daunted, on learning that the Marquis was within, announced himself and friend as "two English gentlemen of Blois who begged leave to kiss M. de Marigny's hand," and they were rewarded by an interview with a chatty old gentleman, whom they found "in the gout and a nightgown, the latter blazing with the Order of the Holy Ghost." Jekyll noticed that the portrait of George III. was alone wanted to complete a collection of European sovereigns in the Marquess' cabinet, and expressed a hope that M. de Marigny would pass a winter in England, when "he would not fail of filling the vacancy." "Ah, Monsieur," replied the Marquess, "I do not despair of seeing London. I was once so near paying you a visit, that my house was hired there, and the wine even laid into my cellars, when my sister, the late Marchioness of Pompadour, sent for me abruptly to Versailles. 'Monsieur, my brother,' said she, 'sell your house in London and all your affairs there, for in less than three months we shall have their Hawke and Boscawen thundering on our coast.'"

With very little recommendation but his own good

breeding, young Jekyll seems to have quickly gained a footing in the best society of the district in which he was living. There are references in his letters to invitations and visits to the Comte de Philepeaux, to the Marquis de Saumery, and the Duc de Choiseul; and the young man seems to have formed a very fair opinion of that gay world which was then piping and dancing to its doom. His father, apparently, grew uneasy at the complacent tone of his letters on these matters, and bade him think of his home, and not try to make himself a complete Frenchman. Money matters probably had their weight in the advice which the Captain sent to his son, for we find the latter rejoining, "I have been fortunate enough to fall into what is called the first company at the expense of what economical young men would call very little gaming, very little dress, and very little gallantry, for such are the prices of *la belle société* in France."

This is one of his last letters, written when he was already making preparations for the return journey. He seems to have quitted France with regret, and to have left many friends behind him. " I cannot tell how it is," said Mdlle. Victoire, a young lady related to the Bishop of Blois, who had been told off with others to try and convert Jekyll to the true faith, "but I always feel sorry to think that our little Englishman is to be damned."

Jekyll returned to England in February 1776, and was not long in deciding to follow the profession in which his namesake, Sir Joseph, had won eminence.

He was called to the bar at Lincoln's Inn in 1778, but he soon migrated from the Chancery Inn, and became a member of the Inner Temple. He was here a fellow-student and near neighbour of George Colman the younger, who speaks well of Jekyll's wit and good nature in his "Random Records." He read and gave his advice upon the plays which Colman wrote instead of reading law, and expressed his sympathy for a pet squirrel in his revolving cage as "a poor devil upon the Home Circuit." Jekyll himself eventually went on the Western Circuit.

The social qualities which had made young Jekyll's path easy in France stood him in good stead in the opening of his career in England. Never was the proverb "Manners makyth Man" better exemplified than in his case. He soon became known as a wit and diner-out; and although, as we shall see later, he attained eminence of a sort, both in his Inn and in his profession, there is no doubt that he owed little of his success to his legal attainments, which were small, and a great deal of it to his mother wit, which was ready and copious.

Jekyll early turned to the newspapers as a means of increasing his income, and his contributions may still be read in the *Morning Chronicle* and the *Evening Statesman* of the last quarter of the eighteenth century. Both these papers were devoted to the Whig party, of which Jekyll himself remained a consistent member throughout his career. So far as his anonymous writings can be identified, they seem to have been satirical effusions

*b*

against the Court party led by Pitt. This was only natural in the circumstances. The Whigs, during a stay in opposition of twenty years, had ample opportunity of perfecting themselves in the art of political invective, and the long ascendency of Pitt left them little other consolation. It is a melancholy fact that jokes do nor preserve their flavour through the centuries; and it must be confessed that much of Jekyll's wit which is supposed to have convulsed the town a hundred years ago, to-day leaves us unmoved. At a time when puns were reckoned funny Jekyll was, no doubt, much admired, both as a sayer of good things and as a writer of smart squibs to the newspapers. But the pun is, to-day, as dead as Queen Anne; and jokes which have little else to recommend them remain unread. Most of the specimens of Jekyll's wit which have survived are of this character, and as such not suitable for quotation. But he apparently enjoyed a great reputation in his day. The bar, we are told, was continually convulsed with his sallies, and men like Abbot have quoted his jokes in their diaries.

Some verses occasioned by Pitt's tax on salt and vinegar, entitled "The Tears of the Cruets," have often been printed as a good specimen of his muse; but we think there is much more humour in the following account of a supposed meeting of the Prime Minister and his colleagues:—

"At a meeting at Downing Street yesterday, Mr. Pitt declared to several of his friends that he found himself destitute of any ideas to meet Parliament with for the purpose of finance, peace, or war. It was held advisable to send to the Duke of Portland's office to enquire if any were to be had there. The clerks returned for answer that they were totally unprovided; the last two ideas that were left in the Treasury had been sent by Mr. Cox to the Emperor on Saturday, which, it was confessed, should not have been done without the consent of Parliament, but that it was thought the safety of Germany depended on it.

"Mr. Pitt then enquired if the Right Hon. Sylvester Douglas had brought any ideas with him when he so lately took his seat on the Board, and was informed that the few he had were, by accident, packed up, and had sailed with Lord Macartney.

"Lord Mornington declared that he had put his whole stock into a pamphlet some years ago; and Lord Hawkesbury and Mr. Canning said they had lost all theirs with their light baggage on the forced march to Paris.

"Mr. Rose suggested a plan for putting ideas in requisition which he had found very successful at the Verderers' meetings on the New Forest Bill, and proposed as the most intelligible mode, the New Cavalry Act. Gentlemen who were supporters of the Ministry and the war might be classed according to the number of ideas they possessed, or were supposed to possess respectively; ten in a class, for instance, where each gentleman had only one idea apiece, and so on in proportion, if any gentlemen happened to possess more. The gentlemen on whom the ballot fell should be bound to furnish one idea for the use of the state, the fitness of which should be judged of by the Deputy Lieutenants of the respective counties. When the whole return was complete Mr. Dundas might be directed to put the ideas in a large decanter, and he and Mr. Pitt might pour them out as existing circumstances might require.

"Sir W. Young observed that such a ballot would fall very inconveniently on many gentlemen, who might thereby be delivered of the only idea they had in the world.

"Sir Gregory Page Turner said he did not pretend to deny having an idea, but he declared to God if it were rejected by the Deputy Lieutenant he should not know where to turn for a substitute.

"Mr. Boyd offered the minister ideas dated Hamburg, and on very moderate discount. They might be drawn on London and accepted by the Treasury.

"Mr. Pitt said it always gave him pain to distress the country gentlemen, as he felt this requisition would do, but he had the satisfaction of adding that very few ideas would be wanting, and those reducible at short date. Seven or eight of any sort would enable him to make six speeches of three hours' duration each, and as the Secretary for War kindly consented not to expend any, he was in no difficulty about the Admiralty.

"Mr. Pybus assured the Chancellor of the Exchequer that the Board had done so well without ideas of late, that he need not give himself any concern on their account.

"Mr. Pitt thanked Mr. Pybus very politely, and observed that in that case, without any violation of the

Appropriation Act, the Admiralty ideas might be put into the Poor Bill. Mr. Pitt then returned the gentlemen present many thanks for their very obliging advice, and directed Mr. Rose to make a minute of the transaction."

Jekyll's success as a writer of light political articles may have attracted the attention of Lord Shelburne; and his introduction to that statesman was an event of vast importance to the young lawyer, which soon led to his entrance into the world of politics. In 1787 Jekyll was nominated for the borough of Calne by his patron, and of course returned, although we are naïvely told by a contemporary that "the right of election is vested in the antient burgesses about twenty-four in number." Calne had previously had the distinction of sending Charles Townshend to Parliament; later it kept up its Whig traditions by introducing to political life Thomas Babington Macaulay.

By this time Joseph Jekyll was a rising man, and he found no lack of candid friends to point out that his talents brought him quite as much as they were worth. He was thought of sufficient importance to be made the subject of a "Political Eclogue" which was attributed to Richardson, and afterwards included in one of the editions of "The Rolliad." How some of these Whigs loved one another may be gathered from the opening lines of "The Jekyll," as the effusion is styled—

> "Jekyll the wag of law, the scribbler's pride,
> Calne to the senate sent when Townshend died;
> So Lansdowne willed, the hoarse old rook at rest,
> A jackdaw phœnix chatters from his nest."

Lord Lansdowne's choice of Jekyll and some others, and his omission to include Jeremy Bentham among his representatives in the House, was the occasion for a very extraordinary letter from that philosopher to the peer. It is the letter of an angry man, and is not worth anything as evidence of Jekyll's relations with Lord Lansdowne or of his rank as lawyer and politician; but it is interesting reading if only as a reminder of the ease with which a disappointed philosopher can forget his philosophy.

"Not a single person," he writes to Lord Lansdowne in a letter seventy pages long, "have I seen who has not obtruded upon me his wonder at your choice. There was but one voice as to those who are in. How came Jervis to be pitched upon of all people in the world? A very good man on board of ship, but what is he to do, or what did he ever do in parliament? What! of all men in the world could he find nobody but Jekyll? How could he think of such a man as that for parliament? Put Jekyll into parliament! It is quite a burlesque upon parliament the very idea of it. With others the last choice was matter of particular surprise, for I found he was understood to be a dull man, and that even by dull men, who speak as they can only speak, from his general character in the profession. They speak your sentiments! You will scarce venture to speak your own sentiments when these men are by. When the beginnings of the French Revolution were on the carpet at Bowood, you scarce durst own your good wishes in its behalf, while Jekyll, who has in general so many good jokes, was exhausting himself in bad ones to endeavour to make it look ridiculous. Jekyll's post in your household is that of talebearer, and in that situation he has been pronounced absolutely necessary; and if the talebearer is to be preferred to me for parliament, the same household does not hold me and the talebearer."

This is only one page out of the seventy, but a dignified letter from Lord Lansdowne healed the soreness, and Bentham replied in another beginning, "My dear, dear lord," as remarkable for its effusiveness as was the first for its virulence. What Bentham chose to call talebearing seems to have been a very natural and innocent occupation in all the circumstances. Lord Lansdowne, who as Lord Shelburne had been an active politician since George III. came to the throne, and had recently been Prime Minister, was now in retirement at Bowood. What more proper than that the man whom he had provided with a seat in the House of Commons should keep him informed of passing events in which he might still be presumed to have some interest? From Lord E. Fitzmaurice's life of his ancestor we learn the names of his political friends and the nature of their services. "Morellet kept him informed of all that was passing in France, Arthur Lee on the state of affairs in America, and Orde of events in Ireland, while Baring and Jekyll supplied the latest commercial and political news in London."

Neither were Bentham's prophecies of political insubordination fulfilled, at any rate, in the sense that he meant. Jekyll was a consistent Whig of the advanced party, and the reaction caused by the French Revolution, a reaction strong enough to turn Burke into a rabid Tory, only drove Jekyll into closer relations with the forward school led by Fox. There is an amusing account preserved in the Croker papers of Jekyll's version of Burke's preposterous dagger scene. Mr. Croker dined at Sir G. Warrender's, where he met Mr. Jekyll, and several other well-known men of the period. Jekyll, he says, was very agreeable, and he and Lord Lauderdale gave them many anecdotes about Fox, Burke, Hare, and Fitzpatrick. It seems that Jekyll went down to the House late on the night of the debate on the Aliens Bill and found it very full. He took a vacant seat by the side of Burke, who, since his quarrel with Sheridan, had sat below the gangway. When Fox spoke Jekyll cheered vehemently, and Burke, much upset, begged of him not to cheer so loudly, as he was nervous and it agitated him. Jekyll desisted, and Burke, regaining his good humour, apologised for the inconvenience which his papers and a mysterious parcel of brown paper caused his neighbour. This parcel contained the dagger. When Burke produced it and threw it rattling on the floor of the House, there were cries of derision, inquiries as to where the fork was, and great laughter from all parts of the House. "It quite failed," said Jekyll, though Croker adds, "Lord Sidmouth told me quite the contrary."

Of Mr. Jekyll's later political life one finds here and there a stray record. He voted for Grey's motion for parliamentary reform at the end of last century, and was lucky enough to live to see the principle embodied in the Reform Bill of 1832. He spoke on the motion for incriminating Lord Melville, and strenuously opposed the claim of that statesman to nominate members of the committee which was to report on his conduct. Later he was associated with Fox on the motion as to National Defence, but he was not a politician of much influence. Lord Colchester, in the notes in his Diary headed "Speakers in Parliament," thus describes Jekyll : "First rate for convivial wit and pleasantry, and admired by all. A frequent speaker in parliament, but absolutely without weight even in his own party. Rancorous in language, feeble in argument, and empty of ideas, few people applaud his rising, and everybody is glad when he sits down." He continued, however, to represent Calne until 1816, when he resigned.

In the meantime Mr. Jekyll had made progress in his profession. He was elected a Bencher of the Inner Temple in 1795, and later became Reader, Treasurer, and a King's Counsel. In 1805 he was appointed Solicitor-General to the Prince of Wales, and this royal patronage was of the utmost service to Jekyll. It led to his appointment in 1815 to a Mastership in Chancery, a post which was well paid, the duties of which were not onerous, and which secured to him a comfortable pension.

The appointment was generally condemned, and it was said that it was forced on Lord Eldon by the action of the Prince. His Royal Highness, it was rumoured, called at Bedford Square, and closeted the Chancellor in his own room. "How I pity Lady Eldon," said the Prince; "she will never see you again, for here I remain until you promise to make Jekyll a Master in Chancery." This may have been a humorous way of presenting the fact; but that the Prince's influence was a reality is plain, from the following entry in Sir Samuel Romilly's Diary:—

"Among other obstructions to the prosecution of suits has been the Chancellor's delay in the appointment of a Master in the place of Mr. Morris. That gentleman died on the 13th of April last, and it was only yesterday that Mr. Jekyll was appointed to succeed him. The Prince's favour has procured him that appointment, and as soon as the vacancy happened it was found that Jekyll was to be appointed. The Chancellor, however, has delayed all this time filling up the office, at very great inconvenience to the suitors, only, as it should seem, to show his sense of the impropriety of the appointment. A more improper one could hardly be made, for with a thousand good qualities as a private man, Jekyll is deficient in almost every qualification necessary to discharge properly the duties of a Master in Chancery. If the Chancellor had meant to show with what deliberation he could make a bad appointment to a very important political office, and with how strong a sense of the impropriety of it he could surrender up to the Prince that patronage which it is a duty he owes to the public to exercise himself, he could not have contrived matters better than he has done."

Of Joseph Jekyll the lawyer and politician there is

little else to record; his latter letters, now printed, best convey the character of the man himself. They begin, roughly speaking, when his official life ended, and continue up to the year of his death. Mr. Jekyll, who married Miss Sloane, daughter of Mr. Hans Sloane of Paultons, in 1801, was early left a widower, with two sons. These letters are all addressed to his sister-in-law, Lady Gertrude Sloane Stanley, the wife of Mr. William Sloane Stanley, his wife's brother. She was the daughter of Frederick Howard, fifth Earl of Carlisle, the friend of Fox and Selwyn, and the cousin of Lord Byron, whose misunderstanding with Lord Carlisle and his atonement for it are well known.

The letters, we think, show the closing years of a happy and successful life. Well endowed with this world's goods, Jekyll, at sixty, found himself in possession of good health (for periodical attacks of gout which enabled him to live to the age of eighty-four must have been nothing less than a blessing) and perennial good spirits. More than usually fortunate in his sons, he seems to have passed through life without trouble which left any enduring pain, except the premature loss of his wife. This indeed is a large reservation, to which he more than once makes touching reference in his letters. He was in a position to choose his friends from the highest ranks of society, and he had enough appreciation of art and letters to make his company desirable to most of the literary and artistic notabilities of his time. His name appears in many of the diaries of the beginning of this century. Rogers always expected him with his boys at his annual Twelfth Night entertainment, and was seldom disappointed ; and he was a frequent partaker of the famous breakfasts in St. James's Palace. Sir Walter Scott records meeting him in 1828 ; and it may have been Jekyll's jokes, which on that occasion, the great novelist tells us, "were fired like minute guns, and with an effect not much less melancholy." He was intimate with the brilliant set who surrounded the Countess of Blessington, and was often of the famous parties which met at Holland House.

Of this period of his life there is a full account in the letters. Mr. Jekyll found a sympathetic friend and correspondent in Lady Gertrude, and the lighter topics of the time are done full justice to. There is something attractive in the youthfulness of spirit which could make a man of seventy complain of being claimed by the dowagers as one of their own set ; and Jekyll's assumed horror of the visitor at country houses and the morning caller is not less amusing. Very pleasant, too, is the picture presented of the old politician noting the establishment, one by one, of the principles for which he and his party had striven for half a century, and, the objects of his life accomplished, thankfully singing his *Nunc Dimittis*, and calmly awaiting the end, which came at last gently, and without suffering.

# LETTERS OF JOSEPH JEKYLL.

## CHAPTER I.

*JOSEPH JEKYLL TO HIS FATHER.*

BRIGHTHELMSTONE, *Monday Evening*, *March* 1775.

HONOURED SIR,—

WE arrived here safely about seven o'clock this evening. The roads in admirable order, the face of the country in general very uninteresting.

The London postboy made us pay ninepence a mile to Croydon, though we understood the agreement was for eightpence. Except from Lewes hither (eight miles) we did not pay a shilling a mile the whole journey.

On our arrival we were agreeably surprised to hear the packet might not sail this fortnight; but the Captain has just informed us she will take her departure tomorrow evening,—the *Princess Caroline*, a schooner of seventy tons.

I took this opportunity to write, as to-morrow is no post day at this sequestered spot, and I find you are not to receive even this till Wednesday.

Osgood begs his compliments. I send my duty to

my mother and yourself, and love to my sister, and am, my dear sir, your very affectionate son.

P.S.—Pray tell my sister we had a runaway mare in the shafts from Croydon to Godstone. I hope my next will be from the Grand Monarque's dominions.

BRIGHTHELMSTONE, *Wednesday, March* 29*th*, 1775.

I HAVE directed that this may be put in the post *this* evening soon *after* our departure for Dieppe, which we expect will take place about seven or eight o'clock.

You may suppose the boisterous weather of yesterday prevented the schooner's going out of the harbour.

I have had time this morning to view the town of Brighthelmstone, which nothing but fashion could give repute to. The Steine, or public walk, is an open green with an orchestra. The neighbouring downs are fine, partly arable, partly sheepwalk, and not a tree to be seen. The streets are not paved; the houses chiefly built of the round sea-pebbles pitched in mortar.

There is a contemptible fort of twelve guns *en barbette*, and the encroachments of the sea are everywhere visible. There is a pretty theatre here, but neither of the two public rooms are equal to those at Southampton. We have *Gallicised* in some measure already, for the master of the packet (Killick) has changed our guineas into Louis d'ors and double Louis d'ors.

You will readily conceive a dearth of subject must shorten this letter. I will write by the earliest means from Dieppe, and hope my mother will allow for the uncertainty of a mail by sea.

Osgood has such a hydrophobia upon him that I ought to conclude this letter like a bill of lading. He begs his respects with my duty to my father and mother, and love to my sister, and believe me to be, dear sir, your obedient and affectionate son.

DIEPPE, *Thursday Morning*, 10 *o'clock*, *April 3rd*, 1775.

THE texture of this paper might stand for a date. We arrived here about half an hour ago after a *very brisk* passage of about twelve hours, in which we both were confoundedly sick, as we met with a great sea in the mid channel.

We are now drinking coffee in a balcony that commands a view of the harbour, and the caricature of dress and the noise of wooden shoes conspire to afford a scene of some novelty to me. This town is old and ill-built. The two piers are stupendous works, and the piazza surrounding the harbour has a good effect.

We had only three French women as fellow-passengers. We are sent for to the Custom House, and then set out for Rouen immediately. I am blundering French with the landlord, and have only time to bid a general adieu.

PARIS, *Wednesday*, *April 5th*, 1775.

WE left Dieppe about an hour after I wrote to you on Thursday last in a *voiture*, or two-wheeled post-chaise, and three horses abreast. We travelled at about *four miles* an hour, and our postillion took snuff from the foot of every hill to the summit.

At Tostes we *fasted* on stinking cod-fish, hard eggs sliced, and swimming in rank butter. This, washed down with sour cider, was our first repast; but we fared better for supper at Rouen, where we arrived by nine o'clock, and took up our abode at the Hôtel de bons Enfans. The two Messieurs Garvey treated us most politely, showed us the curiosities of the place, and more particularly the Council of Commerce during its session, with the nature of process in their actions of bankruptcy, Parliament, and Tournelle, or Criminal Chamber. Mr. Garvey's son was dangerously ill of a fever. Mrs. Garvey is near her lying in, or we should have *domesticated* there altogether. Rouen is a very fine city, the Cathedral; the Abbey of St. Ouen, and its rich Convent (where we met with much civility from Father Wilson, an *English* Benedictine); the old Gothic Church of St. Maclou—among whose reliques we saw the *entire body of St. Verecundus*—the bridge of boats; the public fountains, and Joan of Arc's statue, are worth viewing, and we saw everything in the course of Friday and Saturday. The country between Dieppe and Rouen is a continued cornfield planted thick with apple trees, totally unenclosed, the vales very fertile, the hills very barren; the houses built of mud, latticed and thatched. Upon the whole, though, Normandy is a fine province. The people, particularly at Rouen, murmur at the price of bread, and the Régiment de Penthièvres is now quartered there *in terrorem*.

We left Rouen on Sunday at five o'clock in the Berlin and four, dined at Gaillon, and saw the Archbishop of Rouen's magnificent palace there, built by the Amboise family, passed the limits of Normandy at Vernon, a little village full of Jacobite English, and slept at Bonnières.

On Monday got into the Berlin at four, and, as the rate of three miles an hour will admit of a passenger's caprice for walking, lounged through the forest of St. Germains to that royal château, an old building of brick somewhat like Hampton Court, and only famous for the view from its terrace of the Seine, Versailles, Marli, Paris, and the adjacent country, which from Vernon to the Capital is one continued vineyard. We got into Paris by dusk, and took up our residence at the Hôtel du Parc Royal, Rue du Colombier, in the Faubourg St. Germains. The journey from Rouen has been delightful, and we have not kept a *maigre* day since we were at Tostes.

They give us partridges and hares by wholesale; and, indeed, they will hardly get out of the horses' way in the highroad. They give us eels, and smelts, and frogs, beef, veal, pullets, pigeons, salads, sometimes fresh butter, the best bread in the world; salt that we cannot distinguish from pepper, cider for small beer, the wines of Orleans and Burgundy; desserts of cheese, pears, and apples, clean napkins, though coarse ones, and no knives. The beds (as a French sailor told us) are as high as *Belle Isle*, but soft enough, the floors above and below paved with red tiles, and the joists and rafters unceiled. In each room is a commode, whose drawers receive the fragments of the feast. The roads are incredibly fine, generally causeways as lofty as the Roman ones, nicely paved in the centre, of a vast breadth, straight as an arrow for leagues together, and usually planted with trees on each side.

Now, of Paris. We climbed Notre Dame yesterday in spite of Osgood's *vis inertiæ*; and I am convinced that the city is not much more than half as large as London. Their bridges are all pitiful, the Pont-neuf in particular, notwithstanding the *gasconnade* of the "Nouveau Voyage de France."

The streets are infamously dark, narrow, and ill-paved, and the boasted Seine is scarce a third of the width of the Thames at Westminster. On the other hand, we have seen the noble squares of Louis XV., infinitely larger than any *we* have; the Place de Vendôme, not large, but an octagon, with correspondent sides; the Place de Victoire, a regular circle,—all three centred with statues. We saw the Palais Royal this morning, and the Duke of Orleans' capital collection of pictures. The gardens of this Palais are frequented by the *beau monde* at noon. We saw the Luxembourg Palace, and the Hospital of Invalides, with its church and dome, by much the first building I have seen in point of magnificent finishing. In the evening we walked in the Tuileries, and afterwards went to the fair of St. Germains, which, luckily for us, is held in *Lent*, where we have partaken of the comedy, and a species of entertainment called here *Waux-hall*, something like a very inferior Ranelagh, where chance in a lottery for trinkets is included in the price of admittance. As the odds were ninety-six to four, you may suppose we were more unsuccessful than you will doubtless be in Cox's. I forgot to mention that we were at the comedy at Rouen. The representation consisted of three *petites pièces*. In the last a shepherdess was accompanied in her song by the *bleatings of a lamb* that she led in a riband. The drama of to-night was violated by a very libidinous harlequin, and a very licentious dancing bear.

We have also seen the Louvre, and part of the Boulevards. We have called on Mr. Joullain, the printseller, who will send Mr. Willet the earliest notice of the sale, and the catalogue as soon as it is published. He thought I was inquiring for *Woollet*, the engraver, at first, and asked me if he had *finished the plate*. We have called on Dr. Vamier, who is still at Caen; and I think you will allow we have done and seen a great deal, by the help of our books, our maps, and Monsieur Villeneuve, our *valet de place*. We pay the rest of our visits to-morrow, and hope to get recommendations to a provincial settlement very soon, as we feel no inclination to continue the expenses of Paris at this dull season.

The whole world is full dressed here by breakfast, and I have almost forgot the use of my hat already. The female *ostriches* in London are *mere geese* in comparison of the French women, who, by the help of a circular spot of rouge under each eye, and a cap of wire, large flowers, feathers, and riband as broad as a *child's waistband*, add new caricature to their natural ugliness; for, as yet, we have not seen (I may safely say) half-a-dozen beauties.

I have desired the Prince of Condé to give me the refusal of his Palais de Bourbon, if he should ever let lodgings, as it is built of one storey only, and would suit my mother's gout and your asthma so well, though I heartily hope to hear soon that you are both better than when I left home.

ORLEANS, *Wednesday, April* 12*th*, 1775.

YOU will see by the dimensions of this sheet that I mean to journalise, though I could plead as an excuse that it is almost the only paper I can get.

However, a young traveller sees so many novelties that I trust I shall have more matter to scribble than can be worth any one's perusal. I wrote from Paris on this day s'ennight; on Thursday, the 6th, we visited Sir J. Lambert, who was not at home, called on his mother in the Rue de Gramont, a mighty well-bred old lady, who treated us with every possible civility, advised us to think of Tours for our residence, and promised us a letter of recommendation to the Intendant. We next went to pay our compliments to M. St. Paul, who very politely invited us to dinner the next day, and showed us that kind of attention that I beg my very particular thanks to Captain Barrington for.

We lounged to the Church of the Carmelites to see some famous pictures by Guido, Champagne, etc., and that wonderful portrait of Madame de la Vallière in the character of a Magdalen, by Le Brun. This beautiful woman left the arms of Louis XIV. for the rigour of these cloisters, and died after a penitence of thirty-six years. In the chapel of the English penitents we saw the yet unburied body of James II.,[1] together with that of his daughter Louisa, and the effigies of his dead queen in wax. Round the chapel were the tombs of several English who followed his fortunes. In the evening we saw the École Militaire, a most beautiful structure for the education of cadets, and worthy of royal munificence.

On Friday morning we saw the wonderful manufacture of the Gobelins, the Bastille, the Place Royal, which is a square piazz'd all round, with an equestrian statue; the Place de Grève, "that fatal retreat of th' unfortunate brave," on one side of which stands the Maison de Ville, and another side is open to the Seine; in short, we made, by the help of our map, the whole eastern tour of Paris. We dined at Colonel St. Paul's in company with his lady, a Miss Salwin, a Mr. Wilbraham, returning to England from his travels, and an Oxonian, Mr. James, who is St. Paul's Secretary. In the evening we walked in the Tuileries.

On Saturday we saw but little, from a satiety, I believe, of having seen so much, but received a card of invitation to dinner from Sir J. Lambert.

On Palm Sunday the rage of curiosity returned, and we heard high mass in the beautiful Church of St.

[1] The coffin was broken up for the sake of its lead during the Revolution, and the body thrown into the *fosse commune*.

Sulpice, took leave of Lady Lambert, and dined with Sir John. His sister dined with us, who is more French than English, but a most pleasing woman. Young Glyn dined there, too, who set out for London on Sunday, and told us Angers, Blois, and Tours were most infamous towns, very dear, and full of English. In the evening we went to the *concert spirituel*, performed in the Palace of the Tuileries to a very brilliant audience. Mrs. Arthur Blake arrived with her husband at our hotel in the evening on their way to Bordeaux, and I had an opportunity of paying my compliments to them.

On Monday morning, by ten o'clock, we had pacified the exorbitant harpies about us, got an order from the postmasters, and embarked in a most wretched *voiture* for Orleans, which, as it is thirty leagues, and travelling in France is most uniformly inexpeditious, we did not reach till midnight, the great bell of a convent tolling twelve as we entered the gates, and the last two stages were through a dreary forest. The city of Orleans is of the form of a bow described by the Boulevards or Ramparts, which are most beautifully shaded for walking.

The river Loire forms the string of that bow, and is full as broad as the Thames at Putney; a most elegant bridge of nine arches (much beyond any bridge at Paris) is an arrow to this bow.

The Rue Royale here is infinitely finer for its length than any street I saw in Paris; and in one part of it stands a monument to the memory of the famous Joan of Arc, where the *pucelle* and Charles VII., both habited *en cavalier*, are kneeling to a virgin with a dead Christ. Struck as we were by the beauty and neatness of this town, and considering, too, that we had no recommendations to Blois, a dirty, dear town, still farther off, very slight ones to Tours, where the only house we could board at was to cost us eleven Louis d'ors each per month, at the Abbé Rouèrs, whom we now know to be a great rascal, we determined to settle here if possible. We dressed, walked out, citizens of the world, like the first pair from *paradise* (though the comparison does not hold with respect to our Auberge). "Orleans was all before us where to choose."

I soon thought of Mr. Gerard Plisson, Herries' agent here, who, with all the good-natured officiousness of a Frenchman, formed an establishment for us in a trice, as we think very agreeably, and I believe you will think so too. We have very good apartments on a first floor in the house of M. Risse, a Genoese by birth, but an inhabitant of France since his childhood. We board with him, and sit down to a very good dinner and supper with desserts and as much Burgundy as we choose. Our party consists of a Mr. Ellison, tutor to a Mr. Hamilton and a Mr. Booth, all Irish, the last a *réformé* Captain of infantry and a chevalier of St. Louis. The rest, to the tune of five or six more, are all French, and nothing but French is talked at table. The price of my board and lodging is four Louis d'ors per month, not more extravagant than Picardy, though more so than I expected; but the difference at Blois, Amboise, Tours, etc., considered, Orleans is really reasonable. The most exorbitant charge here is my language-master, who is to have tenpence English per lesson; but he is a poet, and candidate for the chair of a professor in this university. We dine at a quarter-past one o'clock, and sup at nine; we are in bed by half-past ten, so rise early in our own defence.

At Paris we dined at half-past two, the men hand the women from the drawing to the dining-room, and sit down promiscuously, so that everybody carves, and there is no top or bottom to the table. No healths are drunk; and if you don't take care of yourself you may rise without a glass of wine. The dessert follows as a third course, after which all rise, turn to the rightabout, and wash their hands and mouths, then return to the drawing-room with the women, drink coffee immediately, and talk small talk till about five, when everybody takes French leave.

The police of this country is much commended, and deservedly; yet in Paris I was assured murders were so frequent that it is customary to see five or six bodies to be owned in the morning at a place called the *Morgue*, and there are nets on the Pont-neuf let down every night to receive persons thrown over by banditti. The morning we saw the Grève there was a gibbet erected. We inquired if there would be much crowd, and were told "No," for there was generally an execution every day.

The road from Paris hither is full of crosses, with inscriptions to perpetuate the infamy of some robber or murderer. We lodge in a beautiful place or square, and saw from our balcony yesterday evening a criminal broke on the wheel. He arrived at five o'clock in the evening, in a cart guarded by the *maréchaussée* (who constantly patrol the roads). He was attended by a *cordelier*, and held in his hands two laths nailed together in the form of a cross. He had received the tonsure and unction, and, while he was undressing, the crowd around the scaffold (which was far from being great) sang a voluntary requiem. The executioner, a very spruce fellow in a bag and *bien poudré*, extended the criminal's bare arms and legs on a St. Andrew's cross, which had two deep notches under the long bones of each limb; then with an iron crow, bent like the blade of a scythe, struck him nine violent blows, the last across the reins. Thus with two fractures in every limb, at each of which he cried out *Mon Dieu!* the agonising wretch was untied and thrown on the forewheel of a waggon elevated about four feet above the scaffold. The holy father drew a chair near him, and muttered something during his last gasps. At night the body was exposed in the neighbouring forest. Horrible and frequent as these executions are (for there are twelve more now in the Châtelet here under the like condemnation), their effects are as insufficient as ours in England. The crime of the unfortunate creature we saw yesterday was burglary, as we learnt from his sentence, which is posted up at every corner in the streets.

Mr. Martin, the banker's eldest son, has a château very near Orleans, where he resides in all the pomp of a British Nimrod, with his pack of dogs and his stable of hunters for foxes, and we have plenty of boars and wolves in the forest.

We have a coffee-house here, but no English papers, so that all sorts of news will be very acceptable, particularly the proceedings relative to the Perreaus, and Mrs. Rudd.[1] Robert Perreau came to Paris some time ago, in company with some acquaintance of Colonel St. Paul. We have a theatre here, but the comedians do not play during this holy season. I am told the Opera House at Paris is very superb. That, the other theatres, and Versailles, are almost the only sights we did not see. The Cathedral of Orleans is rebuilding in a very beautiful Gothic style. We are just returned from a walk round it, and are of opinion that this is one of the cleanest, neatest, and finest towns of its size we have ever seen. The view from our windows of the Place du Martroy is that of a scene always busy, and we have nothing to lament but a south aspect. The prospect from the Boulevards of the adjacent country covered with vines and fruit trees is beautiful; and if any fault can be found, it is that we want hills to diversify. The Loire is navigable hither from Nantes for large flat-bottomed vessels, runs over a fine sand, which shifts a good deal, and forms innumerable shoals. Every part of France we have yet seen is wonderfully populous, and generally fertile in corn or wine; yet, possibly as a consequence of the former, bread is at the rate of three-halfpence English per pound, and it is the

---

[1] Robert and Daniel Perreau, hung for forgery in January 1776. The woman Rudd was acquitted.

only food many of the poor taste for weeks together. As to keeping Lent, M. Risse is too much the *bon-vivant* old bachelor to suffer us to do it; and we are totally reconciled to, if not pleased with, the French cookery.

The châteaux of the gentlemen are in a vile, stiff taste, with regular vistas of trees leading to them. We saw no enclosures till near Orleans, and very little, if any, grazing grounds at all. The most beautiful part of France I recollect is the country about Pont de L'Arche in Normandy. My old acquaintance, David Kerr, is not here, but at Tours. I have written to him for recommendations, though we don't want society at dinner and supper; and walking and the intermediate hours will be employed by my French, and Osgood's Italian. None of our party are under thirty-five years of age, a circumstance in our favour; for the young Frenchmen are not the most eligible company. We have plenty of fresh fish here, and always four or five heretic dishes, so that we have no reason to complain. I have never yet seen a drunken Frenchman, and, indeed, I believe it is hardly possible their wines can make them so. Besides, all ranks of people drink it merely as a beverage; and the idea of putting the bottle about seems totally uncommon, if not unknown among them. I shall receive a letter from home with the greatest pleasure on every account, though I have not the face to ask for elephant paper in return.

ORLEANS, *Sunday, April* 30*th*, 1775.

In my last of the 14th I made a promise to write in a fortnight or three weeks at farthest, and as with respect to home I had rather overdo than be deficient in my performances, you are likely to receive another long sheet of impertinences. On Easter Sunday we heard high mass in the Cathedral, a most magnificent structure, to which they are adding a new *façade* in the Gothic style, at the expense of a fund established on the profits of something like our firstfruits in England. The solemnity was accompanied with a variety of instruments, among which the *Serpent* supplies a good bass. The next day A. Blake and his wife passed through on their way to Angers, and by a whimsical chance we were in the same inn with them here as at Paris, for my friend Kerr invited us to sup with him on his route to Rheims. A very agreeable old chevalier was in his party, who told us he was taken twice in the course of the late war, and once by Mr. Keppel. He travelled with some excellent Hermitage.

It is the etiquette of France for strangers to visit first, so we paid our compliments to Mr. Martin, who rents a small château within two miles of Orleans. Mrs. Martin, whom he married at Lisle, is of Irish extraction, educated in a convent in Flanders, is very young and pretty, and now expecting her first child. Mr. Martin astonishes the whole country with his chases of the fox, wild boar, and chevreuil, a kind of roe buck, which is eaten here as venison. He has hunted wolf too; but one or two of those animals are still domestic enough to visit his kennels by night for the carcase of a dead mule. Through the means of this acquaintance we read the English newspapers, and in the last met with the petition of the ostriches.

We have dined with Martin once or twice, and always have the best French company in the country, without gaming high, which is so universally the vice of France, that old Lady Lambert told us the term for a young Englishman who would not play was *Le garçon est inutile*. Within a day or two after a dinner it is the custom to pay a visit of compliment; and as another etiquette (perhaps of feudal origin), Colonel St. Paul has told Martin he ought to send the Duke of Orleans every season two chevreuil, as a tribute for his permission to hunt in the province.

My Lord Galway, with his Swiss Governor, arrived here, and visited us on their way home from the South. Lord Galway produced a copy of a *certain* hunting song, which was given him by Lord A. Percy at Marseilles, and which was sung there by the Duchess of Leinster and Miss Dalton. He told us an instance of the disinterestedness of the museum Cox that ought to be recorded. The late Lord had some diamonds to sell, which Cox purchased at £200. A few days after, Cox waited on his Lordship, and owned that upon inspection the jewels were worth £100 more, which he immediately tendered. The nobleman, struck with his behaviour, insisted upon splitting the difference. The £50 was accordingly paid, and in less than a week a very superb harpsichord, directed to the youngest daughter, arrived at my Lord's country house. Lord Galway left us on Friday last. He is a pleasing young man, and was a pupil of Mr. Apthorpe's at Croydon.

Lent has ended for some time, so that we seldom eat fish now but on Fridays. We have very good salmon, salt cod freshened, carp, and the alose or shad, which, with the help of rich sauces, is not despicable. In the desserts we have sweetmeats for which this country is famous, particularly the *cotignac*, or quince marmalade of Orleans, and an excellent thickened cream called the Cream of Blois; so that with near a dozen of these matters at dinner and almost as many at supper, one may make a shift to exist pretty well. As I am on the subject of epicurism at present, I must tell you we were lamenting at not having brought good tea with us from home, when Providence, in the shape of a reverend Irish tutor (Mr. Ellison), wrote to Bordeaux for a couple of pounds of the best and cheapest I ever tasted. Upon the whole, though (as I am to experience from a thousand instances), France is not so cheap as we were taught to expect. The Chevalier Booth assisted me in the choice of my linen, which will stand me in about half-a-guinea English per shirt. They are made at the Convent du Bon Pasteur, an institution like our Magdalen, at twentypence English apiece. I mention these trivial circumstances in order to learn the difference.

You will inquire after my studies. I have a master every morning for the pronunciation; I read the "Spirit of Laws," the other works of Montesquieu, and the "Synonimes François," a work, you remember, was recommended at Lord Despencer's. I fence every day. I have taken a ride on a *bidet* that kicked at every touch of the spur, with a huge demi-pique saddle and holsters. We visited a beautiful château about two leagues off, belonging to M. Boutain, a rich financier. It is called *La Source*, from the little river Loire's rising most romantically among its groves, and was the retreat of our Lord Bolingbroke during his exile. The weather is already too hot for midday excursions, and everybody walks with a parasol. Monsieur Loup, old Risse's favourite dog, was cropt this morning, for the French carry their observance of dress for the seasons down to their curs. This is a piece of news for Finette, who, I suppose, is to wear her spring velvet somewhat longer.

Next to the dogs, the most ridiculous objects are the children, with their bags, hoops, muffs, swords, fly-caps, and parasols at seven years of age. At about five the boys have a most becoming dress, which, except Mrs. Martin's lace cushion, is almost the only ingenious contrivance I have seen in France. As an alteration in dress, I might mention a *stone doublet*, which fathers have a legal right to clap upon their sons for extravagance, and of which there are continual instances. What the girls wear by compulsion at that age I know not. I have only heard their voices behind the grate at the Convent of the Lamb of God. You will forgive the desultory manner in which I write; but it is *Sunday* evening, and I am called away to some Spanish rope dancers at the Comedy and a firework.

*Monday Morning, May* 1st.

I was very agreeably surprised with your kind letter of April 23rd, and thank you for the news it contained. I am sure you have my good at heart so much, that I shall attend to your prepossession in favour of Blois, and therefore my friend Osgood and I are to part very soon. I cannot but allow we have too much English society here, and therefore as soon as my month is up, which will be about to-morrow s'ennight, I mean to go down the river to Blois. Osgood is nearly assimilated to French living, and it has never disagreed with me the least. Your account of the navy promotions has made me long more than ever for a Court Kalendar to see how high you stand upon the list now. I am happy to hear my mother recovers of her rash, which perhaps was a critical symptom in her ticklish constitution. I hope I need not say how glad an account of yours and my sister's health always makes me. The French milliners are plaguing me to buy caps at *twenty sous* apiece for "*mademoiselle my fair sister.*"

When I came from home I believe I forgot to desire that the buttons of my new coat and the waistcoat entirely might be covered with silver paper to prevent tarnishing.

Bunbury's etchings and Sterne's journey are almost as good viaticums in France as the postbook. Two French couriers joined us on the way hither, by which means we met with no delays on the road, and a French courier with his boots, *couteau de chasse*, and nightcap, is no trite figure.

The advocates, proctors, etc., wear black, and their hair loose down their backs, an idea which I wonder did not suggest itself to our young sprigs of the law when they undertook the reformation of wigs. We were a little too late at Paris to hear the Countess of Béthune argue her own cause in the robe of a pleader, and attended by three of her children.

The case is a matter of equity. As the elder sister of three, she received a smaller portion than the rest in marriage, on condition of inheriting solely the estate of her uncle.

The uncle dies without executing an instrument, and the sisters claim under a coparcenary division. Her process has been once lost. Her advocate now lies under an interdict, and she therefore makes her appeal in person.

BLOIS, *Tuesday, May 30th*, 1775.

I AM unable to describe the advantages of my situation here in every point of view, and the triumph I feel in having retreated from Orleans, where my only object in this kingdom was totally defeated. I have but just recovered the regret of having misspent my first month so egregiously, and have acquired a great deal of very creditable abuse from my countrymen on the *sacrifice* (as is it called) of quitting them, and venturing, unknowing and unknown, to Blois.

As to the language, I am so far in the practice of it,

that, except my first conference with Burvill—who makes almost a religious conscience of speaking French—I declare, upon my honour, I have not articulated twenty words of my mother tongue since I left Orleans, where I talked almost nothing else; and as to the theory, I give twenty-four sous per lesson to a canon of the cathedral for correcting my translations, etc., and Lutaine lends me a variety of French authors which he has himself commented upon in point of style and composition with a good deal of taste. The masters for the exercises are good and perfectly reasonable at Blois.

I thank you for your American news, as it is the perpetual question here; and we are told that several experienced officers in the Prussian service have gone over to marshal the insurgents and form them to military discipline.

St. Paul announced the Queen of Denmark's death officially at Versailles, and I heard last night that the Prince de Conti had lost a niece or a daughter.

I am happy to think you are to be so eligibly settled at Epsom this summer, as well on the score of health as spirits; and as to Bradenham, I can conceive that miss would have felt the absence of her fellow-trudge in clambering stiles and scrambling through hedges, and will perhaps prefer the more elegant *déshabillé* of the wells to the leather shoes, short petticoats, oaken stick, and old black bonnet of Bradenham. I am silent on the subject of riding.

From exercise to appetite is no unnatural transition; and as epicurism has hitherto always had a sort of precedence in my correspondence, I must thank you for the recipe to make gooseberry fool, and in return for the fool would send my *song* of the *source*, but shall reserve it for some future scarcity of prose, and in the meantime inform you that our celebrated *Crème de Blois* is a very mysterious process. The hag who brings us every morning half-a-dozen little *pots* of it, covered with grape leaves, tells me that the cream is permitted to form itself in certain caves of a peculiar coolness, and that after it is skimmed from the milk they churn it to the consistence we eat it in. I can only say that it excels the preparation in the West of England, and resembles all that part of a whip syllabub above the wine.

St. Gervais, a neighbouring village, most romantically situated on a rock of vines, is famous for its manufacture, and we make parties continually to drink at the fountain head. In short, I am so reconciled to *soupe* and *boulli*, such a convert to frogs, and so naturalised to the wine (which is excellent here, and never disagreed with me), that I reflect upon tea, porter, and cold boiled beef without a sigh. Mr. Burvill—whose father, I believe, was formerly a captain in your service—has behaved to me with uncommon politeness. He has been here two years, is universally respected, and well received, and has introduced me so effectually already, that I visit all the families of fashion in Blois—the only means of acquiring the best language, and a piece of good fortune I had no reason to expect so immediately on my arrival here, without the least recommendation.

I will name the houses, as you have met with an Englishman that has been at Blois; and first, then, the Bishop, M. le Comte de Monperraud, M. St. Michel (President of the late Conseil Supérieur), M. de Saumerez, M. le Vaste, M. Artabuis, M. la Fosse, M. la Vallière, M. Papin, M. Baudré, M. Rambord, M. Bourdon, and M. Tessie. We have several Canadian families here, who are particularly fond of the English. I am in company every evening, and the *demoiselles* are perpetually asking the most ridiculous questions about poor old England, and laughing at me for my blunders. We dine at one o'clock, we join the *monde*, as it is phrased, somewhere between four and five, and at six they stuff bread and cakes and wine, play at whist, and walk from seven or eight to supper time. This, with my morning studies and exercises, is generally the journal of my time.

On Tuesday se'nnight I was present at the Ceremony of the Veil at a neighbouring convent of Carmelites. It commenced with a preparatory sermon addressed entirely to the novitiate, who appeared at the grate richly dressed "in the pomps and vanities of this wicked world." The Father Guardian of the Capuchins opened the grate, and delivered to her a consecrated taper and the habits of the order on a silver salver decorated with natural and artificial flowers. She distributed these, —and I, as a stranger, got a most superb bouquet,— took leave of her relations, and withdrew with the sisterhood, who were a good half-hour cutting her hair off. On her return in the religious habit the Father

Guardian gave his benediction, and the grate was closed.

I have meditated since on a loss of liberty by no means on the same pious motives. Three hundred wretches, chained by the neck like dogs, passed through Blois on Wednesday on their way to the galleys at Brest, where they were not to arrive till the 14th of June. Some of them had undergone the torture, and could scarce support themselves on crutches. They were fed on the ground in the market-place.

These are not pleasing speculations to an Englishman, but to-day afforded a more joyous scene. Mademoiselle Tessie, a very pretty girl of our acquaintance, was married to a young president of Angers. For two days before the wedding the *monde* visit the bride and bridegroom at the house of the lady's father. The bride is distinguished by an enormous nosegay, and the chamber is almost hung with flowers. We attended the ceremony and mass this morning, and to-morrow the *fêtes* commence for three days of music, dancing, and guzzling, to which I have a perpetual invitation. I see my sister laugh, but the character of a *garçon* is always well received in France.

On Thursday last I saw a wild boar hunted in the forest of Chambord. The furious animal, after killing two dogs, received a wound from the *fusil* of one of the Gardes de Chasse, was finally despatched by their *couteaus*, and the monstrous head carried off triumphantly on a lance. I saw the catastrophe, like Sancho, from a tree, discharged my *fusil* most manfully at a very innocent wolf on our return, with all the guilt of premeditation, and, as usual, without the completion of murder. As my curiosity is satisfied I believe it is the last chase I shall partake of, unless I am invited to Fontainebleau.

## CHAPTER II.

*JOSEPH JEKYLL TO HIS FATHER (Continued).*

Blois, *Wednesday, May 31st,* 1775.

You would have received this scrawl perhaps three days earlier had the impatience of our bride permitted her to postpone the commencement of the *fêtes* to this day. But I was suddenly summoned to the dance yesterday evening, and obliged to break off at my *boar*. We sat down forty to supper, and afterwards danced *à la ronde* with a sort of nuptial song. In the course of the dance a lady or gentleman is successively forced into the centre, and they have the privilege of kissing whom they please. You may suppose the Messieurs Anglais kissed the bride, and were in their turn kissed most outrageously.

The seditions here are partly suppressed, and His Majesty will put on at Rheims on the 10th June a diadem valued at eight millions of livres.

An English adventurer, Mr. Soames, who says he came down the Loire with Captain Kempenfelt,[1] has pestered us here with a project to supply his wise countrymen with the manufactures of Lyons, on the

[1] Rear Admiral Richard Kempenfelt, lost in the *Royal George* 1782.

*advance* of the annual subscription by way of commission. But as the chaff was ineffectual he commenced absolute beggar, and we scouted him to Orleans with some difficulty.

I am ashamed of the dull detail of churches, processions, châteaus, prospects, and pictures, and yet it is all I can send, for you don't expect politics; and as to the manners, I am at present but a mere superficialist. Next to the language, the million etiquettes are the most difficult for a stranger to acquire. They are precise to a degree. For example, I will allow that the single circumstance of *taking French leave* (which gains ground even among us at present) is easy and natural. But, on the contrary, I will maintain that there is more formality of compliment in *entering* one assembly here than in taking the round of routs for a whole winter at London.

It is a ludicrous reflection, too, that a journey of so few hours should influence the *petty manners*; but I have frequently laughed of late at my own caricature, a hat and feather, white shoes, a shirt like Falstaff's present to the bakers' wives, a bag, sword, and parasol at eight o'clock in the morning. But this is moderate in comparison of the figure *en cavalier*.

*June 9th*, 1775.

I AM much obliged to you for the news in your letter of June 6th which arrived this evening, and I wish I could send you in return an account of the coronation of *our* King, which was performed yesterday at Rheims.

To-day he touches for the evil, and to-morrow goes to Compeigne for the *Fête de Dieu*.

I believe I once gave you a sketch of Blois, but I am now able to finish it with the accuracy of a Flemish painter. To begin, then, after the manner of Plutarch, by comparison, Blois is about the size of Windsor, and has a wonderful similitude to it in every point but vicinity to the capital. It is situated on the side of a hill, the foot of which is washed by the Loire, over which is thrown a most beautiful bridge of eleven arches, ornamented at the centre by a magnificent obelisk and cross. Louis XV. struck a medal on the occasion, which I saw at Paris.

The château, where several kings have resided, is very considerable, and much embellished with paintings of the time of Henry II. The *new* voyage of France recommended by the sea officer whose tour you gave me describes this palace as the fragment in Toland describes Nonsuch in your neighbourhood. (By-the-bye, that voyage-writer has either translated the work he speaks of, or borrowed upon hearsay, for I am convinced from his descriptions he never saw Orleans, Blois, or the Loire, within these fifty years.) The modern part of the château, which never was finished, is the work of Gaston, brother to Louis XIII., who also built the Jesuits' Church here—the *façade* and high altar of which are models of taste—as well as an Ionic corridor in the front of the old palace. I have remarked everywhere dispersed through the ornament the relief of a porcupine, and am told it was the device of Louis XII., whose grandfather, the Duke of Orleans, had established a knighthood of that order, with the motto "Cominus et Eminus." Henry III. held his estates here, and the *ordonnances* of Blois about the year 1579 are well known in history. From history, too, I have collected that Blois has been as well the retirement of misfortune as the seat of royalty, particularly to the family of Medicis. Catherine of Medicis died here in the midst of those distressful times about the year 1588, and Mary of Medicis (wife of Henry IV., and mother of Louis XIII., Gaston, Duke of Orleans, and the Queen of our Charles I.) was confined here, and effected her escape to Angoulême in 1619. Monsieur le Duc d'Orleans fled hither after the Rebellion in 1652, and the Capuchins showed me a wretched chamber in their convent where the unfortunate King of Poland passed several years of chagrin.

The Cathedral of Blois, dedicated to St. Souleine, is situated on the highest part of the town, which abounds in inequalities.

The garden of the Bishop is one of the most enchanting spots I ever saw, and commands a delightful prospect of the adjacent country diversified with corn, vines, and villages, skirted by the forests of Russie and Chambord, with the château of the latter and that of Menars in view; commands, too, the course of the Loire, with groups of sails, fishermen's huts, and floating watermills of a very peculiar construction. This garden is free of access to all who know the Bishop. I was reading there one evening, and was much pleased with the effect of a storm of thunder at a distance, which is usually very violent in these parts of France.

Blois was formerly in the Diocese of Chartres, but Pope Innocent XII. erected it into a See in the year 1697, and united here the Abbeys of St. Laumer, Pontlevois, and Bourgmoyen. The *Prieurs* of the former furnished the Chapter with Canons, and the Dean is a regular Canon of Geneviève. Blois has a Chamber of Accounts, as being of the Dukedom of Orleans, and a *Presidial* of Special Judicature. The Superior Council, too, is but lately abolished.

I was twice at church on the *Fête de Pentecôte* to see the *bon Dieu* carried in procession with a canopy and torches. The most singular circumstance to a stranger was the collection for the poor. The plate is always carried about by some young lady of fashion, full dressed, with a most immense nosegay, and preceded by the *suisse* or beadle of the church bearing a halbert. The young lady was accidentally of our acquaintance, and I was much surprised to see her sitting at a distance from her family in a place appropriated with all the splendour of a churchwarden. The congregation sit on chairs.

Burvill and I made an excursion on Friday last to Corbrand, an estate lately purchased by Mr. O'Donnell, an Irishman, who formerly served in the brigades. He married the daughter of Sir Astley, a sister of the Ladies Tankerville and Vincent. We met there Mr. Webb (son of P. Carteret-Webb), who is in France during his law-suit with his stepmother, Mrs. Bever, and for the education of his son.

The country about Corbrand abounds in lakes of a great extent. Mr. O'Donnell stocks them with carp at a louis per thousand, and sells them again at a louis per hundred. Soin, a neighbouring village, as well as Romorantin and Blois, were Roman stations. I saw several Urns of the Seventh Legion at the former, and Mr. O'Donnell means to open some barrows in Dr. Stukeley's manner. We have two famous Roman bridges or causeways at Blois, and I am hunting Cæsar's Commentaries to account for them. On our return we saw the Château of Cheverny, belonging to M. Dufour, which is very magnificent. He has a theatre there, and enjoys life in every respect perfectly.

The peasants of this part of France are miserably poor. The girls who herd the cows are always at work with their distaffs, and the cap is always clean and perhaps laced, while the feet are without shoes and stockings. Ignorance, too, approaches so near to barbarity, that I declare when we inquired our way the children kept aloof, for fear, as they said, that the strangers would hurt them.

The earth is covered with aromatic herbs, which produce most excellent mutton; the trees abound in wild productions, particularly a sort of flowering ash that bears a fruit like the Catherine pear.

I am just returned from dining with my good friends the Benedictines, who showed me in their sacristy two arms and a head in gilt silver, containing the skull and limbs of St. Bonaventure and St. Colomban. One of them told me that my friend, David Carnegie, will have the honour of showing England to the son of the great Buffon.

My duty attends my father and mother, and my love to my sister.

*July 1st,* 1775.

"THIS comes hoping you are well, as I am at this present writing," an exordium I must confess somewhat fallen into contempt, but nevertheless totally Roman, and full of the very pith of correspondence. I hope you received my last letter directed to Epsom, and dated June 13th, in answer to one of yours which arrived here the night before; and as "*to rush into the midst of things*" may be as good a rule for an epistle as for an epic poem, I shall recommence my journal without farther prelude. On Tuesday, June 13th, at sunrise, Burvill and myself embarked in a *cabane* for Amboise. The party consisted of an old French flirt and her daughter (who, in spite of our remonstrances, was destined for the veil, because she was handsomer than her mother), and a young Capuchin, who stunk like a polecat.

We arrived at Amboise by noon, an ancient town of the Touraine, on the banks of the Loire. I presented Newnham's letter to the family of Hennesy. Burvill was at home at Mr. Ryan's; and we met with such universal hospitality that we neither ate nor drank at our own expense during our stay there. In the evening we viewed the town, and the castle built by Charles VIII., who afterwards repaid himself by running his head against the door of a tennis court they showed us, the immediate consequence of which was an apoplexy. They carry on a small manufacture of silks, buttons, and casques for the soldiery. In the principal church we saw the arm of St. Denis. It is set in silver, and richly ornamented with jewels. They told us a robber attempted to steal it, but the great bell began to toll of itself during the attempt at midnight, and he fled with precipitation. It was carried in procession on the *Fête de Dieu*.

On Wednesday, the 14th, we rode to Verrât, the seat of the Duc d'Aiguillon, a magnificent château newly built on the banks of the Cher. The house is ornamented in the rural taste, and the neighbouring country is wonderfully beautiful, the prospect a vast sheet of cornfields and vineyards, interspersed with walnut trees, finely watered, and terminated by the town of Tours. I was fortunate enough to encounter the Duke and Madame du Barry on the road in their way to Aiguillon, where he intends to pass a good deal of his time. The Duchess makes her own butter every morning at breakfast with a little mill I saw on her toilette, which pleased me mightily.

Thursday was the *Corpus Christi*, or *Fête de Dieu*; and after the processions we walked to Chante-loup, the superb palace of the Duc de Choiseul,[1] situate about a mile from Amboise. The centre is very long, and joined

---

[1] The minister who owed his power to Madame de Pompadour, the mistress of Louis XV. The Duc d'Aiguillon was the nominee of the new mistress Madame du Barry, de Choiseul having refused dealings with her.

to the wings by a Doric colonnade, and on the back front is a cascade of a quarter of a mile in length, supplied by an immense basin. Orders had been given that the house should not be seen, but Englishmen were excepted in the proscription. The ornaments, the gildings, the glasses, the library, the theatre, and the concert-room are exquisite, but the little cabinet of madame is a work of witchcraft. It is about ten feet long, totally inlaid with ivory, ebony, and every elegance in miniature. The Duchess herself is the prettiest fairy imaginable, and the chairs and tables in the cabinet are so adapted to four foot five, that I had some doubts whether I was in France or in Lilliput. The stables contain one hundred horses, and many English ones ; and the dairy, the cow-house, and even the dog-kennel, are elegant to a proverb.

On Friday, June 16th, at four o'clock in the morning, we rode to Tours. I inquired for my Lord Castleconnel at M. l'Abbé Solas'. I was told M. l'Abbé was in his bath, but might be spoken with. I entered a bed-chamber, in the corner of which was a tub covered with blankets, and terminated by a meagre yellow French face in a nightcap. In the course of this literal *tête-à-tête* the *head* told me " My lord was in the country, but that there were two Englishmen in pension (with *it*, the aforesaid ostensible head), who would be happy to meet their countrymen at dinner." I acquiesced almost from curiosity, to see whether the *head* had a *tail*, and was agreeably surprised to stumble upon Welldon, an old college acquaintance, in the person of one of his boarders.

We viewed the new bridge of fifteen arches, not yet finished, and designed on the same noble simplicity of style with those of Blois and Orleans. The walk on the Boulevards, or Mall, is a mile in length. The Church of St. Martin is one of the most ancient in Christendom, situate deeply in the rock. While we were viewing it a priest offered to say a mass for us *as travellers*. The Palace of the Bishop is a fine structure, and the head of St. Benoit is to be seen at the Benedictines' convent. I reconnoitred Newnham's old lodgings in the Place de Bâune, and lounged away an hour or two in the magazines, where they wind the silk from the cocoons. On the mountain facing the town is an immense convent of Capuchins, and another of Benedictines, called the *Marmoutiers*, and said to be one of the richest of France. Among other reliques and treasures we saw there a little of the holy oil of the Sainte Ampoule of Rheims, used for the anointing of kings, and brought to St. Remy by an angel at the Coronation of Clovis I., A.D. 484.

The prospects on the banks of the Loire from Amboise to Tours are highly picturesque. Immense rocks on each side, excavated into dwelling-houses of three, four, nay, five stories, tapestried with vines, and here and there an old feudal castle in ruins, hangs over the summit. We enjoyed this scene heightened with the sublimity of a dark thunderstorm. It was a subject for the pencil of Salvator Rosa; but it wetted the connoisseurs to the skin.

On Saturday we returned to Blois, having seen in

our way the château of the family of Chaumont, situated most romantically. The ancestor of this family (Chaumont d'Amboise) put Francis I. in possession of Franche Comté, after the Emperor Maximilian had broken the truce, A.D. 1479.

Mrs. Hennesy is one of the most agreeable women in the world, and speaks the best French and English I have heard. Her daughter, a pretty, pale, melancholy girl of seventeen, told me in bad English, though good Irish, "how happy she should be to see her *own* country, for that she was born at St. Germains." Hennesy was in the Brigades, and I met an old Colonel Morris there who had been a prisoner at Hull in the year '45.

We have had processions by dozens of late. On the *Fête de Dieu*, the houses were hung with tapestry, and at every corner altars or *reposoirs* were erected, with a variety of flowers, pictures, etc., etc., shaded with a sail-cloth extended across the street.

On Monday last ·the children who had received their first communion preceded the *bon Dieu*, habited, according to the French idea of angels, with wings and coronets.

On Tuesday the *Train Bands* of Blois were under arms. Two new pairs of colours were solemnly carried to the cathedral, and received the benediction of the Bishop.

On Wednesday we had a fair of beasts; and I was much pleased with the gaiety of the peasants, who dance *cotillons* with more natural ease than even Mr. Villeneuve's scholars.

Osgood wrote me word he was to quit Orleans on

Tuesday with Ellison and Hamilton. He is by this time at Paris, and where to go next, to use his own melancholy words, "the Lord only knows." To say the truth, he appears to be heartily chagrined at his tour, the natural consequence of an inactive residence at that stupid town of Orleans, where an Englishman never got into French society.

But I must not forget the chapter of cookery. We have made punch of the brandy of Cognac, a town in our neighbourhood, and more famous than Nantes. We have had excellent syllabubs, and beg the receipt of your gingerbread nuts.

To-morrow we are to have a *fête*, a procession, and a firework in honour of the Coronation, and the evening is to conclude with a masked ball.

There are two young Englishmen arrived here; but as we observe the French etiquette in expecting their visit, and they, perhaps, preserve the English one in expecting ours, it is possible we may not be acquainted. I hope I have given an instance that it is the sort of society I do not seek in France.

I have just received a letter from Burland with a very vague direction. I have just answered one of Isted's in most execrable French; and I must put a period to this.

With duties and loves respectively to my mother, father, and sister.

*July 29th*, 1775.

I DID not receive yours of the 16th instant till yesterday, in consequence of a little tour I had made for a week, and which I shall journalise after I have thanked you for the entertainment your two last letters afforded me. English politics and English gingerbread are highly relished in France, and when you have leisure to descend to a more confined circle I shall be happy to hear what society you have at Epsom.

I am pleased to hear my sister admits Cardinal de Retz and Bishop Latimer to her toilette, and hope she recurs sometimes to the little sketch we made last summer among the solitudes of Bradenham, since history, without chronology, is the merest chaos imaginable, when she has a mind to discard cardinals and bishops for fossils and minerals. I am sure the translation of the "Spectacle de la Nature" will afford her more useful entertainment than all the אשובאבה of Monsieur Catcott. Philosophy ought to be dressed in a slight French *déshabillé* to please the ladies, and not stuck up in the formality of system and hypothesis.

But now (as Robinson Crusoe says) to my Journal. June 2nd was observed throughout this kingdom as a *fête* in honour of the Coronation, and in consequence Blois had a bonfire, a firework, and a procession. We had a masqued ball at night, where your humble servant appeared as an English jockey, and the streets were filled with serenades till sunrise.

On Thursday, the 20th, I accepted an invitation *to assist at a fête* at Pont-le-voy, a neighbouring convent of Benedictines, who superintend the education of near three hundred boys in all the languages and exercises. This community has succeeded to the charge formerly held by the Jesuits throughout France, and does a great deal of honour to its establishment. The boys wear a uniform, and are lodged, boarded, and instructed in classic learning, drawing, fencing, riding, dancing, and music for about thirty guineas per annum. I found there a little boy of the name of Bagly, who said he was a nephew of my Lord Sandwich. I found there, too, a wild Irishman, who, under the title of L'Abbé M'Carthy, taught a jargon he called English. The *fête* was given in honour of the prior on the Feast of St. Victor, his patron.

The good old man is much beloved by the children, who run for his benediction whenever he appears among them. After we had heard mass and dined most elegantly, two comedies written on the occasion were presented in a theatre constructed with a great deal of taste. After supper a monk conducted each stranger to an apartment, and mine was so inquisitive about Monsieur *Vilkes*,[1] that I got no sleep till one o'clock.

We were waked by three volleys of musquetry by the scholars under arms, with drums beating, and colours flying. From ten to twelve they appeared in the *manège*. At one o'clock we dined with the prior, and the ladies of the neighbouring country from five to eight were again entertained in the theatre, and the evening concluded with a firework. The young French ladies laboured hard for a dance; but as it could not be permitted in the convent, we seceded to the green

---

[1] John Wilkes.

before the village, and played at blind man's buff (for it was little better) till daybreak.

On Saturday Lutaine and myself left Pont-le-voy, and crossed the river Cher at Montrichard, a pretty village brow-beaten by an old feudal castle, and arrived at Aigues-vives, a convent of the Chanoines Réguliers situated in a deep valley and screened by woods.

There was an air of religious melancholy without, but within there were merrymaking, good wine, and great hospitality. In the evening we rode to Chenonceau, a château singularly constructed across the river Cher. It is absolutely a bridge of seven arches, and was built by that restorer of the fine arts, Francis I., and given to his favourite mistress, Diana of Poitiers, afterwards Duchess of Valentinois. The scenes around it are the most picturesque imaginable, and her name has afforded a thousand devices in the palace and gardens. On our return to Aigues-vives we contrived to lose our way, and if I had not recognised a broken crucifix by the roadside we might have wandered all night.

On Sunday we paid our respects to a monastery of Chartreux. Every monk has a separate cottage and garden, lies on straw, and wears no linen. They never eat flesh, and observe a perpetual silence. Our conductor talked, but his brethren covered their faces with hoods on our approach. He gave us a good dinner of fish and roots, a supper of milk and fruit, and lodged us in a handsome apartment.

I withdrew myself the next morning from the gloom of a cloister to the racket of a squad room, having received an invitation to Celles from a young cornet in the late Dauphin's regiment of cavalry.

The Château of Celles is superb, and was built by Maximilian de Béthune de Rosni, in 1641. He was Prime Minister to Henry IV., and ancestor of the Countess, who is now pleading her famous process at Paris. I found in the great gallery a profusion of Greek, Roman, Etruscan, Egyptian, and Indian antiquities, most whimsically confused—Lachrymatories crowned with sphynxes, and Dianas grouped with pagods. Europa, too, had mistaken the bull Apis for Jupiter, and had almost got astride his Egyptian godship. But the enormities in the chapel were still more amusing. Cicero's head (by the sympathy of eloquence, no doubt) had got upon St. Paul's shoulders, and a Messalina, without the process of penitence, had been converted into a Magdalene.

On leaving Celles I repassed the Cher in a ferry boat at a village called Theseé, and visited an immense Roman work at the distance of half a league, supposed to have been built by Labienus, as a station for his cavalry.

The Curate of Soin, who is a perfect Vicar of Wakefield, received us with the greatest hospitality, and we spent the next day in reconnoitring the Roman camps, etc., in his parish. We fished in the evening on the great lake, and were forced into shelter by one of the most terrible storms of thunder, rain, and lightning I had ever seen. On these occasions the peasants fly to the church and ring the bells—a principle so totally unphilosophic, that I expected we should have had the steeple about our ears in an instant. At midnight the old curate went out, in spite of the inclemency of the weather, and recited the Passion of our Saviour before the image of St. Fiacre, amid his trembling parishioners, the result of which was, as you will believe, an immediate calm.

We left Soin yesterday, passed Brasseux, and arrived at Chambord, a vast palace belonging to the King, in the midst of an extensive forest. Mareschal Saxe retired hither after the Peace of Aix-la-Chapelle, and died here about twenty years ago, from whence his body was transported to Strasbourg. His two regiments of horse and infantry were always stationed here, and disciplined in camp under his eye. He was allowed a bodyguard, and, in short, maintained the pomp of a king in this princely retreat. The château is very old but regular, and totally unfurnished, which is always the case where His Majesty does not actually reside. The grand staircase is a double screw, by which means two persons may ascend and descend without meeting each other. There is an idea of this kind in miniature at my Lord Bessborough's at Roehampton, but the construction is totally different.

The Province of Berry is beautifully fertilised, well watered throughout, and ornamented with a profusion of poplar, walnut, and acacia. The Sologne is sandy, but very populous, and the good old curate assured me he had frequently married peasants when they had begged the twenty-four sous for the surplice fees.

The heats have been excessive, and I am burnt to a good French complexion. The wheat harvest is over, and we have had a plentiful one of hay, which is brought from the fields on mules, which are so entirely covered as to appear like walking haycocks. I often think of Birnam Wood, when I see a field stalking very deliberately up the High Street.

I had the curiosity to ask the price of poultry at Brasseux, and found a fat goose was fifteenpence English, and a fat fowl fourpence; yet in spite of fat geese and fat fowls the poor live upon bread and water from Monday to Sunday.

If you encounter the family of Talbot I beg you will present my compliments, as well as to all other inquirers.

BLOIS, *August* 19*th*, 1775.

THE posts of France are very capricious; for your last letter, though on paper of the usual size, was charged double, as I suppose the words "single sheet" lost their efficacy at Calais. But the contents were too precious to be overrated, as I had no authority for the American news but the Republican fury of an Amsterdam Gazette.

With respect to Mr. Ratcliffe, Lutaine has no apartment for a second pensioner, and I know of no other establishment in Blois either decent or agreeable. I do not say this because I am interested in preventing the arrival of an Englishman, as the only circumstance to retard and perhaps totally defeat the progress I begin to make in the language, but you will remember that I quitted even Osgood on those reasons. I avoid Burvill in company, for it is not the French of an Englishman that improves the style, though it supports the practice. I have avoided, too (by perhaps too nice an etiquette), the acquaintance of Sir Harry Gough and a Mr. King, who pass the summer here; but I find my account in not having articulated my mother tongue for nearly three months. I trust you will give a delicate colouring to these ideas, in order to divert Mr. Ratcliffe from Blois.

Amboise has very little French society. Angers is full of young English, and is perhaps the most dissipated provincial town in France. Bourges, the capital of Berry, has a thousand *agrémens* for an Englishman. I may mention Auxerre in Bourgogne, where Osgood is agreeably settled at present with a Mr. Pallet, an Italian. I believe he will leave it in the vintage to continue his tour towards Provence and Languedoc, and he is the only Englishman at Auxerre. They speak French in as much purity in Burgundy as here, and indeed Dijon has a prevailing character.

The pensions in France run from ten to three Louis d'ors per month. Those on the banks of the Loire are perhaps the dearest, as most usually filled by the English. Perhaps you will feel the truth of this observation when I desire you will enclose me one of Mr. Herries' bills in your next, as by the 10th of September my stock will be reduced to about one hundred and thirty livres.

I do not forget the preliminaries we had settled with respect to entering upon the little legacy of my aunt for the extra expenses of my tour; for while I am conscious of no misapplication, I cannot be chagrined at such an arrangement.

I passed four or five very agreeable days last week at the château of M. la Vallière. 'Tis in these domesticated visits one Frenchifies most. The house was full of company; and as Mademoiselle Chartier, a very pretty girl of seventeen, was to sleep in the room we supped in, and as Messieurs liked their Burgundy too well to leave it very early, she very fairly retired to the other end of the apartment, undressed, went to bed, and after having sung us two or three songs in her nightcap, fell asleep with all the politeness possible. I believe all this may be right; but such is the affinity between exquisite refinement and exquisite barbarism, that Paris and Otaheite are nearly on a level.

We have as yet had no rejoicings for the birth of the Comte d'Angoulême, and are perhaps to have none, as the royal bed has not yet been blessed with a Dauphin. However, at all events, Blois is going to be very gay, for the fair will commence in a fortnight, and the managers of the *comédie* and other spectacles are already making their preparations. We expect to see even the more distant neighbourhood, though the town, as on the great highroad to Spain, is in a continual fluctuation of new faces. Among others, I had the satisfaction of seeing that of the famous Miss Cardière, whose process made so much noise in Europe many years ago. She was on her way to her house at Tours, and has the remains of a beauty.

The Duc de Chartres, who is now making the tour of

the ports on a kind of naval review, purposes to institute, on his return to Paris, a race of French horses, on the plan of our hunters' plates. I have as yet seen no breed fit for the turf. The cavalry are decently mounted, and Normandy supplies a tolerable sort for draught, but the ordinary labours of agriculture, etc., are performed with oxen, asses, and mules, the latter frequently fifteen hands high. The French ladies, who have no ideas of an English huntress, don't scruple to mount an ass in the country. They often ride astride, and with cotton in their ears, for the amiable animal brays during the whole afternoon. You will coincide in the transition from asses to *petits maîtres*, of whom we have just received a fresh importation from Paris.

The ladies are never behindhand. Their head dresses are more extravagant than ever. The cap is a frame of wire erected on the back of the head, and covered with flowers in the form of an espalier. The hair is cut short on the forehead and temples for two inches before the *toupée* commences, and a curl, called the *sentiment en bas*, descends to the collar bone. Add to this rouge and patches, and the *tout ensemble* is not human. But such is the force of custom that I begin to regard it even without horror.

I am ashamed to have said so much and so little; but, to use your own expression, "there is no honey in the hive."

BLOIS, *Tuesday, September 5th,* 1775.

YOUR last kind letter which I received (undated) last night was an "Iliad" in a nutshell. Your own descriptions, the florid manner of my Cousin Charity, and the less luxuriant, though not less emphatic, style of Sir Robert Herries and Co., have an equal claim to my acknowledgments.

I am obliged to you for every *finesse* that may prevent an Englishman's joining me at present; and in answer to your kind intentions of sending me a Court Kalendar, I hope to receive one by Mr. Burvill's nephew.

Sir Harry Gough and Mr. Keen (son of the Bishop) lent me the two last magazines, a detail of the killed and wounded in America (among the former of whom I see the name of young Gardiner, whom I knew in the Marines at Portsmouth), and the defence of Perreau.

They have spared me some English tea, though I am naturalised at present to a French breakfast. They have a packet of James's powder; but as they have lost the directions, we are ignorant how to administer it in case of necessity.

Mrs. Whatman's death shocked me greatly. I saw her husband's name lately mentioned in the *Paris Gazette* as the manufacturer of those immense sheets for Edwards' print of the interview between Francis I. and our Henry VIII. near Calais.

In return for the gaieties of Leatherhead and Epsom, I shall chronicle those of Blois, which began on the Vigil of St. Louis, August 29th.

St. Louis is the patron of the Cathedral; and the *fête* was really magnificent. The church was richly tapestried, the most costly relics exposed, and a concert of instrumental music accompanied the whole service.

In the evening we danced quadrilles at M. Girot's, and paid our compliments to Mademoiselle Louise on the anniversary of her patron. They present nosegays on these occasions, and my Muse made a very awkward attempt for the first time in French verse.

The fair commenced the day after, and is, at present, in its meridian. The grand square and principal street are covered with booths and bedizened with tapestries of a thousand colours. The shops are baited with every kind of trinkets; but as a fairing extends no farther than a box of bonbons, one may keep female company with impunity. At five the spectacles commence; and first the comedy, which is very respectable. They have already played nearly all the best pieces of Voltaire, Molière, Diderot, Piron, and Belloy; and it is with shame I feel how universally we have plagiarised in our modern productions.

The French tragedy is reformed almost to coldness; but the conduct is pure and regular. Their after-pieces are the merest farces imaginable, and nothing is too trivial for their intrigue. The subject of that of last night was a man who walks in his sleep. The situations produced by the sleep-walker were highly ridiculous, but too pantomimical for the caprice of the British theatre, who sometimes cite Mr. Foote to the tribunal of Aristotle; while honest Shakespeare is even adored for his breach of the unities.

The comedy closes by supper time. At half-past ten you whip on a domino, and run your nose into the first house where you hear a fiddle, or amuse yourself in the fair (which is covered with an awning and illuminated) till midnight. The *maréchaussée* patrol the streets till sunrise, to the no small molestation of sundry amorous scrapers who serenade their mistresses.

My friend, Lord Lewisham, and Mr. Legge, his brother, passed through Blois about ten days ago in their route to Tours, the former on his way to Italy, etc.

I find, for the first time, a want of subject; and I am proud of the symptom, since it is a hint that I am naturalised a little.

I could, indeed, send you instead of news the King's economical regulation of the posts; instead of anecdotes the wicked life and conversation of a French punch, who is no ways inferior to that reprobate our countryman; and for descriptions, I could paint the banks of the Loire clothed, as they now are, with grapes.

In short, and you will believe it readily, I could write you a great deal of nonsense, but I am persuaded you had rather I should go to the comedy, which is always a lesson in the language.

I would take French leave if it did not deprive me of an opportunity of expressing my duty to my mother and father, and my love to mademoiselle, and of assuring my dear sir that I am his very affectionate son.

COLLIVEAU, NEAR BLOIS, *Tuesday, September 25th,* 1775.

I SNATCH half an hour from the singular dissipations of the vintage to thank you for the packet I received by Mr. Rockliff, who arrived here this day week. He is totally fresh, and promises to be decently tiresome. He is at present in my room at Lutaine's, in spite of a thousand resolutions to fix elsewhere in the town. However, I shall return to Blois in two or three days, and make a point of finding a pension for him; for speaking even French with an Englishman is but miserable work. You will disguise all these sentiments to his family and Mr. Kentish under the profession of a real readiness to serve him in many essential points.

Jean Jacques Rosseau has said that to see mankind one must prefer countries to cities. I have done still more than this. I have been dancing with the peasants for these five days. " Monsieur Anglais," as a novice, was an object of amusement. He was stript naked to tread the grapes in the wine-press. He was forced to *bleed* the *reservoir*. He was crammed with the *galette* or cake of the vintage. The men crowned him with vines, and the girls smeared his face with the lees. He was obliged to dance in wooden shoes, and was as gay and as dirty as possible.

Our fair closed, after my last letter, which, as I think, I wrote in its meridian. The town of Blois was instantly deserted for the autumn, and at present wears the face of contagion. I took the occasion of flying hither for a few days to the house of M. Pecqureau, a friend of Lutaine's, where I see the process of the season, and amuse myself in a very agreeable society, chiefly of females, the only pleasing, and perhaps the most edifying, mode of acquiring the language in any degree of delicacy.

In England it is possible to have even the whole morning to yourself when upon a visit in the country. In France it is so indispensable to be always together, that I write in continual apprehension of interruption from these same sprightly misses, who are dressed by six in the morning, and never quiet but when asleep. As for Rockliff, who is still less a Frenchman than I am, they call him Huron, Iroquois, Algonquin, and Albigeois.

BLOIS, *October 10th,* 1775.

I AM ashamed to pester you with another stupid scrawl so immediately upon the back of my last, and which promises to be equally barren of incident; but the receipt of yours of the 19th of September calls for my acknowledgments. The gloss of novelty is gone off; yet as you have agreed that these same scrawls, shabby and threadbare as they are, shall amount to a proof of health and good spirits, I scribble on with that providential maxim laid down by Mr. Shandy. "I begin," says he, "with inditing one line, and trusting to heaven for another." I reflect with contrition upon sundry enormous sheets I retailed to the broad sanctuary on my first arrival in these distant and hitherto unknown parts. The guilt was more flagrant, inasmuch as I came abroad with Horace's "Nil Admirari" in my head, and as you had warned me of (to use a word of Mr. Shenstone's) the Flocci-nauci-Nihilipification of your own sea journals. Beau Clincher's "June 1st, saw a whale," was but a type of the gorgons, hydras, and chimeras I met with between Blois and Brighthelmstone; but I may congratulate you on the tone of my correspondence at present, for the bitterness of description is surely past.

A young Englishman for his first four or five months here is upon the broad stare. Staring is over with me, and I begin to grin; so that between grinning and staring I make a plausible figure. Your opposition of turtle and *grenouille* is somewhat tyrannical. In point of epicurism Old England excels this country. I speak as to rarities; for it must be confessed the French are profound mannerists. The luxury of the table among us consists in its expense, whereas here the whole merit of the kitchen is a disguise.

I have seen but two pine-apples since I have been in France; and as for the turtle kind, they have not an idea beyond the lining of their snuff boxes.

I may say I was pleased to see the name of Edward Jekyll so advanced by the late promotion. *Apropos* of Mr. Rockliff, I have settled him in a separate pension, and had happily *finesse* enough to displease neither him nor Lutaine. He is as English as he can be, and of course I see very little of him. I should pay Osgood a very bad compliment to unite myself with an Englishman at Blois. He writes me word from Auxerre that he is very agreeably settled, and washes his feet in Burgundy.

The hangman is passing under my window; and as a modern biographer has thought it worth while to chronicle that character as it exists in Corsica, it may amuse you to define it in France, and then to draw the comparison (after the manner of Plutarch) with the Ketch of Great Britain. The post is sacred here, and approaches the *noblesse* in the right of using a sword, and the priesthood in being proscribed entry at all spectacles but that of the profession. If blood unsullied by improper alliances can ennoble, then I know of none so pure and uncontaminated, for a French hangman can marry none but a French hangman's daughter. Add to all this a bag, ruffles, embroidery, and (at Paris) a coach, and the Cham of Kamschatka is not so refined a personage. Thus much of hangmen.

The Bishop baptises to-morrow in all the pomp of Christianism six bells, newly cast for the cathedral. The *Te Deum* was chanted while the metal was in fusion; and as the Marquis and Marquise de Saumery stand godfather and godmother, I shall assist at the ceremony, and dine with the good Catholics. I have received the most singular civilities from that family, and have an invitation to pass a week at their château. Monsieur is governor of Chambord, and upon a firm footing at Versailles. Madame is the best-bred woman in France, and Mademoiselle has learned of somebody to say "God damn ye!" in English.

Barnard has no right to complain of me at present. I shall give good cause to Burland, Sneyd, Onslow, and Isted. I cannot give a stronger symptom of sterility than that I am about to write, the only interesting part of my letter—that of presenting my duty to my father and mother, and love to my sister.

BLOIS, *October* 24*th*, 1775.

YOUR letter of the 8th instant reached me in the country, where I had seen the close of the vintage in this part of France. My sister may ridicule our *orgies*, but I will answer for it she would not be better amused as a belle at the wells than as a *Bacchante* in the Blaisois. I am extremely sorry for the loss of Captain Bentinck, which is really a national one. I communicated your observations on James's powder to Sir H. Gough, and his servants have already profited by them. Those ingenious gentlemen had substituted Cognac brandy for the "d—d French wines," as they were pleased to term them, and the consequence was a fever, heightened by the dog-days. Their masters are now at Paris, on their way to England, with almost as little French as if they had passed their summer at Brighthelmstone.

Mr. Rockliff and myself are nearly in sole and peaceable possession of Blois, and I wish I could say he is as content with his situation as I am. We are upon the best terms in the world, and I do not see much of him. When the town is fuller of amusements I hope to see even less, as he speaks French so much worse than I do, that it is equivalent to talking English together.

I am glad to hear Barnard acquits me of neglect, and I wish I could persuade many of my other friends to be as reasonable as he is. They should remember that I am not in France to write memoirs; and yet whenever Burland has a rainy morning in Somersetshire, whenever Isted has seen a new flame, or scraped acquaintance with a new title at Kettering Assembly, whenever Onslow has a brilliant thought for a new phaeton, the consequences fall upon my shoulders. Jekyll must write to all these miscreants. He must indite Hudibrastics to Onslow, he must mangle the French tongue to Sambo, and he must be comical to make the sergeant show his teeth.

I have returned my compliments by letter as politely as possible to Messrs. Rockliff and Kentish, and have seen transcribed by the former to his son (for he writes volumes) copies of those which passed between General Gage and *Generalissimo* Washington. I *exhausted* in my last epistle my animadversions on being *exhausted*. I have as ingeniously filled this *letter* with a recapitulation of *letters*. I am conscious of having said much and of having said nothing. But I am going to say what I hope will be always acceptable at home—my duty to my father and mother, and my love to my sister.

BLOIS, *November 7th,* 1775.

OUR letters have of late crossed each other on the road, but the consequence is not very material where the style abounds more in the relation than the dialogue. You mention a touch of my mother's gout. I should hope this will find the family in better plight. As for Mademoiselle, she can hardly have time to be ill amid the brilliances of the toilette, the course, and the ball. I agree with you on the risk our fair countrywomen incur in adopting the modes of this volatile kingdom. There is that sort of heroism in dress about a Frenchwoman that dares at singularity, while, on the contrary, the amiable tameness of a female spirit among us shudders at the attempt, and hardly enjoys the success. I seem to be writing to my sister at present, and right sorry am I that I have nothing new for her in the convent or matrimonial way. The latter is an universal topic at Blois; and the former, with the imagery of "sweet young virgins all in white, wax candles, and chastity," never fails to amuse the damsels of our little heretic island. I can only tell her that all the world here is running mad after a new undress, called "a Circassian," which is too pretty and too ridiculous for me to describe, if I was able.

I turn to more essential objects in addressing myself to you, sir; and I am sorry to say, that as you wish to see me complete in my exercises (the only point where the regularity of an English education is defective, and that a material one in public life), we have no academy, and consequently no *manège* at Blois. With respect to all other exercises, I have made such application that I hope you will have no reason to complain of my performances. I own it would please me much to ride with grace and dexterity; and, indeed, the want of instruction in that line, joined to that of the theatre, are the two only ones young Englishmen feel at Blois. But something must be always sacrificed; and perhaps the circumstance of being even intimate in a numerous and polite French society, which does not always happen, may be regarded in some degree as an equivalent. I agree, then, so far with Mr. Price, who tells Barnard he is sorry I am not in the *true way*, but we differ in definition, a material point in Polemics.

The Palace of Menârs, built by the late Marchioness of Pompadour on the banks of the Loire, at the distance of two leagues from here, and now in the possession of her brother-in-law, is one of the first in point of splendour in this kingdom, as you may conceive from its foundress, who, as the favourite of a great king, had the means, and joined to an exterior the most exquisite, that constitutional love of beauty which produces taste and order.

There had been a prohibition of seeing the apartments in consequence of some impertinences similar to those committed in the Queen's Palace at London. Mr. Rockliff and myself were informed of this by the *suisses* at the gate. Sap was impossible, and I changed the manœuvre to an assault. I inquired for the Marquis, and announced some English gentlemen of Blois who begged to kiss his hand. We found him in the gout and a nightgown, the latter sparkling with the Cross of the Holy Ghost. I blundered out, " How fortunate we were in having an occasion of paying our court to M. le Marquis de Marigny, on begging permission to see the most elegant château in France, which was the *universal topic* of travellers in *London*." The reply to this was in an excess of politeness ; and had I not urged the gout he would have stumped about the house with us. " This, gentlemen," said he, " is my library. Here is an edition of Terence, printed and given me by Walpole of Strawberry Hill. These chairs are English.

How beautiful is your manufacture of horsehair for the bottoms! This is the Hall of Kings. There are the portraits of Louis XV., Christian of Denmark, and Gustave of Sweden, given me by their own hands." I observed that "there was a panel vacant for George III., and that if Monsieur would honour London with a winter's residence he would not fail of filling it." "I do not despair of seeing London," replied Monsieur. "I was once so near paying you a visit that my house was hired there, and the wine even laid into my cellars, when my sister, the late Marchioness of Pompadour, sent for me abruptly to Versailles. 'Monsieur, my brother,' said she, 'sell your house at London, and all your affairs there. In less than three months we shall have their Hawke and Boscawen thundering on our coasts.' Amongst the infinity of fine objects you will see at Menârs, don't overlook the hydraulique machine I have lately constructed on an improved plan of your affair at Chelsea. The first agent in mine is water, and it is a masterpiece of mechanics that would do honour even to an English artist."

We took leave of the Marquis in the Hall of the Bourbons, hung with the portraits of that illustrious family from Henry IV. down to Louis XVI., and retired to the gardens till dinner-time, when the Marchioness usually rose, and when we might enter her apartments, for we were too undressed to assist at her toilette. Amidst a multitude of the most exquisite ancient and modern statues, I was peculiarly taken with the production of a young Languedocian, the figure of Phaëthuse turned into a poplar or aspen. The statue is colossal, and of the finest marble. The feet are rooted, the left side already enclosed by the bark, and the whole frame agonising. I was more touched at it than by the famous Daphne of antiquity. We entered the bed-chamber of Madame a few moments after she had left it. The bed was still in an interesting disorder; and while I was lost in the comparison of beauty which arose between the portraits of the Marchionesses de Pompadour and de Marigny, and the contemplation of a group of the most amiable pugs imaginable which belonged to the latter, the ideas of my friend had been swift enough to discover various articles of toilette. As there would be then no end of recapitulating all the striking objects we saw at Menârs, I cannot break off too abruptly.

BLOIS, *November* 21*st*, 1775.

I HAVE seized a half-hour before the departure of the post to give you some particulars of one of the most agreeable weeks I have yet passed in this kingdom. M. le Marquis de Saumery had invited me to pass a few days at his château. I believe I have already boasted of this acquaintance. He is Field Marshal, Governor of Chambord (the Windsor of the Blaisois), and reckons a descent from the ancient counts of Champagne, if not from Clovis himself. As it is not the good fortune of every young Englishman to fall into the best company in France, where only he is likely to get the best French, I embraced the occasion most readily.

I will not enter into the detail of etiquette observed in a French family of rank in this ceremonious country. Suffice it to say that *Monsieur* had a suite of five apartments allotted him, and was always preceded to table by an officer of the household.

The house was full of company. The morning is usually passed separately in the respective apartments. At one o'clock the young men assist at the toilette of Madame la Marquise; at two dinner is served; at five cards commence; at nine we supped; and after supper we had usually the *Comédie Bourgeoise*, or *Allemande*, till midnight.

The Duc de Choiseuil honoured Saumery with his company two days during my stay there. He appears to be the most agreeable of Frenchmen, and that is to say a good deal.

You may suppose I left this circle of gaiety and politeness with regret, and fortunately not without an invitation to pass my Christmas holidays in the same agreeable manner.

My last and this letter seem to have caught the contagion of the pride of French nobility; but I shall go on to tell you that in consequence of the credit which my footing at Saumery has given me in this country, I have been invited to pass a week with M. le Comte de Philepeaux at Herbault. Perhaps I need not tell you that this family has given fourteen ministers to the State. The Comte is nephew to the Duc de la Vrillière (the late Mr. St. Florentin), and brother to the Archbishop of Bourges.

I am almost led to recapitulate the advantages which result from good company in France when I reflect on the life my young countrymen lead here. All the morning on horseback, and all the evening gaming with low Frenchmen or lounging with strolling players. As to their exercises, it is a fact that we had an Englishman at Tours who took a lesson of whip-cracking every day from a postillion.

After so many dukes, counts, and marquises, you will not be surprised to hear the name of Sir Robert Herries mentioned.

At least, I will hint that December 10th is not far off, and that the keeping good company never made me lose sight of economy.

BLOIS, *December 12th*, 1775.

I WITHHELD my pen till I might be able to acknowledge the safe receipt of Sir R. Herries' bill for thirty pounds sterling, and am much hurt at the other contents of your letter. It found me in a round of gaiety, as you will naturally suppose, in this the gayest of countries, and you will as naturally conclude that it threw a damp upon my pleasures.

I did not want so unpleasing a motive to bid me think of home, especially as I am convinced that to become absolutely a Frenchman is the work of a much longer period than my future views can afford. I have been flattered—nay, perhaps, I had begun to flatter myself— that I should speak the language more fluently than the generality of my countrymen. I have not neglected my exercises. I have made myself acquainted with the history, customs, and government of the kingdom.

As to the present favourite point of travel, I can say that I have been fortunate enough to fall into what is called the first company, at the expense of what less economical young men would term very little gaming, very little dress, and very little gallantry, for such are the prices of *la belle société* in France. In the meantime, I must own that a stranger has but few occasions to be frugal. He is imposed upon by all the world, and without a certain expense can keep no company.

You seem to think with me that my visits to Saumery and Herbault ought not to be neglected. When they shall be paid, with all my debts, up to the middle of January, I do not believe I shall have a *sol* left for my journey to Paris. You seem to apprehend as much. I need not add that one does not see sights for nothing.

I dare not make the transition from money matters to America. The two subjects are too dismal, and I would willingly divert you if I could. I do not know whether you received my account of Menârs written in a livelier style than this can be, for I had not then heard of your illness.

The Bishop has shown me the most particular attentions of late. I translated that long letter of Burgoyne's to Lee for him, which pleased the old man so much, that I have dined twice a week at the palace ever since. The society is generally ecclesiastic. The Father Guardian of the Capuchins labours hard to convert me all dinner-time, and the Mesdames de L'Orge, who are let out of the Convent on Holy Days to dine with their uncle, attack me during the dessert. We contrive to steal a dance sometimes in a *salon* in the garden. "I don't know how it is," said Mademoiselle Victoire the night before last, "but I always feel sorry to think that our little Englishman is to be damned."

BLOIS, *February 6th*, 1776.

YOU will have learned from three importunate letters how much your silence had concerned me. I am to thank you for the bills and letter dated January 22nd, though the ill news of your health are still worse than my late suspense. I know the prejudice in favour of old practitioners, but I should be very happy if Dr. Parsons could be made acquainted with your case.

I hope you will not suppose I can amuse myself at Paris; and as to mere sight-seeing I am very expeditious. I stayed five weeks with the Marquis de St. Herem. We hunted the boar and the wolf very successfully till the snows came on. They have been prodigious. The thermometer of the Observatory of Paris marked three degrees of cold more intense than the winter of '49. Four couriers have been expected these three weeks from the North, and all travelling towards Germany and England has been obstructed.

An epidemic cold seems to have spread itself from London to Barcelona. In passing through this kingdom it has obtained the name of "grippe"—a term significant enough from the nature of its attack on the throat. I saw nothing but extreme unction at the Marquis' for the last four or five days.

I am very well at present, and hope to find you all so soon at London. I have letters to the Marquis de Montmorin at Versailles, Cordon Bleu. La Marquise is *dame d'honneur* to Madame d'Artois, so that I hope to see the court in its splendour, as the Carnival is not yet over. And I will carry home, if I can, some of its native vivacity to put you into good spirits.

My duty and love attend respectively my dear father, mother, and sister, and I rest theirs most affectionately.

Hôtel de la Dauphine, Rue Cocqueron,<br>Paris, February 14th, 1776.

NOTHING less than the delay of my passport permitted me to stay long enough to see Versailles and the raree shows of this volatile capital. My Lord Stormont sent it me express last night at eleven from the minister, and I shall set off in four hours for Lisle.

You will not be surprised that I take that route to Calais, when I tell you that I shall perform it in as little time, and shall have the company of M. de Rancoigne, a young *mousquetaire* I knew in the Provinces. I left Blois a very few minutes after the reception of your last letter, and nothing but bad weather shall retard me at Calais.

I hope to embrace you all very soon, and to see my dear father's health re-established.

# CHAPTER III.

## MR. JEKYLL TO LADY GERTRUDE SLOANE STANLEY.

SPRING GARDENS, *January* 13*th*, 1818.

WITH the Methusalems[1] I shall be in disgrace, for I have excused myself from three dinners—at Lord Malmesbury's, Hatsell's,[2] and Grenville's. My lungs were not equal to the first, nor my punctuality to the second, nor the drums of my ears to Lord Glastonbury at the last. Mrs. D'Oyly[3] has given them a dinner also, to which I was not invited, I suppose on the score of my *youth*. The poor old soul seems in her last dotage, though Mr. Sloane does not perceive it. "Sans eyes, sans voice, sans sense, sans everything." I do not understand one word she says, and I believe she is in the same state as to what she says.

---

[1] An expression often used by Mr. Jekyll in writing of his older acquaintances. The chief of the Methusalems were the first Earl of Malmesbury, who died in 1820; the first Lord Grenville, died 1834; the first Lord Glastonbury, died 1826; the sixth Earl of Stair, died 1821; and the Dowager Countess of Essex, died 1821. Some of these were only Mr. Jekyll's contemporaries, but they apparently did not preserve the same youthfulness of spirit.

[2] John Hatsell, Clerk of the House of Commons, author of "Precedents of Proceedings in the House of Commons, 1794-6."

[3] The daughter of Mr. Hans Stanley of Paultons. Her mother was daughter of Sir Hans Sloane.

You had no loss in Foscolo,[1] with all his learning and talents; he is what Dr. Johnson called a "tremendous companion," uttering with the clamour of a speaking trumpet a jargon composed of every language under heaven, and never combined before since the Tower of Babel. At Holland House they grew dead sick of him.

There is a gentleness and almost infantine innocence in the look of your poor little sister-in-law. You and I know ladies who take the *ton* of the tigress and hyæna; she takes the Lamb-*ton*.[2]

As I am, you know, a bad Picton, I borrowed Blomberg's cabriolet at the Pavilion, and an equerry drove me out daily, and one morning I visited my old school-fellow Lord Chichester, four miles off. We had Bishop Pelham and his wife at the Pavilion dinners every day. It seems in his Palace at Exeter she never rises from her seat to receive his visitors. The fat wife of a prebendary came to dinner one day about dusk, and as Mrs. Pelham was in white, and sitting motionless on a white dimity sofa, the reverend Fatima sate down upon her.

If it were not for the eleemosynary toast and butter of Paultons I daresay old Phil had rather be at the twopenny gossip, the threepenny Loo, and the sixpenny

[1] Nicolo Ugo Foscolo, author of "Ricciarda," and a commentator on Dante.
[2] The wife of Lady Gertrude's brother Frederick, who fell at Waterloo, the "Gallant Howard" of "Childe Harold." She was a Miss Lambton, and made a second marriage with the Hon. H. C. Cavendish.

balls of Southampton. My excellent old Birdy delights in it also, and these old creatures are as fond of dressing themselves out as if their shrouds were not likely to be their next garments.

God bless you and the dear children; remember me to William sincerely.

P.S.—Lord Erskine[1] almost quacked himself to death at Oatlands last week with hemlock pills, fainted at dinner, was bled profusely, and would have been bled more profusely if Yarmouth, who turned doctor, had been listened to. I believe they recovered him with difficulty; and to survive hemlock and such a physician's advice was no mean struggle of nature.

Spring Gardens, *February* 19*th*, 1818.

By the time the celebrated residence is to be taken for you in town I hope we shall have something better to amuse you here than daily murders and suicides. Yesterday died the unfortunate Mrs. Thackeray, whom Sir R. Croft[2] attended, and at whose house he shot himself. That catastrophe has never been known to her.

"Hat Vaughan"[3] has been nearly murdered in the street, and his illustrious hat stolen. The thieves have been tried and acquitted. It is supposed the jury

---

[1] Thomas, first Lord, the eminent lawyer. He lived till 1823.

[2] The accoucheur who attended the Princess Charlotte at the confinement which ended in her death. There was an angry outburst of public feeling against Croft, which drove him to suicide on February 13th of the same year.

[3] John Taylor Vaughan.

thought they took it only "as a matter of curiosity." Tom Stepney will now live in alarm if the *dilettanti* are collecting specimens.

On Saturday last Lord Morpeth and I dined at Mr. Sloane's, with sundry Methusalems. The hand of Cowland was manifested in the cookery, and the fingers of Joseph[1] in the glasses. Smith gave Mr. Hailes a knock on the pate with "the Infernal Machine" he burns one dish with while the rest are freezing; and as he took it back he nearly singed off the only nine hairs General de Bude boasts of on the side of his left ear.

Lord Holland[2] will not benefit much by Lord Ossory's Ampthill estates, from what he tells me. It will maintain the residence there; but as *Miladi* will probably proceed to decoration and furniture, her inauguration may be costly.

Pinney's father, who was the image of Sinbad's Old Man of the Sea, is no more, and "the fortunate youth," now at Rome, inherits from him I know not how many millions. They speak seriously of £25,000 a year; he may buy the Coliseo.

There is no enthusiasm in the public about *Fazio*;[3] and the author complains they have cut out his best

---

[1] Two of Mr. Sloane's servants. Mr. Jekyll found much to criticise in his father-in-law's *ménage*.

[2] Henry, third Baron, the nephew and pupil of C. J. Fox.

[3] By Milman. The play was acted without his permission, and he disclaimed the alterations made in the acting version. He had no reason to complain, however, as the representation resulted in the sale of three editions of his play.

poetry to give time for starts and attitudes and screams and hysterics. Lord Byron, too, in the "Bride of Abydos" has been sacrificed to processions and elephants of pasteboard. So I have nothing good to report in the higher walks of the drama but a French puppet show in Spring Gardens the boys dragged me to t'other evening. And so ends my prose.

SPRING GARDENS, *Saturday, October* 31*st*, 1818.

THE Duchess of Devonshire[1] is returned to Italy. The Bessboroughs asked me to meet her at dinner, and I saw her one day at Lord Guilford's. She is grown quite a hag. I believe I told Mr. Sloane there is a good story of Lord Melbourne's marrying Lady E. Monck.

Nothing can be more critical than the state of Lord Ellenborough.[2] It is supposed that while in his carriage on Wednesday last he was visited by palsy, as on quitting it his leg seemed nearly useless. Lady E. has been told by the medical men that she must prepare to expect the worst, and speedily, if these symptoms proceed. I have chiefly lamented my confinement, as it has disabled me from rendering her some consolation and support, for I have lived intimately with them many years. Their eldest son, however, is come from his poor sick wife in Ireland.

I have been disappointed at the "New Tales of my Landlord,"[3] but pleased with some of Mrs. Opie's[4] last

---

[1] The second wife of the fifth Duke, *née* Lady Elizabeth Hervey
[2] Edward, Lord Chief Justice. He died two months later.
[3] The second series containing "The Heart of Midlothian."
[4] "New Tales."

published series. You may suppose I have devoured much trash during my imprisonment. A single volume of the entire "History of France" for young persons is advertised.

We know of no successor[1] to the Chief Justiceship. I suppose Sir Claude Hunter[2] will ask for it, as he was disappointed about the Governorship of Cowes Castle.

Horace Walpole says "Miss Chudleigh cried." George Selwyn said, "Oysters?" Dr. Johnson has the same joke, I find.

> "If the man who 'Turnips' cries
> Cries not when his father dies;
> It is plain that he had rather
> Have a turnip than his father."

And so, my dear Lady Gertrude, I will put a period to this piebald epistle, which looks like a harlequin's jacket.

SPRING GARDENS, *December 7th*, 1818.

THE system of poisoning the guests who infest country houses I do not disapprove of; as, generally speaking, these animals invade any hole or corner where they see an opening, and by their talent at boring know how to make one. All I object to is killing them like Polonius "behind the arras," because then, as Hamlet says, "you may nose them in the lobby." Some of

---

[1] Mr. Justice Abbot was appointed the following November.

[2] Alderman Sir Stephen Claude Hunter, Bart., son of Henry Hunter of Reading, a connection of the Sloane family through his mother, who was a great-niece of Sir Hans. He was a very prominent solicitor, and Lord Mayor 1811-12, when his show was exceptionally elaborate. Died 1851.

them who must have been Lord Mendip's[1] contemporaries, I take it for granted were found full dressed.

They speak of an entertaining book not long published, "A Tour to La Trappe and through La Vendée."[2] Those fools[3] are grown more austere since they starved at Lulworth. Is Baring converted that he builds hermitages? He must emaciate considerably before he can personate an anchorite himself.

Lady Morgan's[4] "Florence McCarthy" I have not yet read, but languish for the portraits of the Irish Chief Justice Norbury and Mr. Croker.

*Les ouis dire* in politics for the last week have been plentiful and extraordinary; but as through life I have uniformly disbelieved, in the first instance, whatever is told me as curious, singular, and remarkable, and have as generally found such incredulity, five times out of ten, well founded, these reports have gained little credit with me. It is not the pure love of lying that generates these wonderful anecdotes, nor always the natural propensity

---

[1] Welbore Ellis, first Lord Mendip, the well-known politician of the school of Henry Fox. He married, in 1765, Anne, eldest daughter of Mr. Hans Stanley of Paultons.

[2] "A Visit to the Monastery of La Trappe," by W. W. Fellowes.

[3] The members of the Order of La Trappe. A number of these monks, who fled from France at the time of the Revolution, were received by Mr. Weld of Lulworth Castle, who gave them land, and provided habitations. They remained at Lulworth till 1815.

[4] An Irish lady whose maiden name was Owenson. She married Sir Charles Morgan, and was often spoken of by the title of one of her novels, "The Wild Irish Girl." Two of her works, "France" and "Italy," made some stir at the time of their publication. Their sale was forbidden in Sardinia, Rome, and Austria, and the authoress prohibited from visiting the latter kingdom.

to exaggeration; but a newsmonger thinks he increases his self-importance in communicating what another has not yet heard. As for political changes, like changing partners, it will probably only be among themselves, unless they can bait the hook for Lord Wellesley with his brother, the Duke;[1] and as for worthy gentlemen who may retire, I should think there will be some mouthing against pensions by our economists.

The Thane of Cawdor[2] and a full meeting in Pembrokeshire have, I see, published two discoveries of some novelty—that my countrymen are too prone to litigation, and that some attorneys are great rogues. Now "we did not want a ghost to tell us this." I hardly believe the Reformers of all things at Aix-la-Chapelle could prevent Welshmen from quarrelling, or make all attorneys honest; but the Lord have mercy upon the squires of the meeting if they should hereafter be forced into any Welsh law suits themselves.

The times have been gloomy to me—Lord Ellenboro's state; Romilly's[3] door I passed yesterday with a ring at seeing the two achievements side by side. Poor Disbrowe, too! The boys and I were under promise to visit him at Windsor next Christmas. A better husband and father never lived.

[1] The Duke of Wellington joined Lord Liverpool's Government in 1819.

[2] John, first Baron Cawdor. He married Lady Gertrude's eldest sister, Lady Caroline Howard.

[3] Sir Samuel Romilly, the eminent lawyer. He committed suicide on November 2nd, 1818, from grief at the loss of his wife a month earlier.

In spite of their losses, I find Opposition in high spirits as to their operations next campaign. Tierney was here yesterday. Brougham has just left me; and to show you I am not the only man of letters who writes an infamous hand, I made him frank this cover.

Kean surpasses himself in the new Brutus. Farren,[1] a comic actor, is highly spoken of. The lady *débutantes* are numerous, but not of great promise.

It is said Romilly left £150,000 to be divided into eight parts among his seven children, the eldest taking two parts.

Lord Ellenborough can no longer articulate nor keep anything on the stomach, so the crisis is nearly at hand. Lord Kilmorey followed his wife with a broken heart in four days, like Romilly. Want of conjugal affection does not seem the reproach of our days.

At a ball at Brussels given to the Sovereigns I read that the Dowager Empress of Russia danced with her son the Emperor, that at the end of the dance they fell into each other's arms, embraced tenderly, and wept. "Every one," says the *Moniteur*, "sympathised in this interesting scene." Woronzow[1] and his daughter must do the same at Almack's. As by the Holy Alliance the practice must come here, I can imagine many picturesque couples—Lady Liverpool, Lady Salisbury, Mrs. Bankes—waltzing and weeping with their respective offspring, Viscountess Dudley and Ward in a *reel* with John William, and shedding maudlin tears.

---

[1] William Farren made his *début* at Covent Garden this season, as Sir Peter Teazle.

[2] The Russian Ambassador, Count Woronzow.

Some few years hence your ladyship may suppose you have only to chaperon your daughters to balls. "Lay not such flattering unction to your soul." You must dance with Willy, and weep. Then you must dance with George, and at the close of "Molly, put the kettle on," you must clasp him to you, and pour into his bosom the residue of the tears unexpended upon Willy.

*Monday, December 28th,* 1818.

LORD LAUDERDALE has brought over a spick-and-span new poem[1] of Lord Byron's from Venice, sealed up, so the Scottish bearer, no great critic in works of genius, knows nothing of its merits. But Murray the bookseller has volunteered a great price for it. He says the poet is grown fat and cheerful, and comes to England next spring.

The great Rogers has also a poem of length ready for publication, entitled "Human Life," which his perpetual enemy Ward[2] will say can only have been composed impartially by a dead corpse.

Crabbe has also a poem coming out,[3] for which Murray, the Mæcenas of booksellers, has given him £1,000.

[1] The first Canto of "Don Juan."
[2] J. W. Ward, Lord Dudley. He wrote an unfavourable review of "Columbus" in the *Quarterly* for March 1813. This caused a coolness which was never removed, although Ward apologised. Rogers took his revenge in the epigram—

"Ward has no heart they say, but I deny it.
He has a heart, and gets his speeches by it."

[3] "Tales of the Hall."

A lawyer of eminence went to Milan last summer on a particular cause. This has been magnified into an investigation of the Princess of Wales' misconduct at the Lago del Como. The whole is a fable.

Lord Holland says Lord Morpeth never admired Crabbe, nor do I, so morbidly as Brougham and others do. I think also in private the man overacts simplicity of character; still I think he has vast talents at minute and characteristic scenes. If Rogers had not made him put his first payment from Murray of a third of the money into a banker's hands, he was going to carry it with him in a stage coach to show the banknotes to his son, and would probably have been robbed of the whole of it.

If in your accidental communications with Southampton you can inform poor Birdy,[1] without the expense of postage, that the boys and I are in perfect health, I shall thank your Ladyship, inasmuch as I cannot give her a line till I return from the Regent at Brighton a week hence.

Spring Gardens, *January 17th*, 1819.

As you have so amply atoned by a long and charming letter just received for all former sins of omission, I am determined to issue from my fireside an immediate absolution, especially as it will not cost tenpence, and the Pope sells one for half the money. Though I was nearly converted to the Romish Church

---

[1] A lady who had acted as governess to Mr. Jekyll's wife, Miss Maria Sloane

by seeing Harry Howard carry the Duke of Norfolk's *Baton de Mareschal*, which so clearly manifests the truth of transubstantiation.

W. Howard will tell you of a Methusalem feast he had yesterday, of which I have tasted plentifully within this month. Like Macbeth, "I have supped full of horrors." I upbraided Lady Stafford with adding to her climb-ax of antediluvians by inviting the Earl of Stair and the Countess of Essex. The latter I comforted with a glass of champagne, and Lord Stafford made her mouth water by producing the original warrant for beheading an Earl of Essex signed by Queen Elizabeth. However, Lady Stafford *en dédommagement* gives me a dinner again to-day with Ellis and Ward, and people born within the last century.

It is not only from Harley Street and General Grenville, but I have been dragged to these "Old Mortalities" at Fagel's, Carleton's, Henley's, Antrobus's; however, I am determined to emancipate myself from the catacombs and be pre-engaged for six months. On Sunday I dined with Lord Hertford, where we had only the Regent attended by Nagle. The Regent whispered me that the luminous equerry, who had been forced by "Chic" Chester to drink five glasses of brandy last summer at Cadlands, mistook the said Chic for me the whole time. To support this delusion I continued all Sunday to personate Chic, to remind Nagle of the brandy we tippled so freely; and finally persuaded him that nothing but a violent cold prohibited my renewal of the libation.

The robbery and ransom by banditti of Chantrey is all a fable. He told me that at the instance of Lady Davy and poet Moore on their knees, the Princess Borghese put her foot out of bed for his admiration as a statuary.

Walter Scott is to be a baronet; his "Ivanhoe" is said to deserve it.

I am interrupted, so this shall not pass for a letter.

Spring Gardens, *June 22nd*, 1819.

The most solemn ceremonies are held to be incomplete and unsanctified unless I assist at them. An infant named Louis Frederic Xavier Spiridion de Luzy could not be christened but by my attendance at its grandmother's dinner, the Marchioness Dowager of Lansdowne.

Parliament, it is thought, may end by the 15th of July, and in fact the political campaign is closed, and people are quitting town early. If there be not ratting, alas! there is rotting among my Opposition friends,—Lord Holland, still unwell with a lingering gouty debility, Tierney[1] obliged to abstain from debates, Brougham too much of an invalid for great exertion, and Mackintosh not the stoutest of men, though confessedly one of the most able and eloquent.

We had a profusion of boxes from Mrs. Coutts[2] at

[1] The Opposition led by Tierney had been recently defeated by a majority of 179 votes, in a trial of strength with Lord Liverpool's Government on the motion to inquire into the disturbed state of the nation.

[2] The wife of Mr. Thomas Coutts the banker. She was an

the close of the theatres. Mr. Sloane came to us in high glee several times. One night between the acts he made me a vigorous proposition: "If one could get a good packet," says he, "I should not dislike a trip to Bordeaux." It was in vain to ask why or wherefore, so I contented myself with the silent admiration of fidgets eighty years old. Robinson gave us a catacomb dinner on Saturday last; among other mummies Malmesbury and his sister, who are leaving town for Hants, Lady Malmesbury squalling that she has no country house of her own, and is therefore driven to Tunbridge. The Granthams are going to Spa.

Last night the Regent gave a ball to children, and the boys and I did not leave Carlton House till near three o'clock. An immense party of Lilliputians sate down to supper, so I suppose the apothecaries are by this time sending in all the old rhubarb and magnesia they are possessed of. Elderly fools began waltzing when the babes were exhausted. The Staffords, Morpeths, and Lady Carlisle were there. My boys and a dozen of their schoolfellows, the Russells, Pagets, Pelhams, and Amhersts, seemed to abandon the small misses, and bestow their tender attentions on chickens of a more eatable character.

Lord Yarmouth again takes the Duke and Duchess of York and a large party of us in the Admiralty barge

actress, Miss Mellon, and succeeded to his vast fortune on his death in 1822. In 1827 she married William, ninth Duke of St. Albans. She died in 1837, and bore the reputation of great charity. There is a most interesting account of a visit she paid to Walter Scott, at Abbotsford, in 1825, in Lockhart's "Life."

next week to stuff whitebait at the "Artichoke"¹ beyond Greenwich.

P.S.—Poor Dr. Latham.² It makes one quite miserable to think of his misfortunes. But I will say nothing more of calamities, for this letter is already blotted like an elegy.

Spring Gardens, *July 7th*, 1819.

Mrs. D'Oyly is still alive, and the fidgets of our young heir-apparent in Harley Street are indescribable. To the utter dismay of her servants, and with more caution than taste, he goes to Twickenham every other day armed with an attorney in his carriage; but it would be no miracle if she still lives another century, for Sir Henry Halford³ told me on Sunday at a dinner the Duchess of York gave us, that she had recovered her intellect, and that all disease was subdued.

On Monday last Yarmouth⁴ gave us his aquatics. The Duke and Duchess of York and a considerable crew of us embarked at the Tower in two Admiralty barges

---

¹ An inn at Blackwall noted for its fish dinners.

² John Latham, M.D. Physician Extraordinary to George IV. Mr. Jekyll probably alludes to his health, which was bad. He was a voluminous writer in medical subjects, and died in 1843, aged eighty.

³ A very successful Court physician. He was accused by his professional brethren of servility to his superiors and of rudeness to his inferiors, and was known as the "eel-backed" physician. When the coffin of Charles I. was opened he possessed himself of the cervical vertebra which had been severed by the axe, and was accustomed to exhibit it at his dinner table.

⁴ Francis, afterwards third Marquess of Hertford.

and two Royal Standards flying, for the "Artichoke" at Blackwall. As the digestion of whitebait exhausts the whole day, Lauderdale and I had ordered post-horses in the evening, so left the squadron to proceed up the river in the dark and contemplate the comet.[1]

From what one sees on Mondays and Saturdays at Lady Jersey's and Lady Castlereagh's, London does not yet feel its various departures. The Prince Regent gives us a Fancy Ball on the 15th in honour of St. Swithin. I heard two women last night, nearly of Philly's age, debating whether they should go in Spanish or Circassian dresses.

On Saturday the boys and I go for a couple of days to Holland House, as they visit Bowood the ensuing week. The Lansdownes meditate a month's stay at Paris in the autumn, and leave the partridges to amuse my former constituents at Calne. Lord Holland is quite well again.

It is believed Parliament will be prorogued on Monday next, I should think certainly not later than Tuesday, as Vansittart invites some of us to dine with him that day.

The brother poets Rogers and Moore were here to-day, and did not seem to think "Mazeppa" had added much to Byron's bays. I am charmed with it, and as much with the verses on Venice, which he strangely entitles "An Ode." At the tail of the book is an unintelligible piece of prose he calls "A Fragment."

[1] Encke's Comet.

In "Mazeppa" I think I discovered an anachronism. His hero alludes to "the electric wire" in a speech to Charles XII. of Sweden. Now I believe the Leyden Vial and its wire were not discovered till the year 1745. Crabbe's new tales I have not read.[1] A critic tells me the new series of "Tales of my Landlord"[2] surpasses the former.

A week ago, when we were dining with the Duke and Duchess of York, Erskine sent a sudden excuse. We learned afterwards he had run away with his illegitimates from their mother, who next day had the impudence to come to York House and inquire where her babes were secreted.

A splendid house is taken in Waterloo Place for a new club yclept "The Travellers." A candidate must have travelled five hundred miles from London and by land, or convicts from Botany Bay might have been qualified. To prevent any desertion from the club, I proposed they should elect Sturges[3] as president—" A bourne, from which no traveller returns."

I saw the last of Lady Stafford on Saturday at Lady Castlereagh's. She very kindly asked me to travel to Trentham this summer. I told her I should always

---

[1] "Tales of the Hall."
[2] The third series, comprising the "Bride of Lammermoor" and the "Legend of Montrose."
[3] William Sturges, who assumed the name of Bourne in succeeding to the property of an uncle in 1803. He was a political follower of Canning, and was Home Secretary in that statesman's administration in 1827. Although a bad speaker his advice was much valued in the House of Commons. He died in 1845.

travel to you; and when I have done that you know I never lengthen my tour beyond the great elm. Harry Wrottesley is named as one of the candidates for the vacant Welsh judgeship. As Leach, Sergeant Copley, and Warren have been successively appointed to the Chief Justiceship of Chester, they have christened Chester "The Rat Trap," and Cheshire Cheese enhances the value of the joke.

Among other miseries of Opposition, poor Perry of the *Morning Chronicle* appears to be quite broken up in health, and cannot last. Mackintosh[1] advanced daily in popular estimation, as much for sagacity and moderation as eloquence.

Spring Gardens, *October 15th*, 1819.

His excellency the Persian Ambassador, with that laudable curiosity which ornaments the functions of diplomacy, suddenly popped his black beard and turban, on Wednesday last, within the door of Westminster School. The boys ceased to gabble their Greek, and on the irruption of this formidable spectre burst into a fit of that immortal laughter which their Homer gives credit to the gods for. The master was indignant at this seeming insult to the Court of Persia, as it might tend to a breach of that peace and amity which fortunately subsists between the two empires, and the boys escaped whipping by miracle.

Mr. Sloane is in the height of his favourite element:

---

[1] Sir James Mackintosh. He had recently carried a motion for mitigating the law as to capital punishment.

a scrambling life, Mary's cookery and hackney coaches, and a *tête-à-tête* for picquet at night. I dined with them on Wednesday last, and cleaned my own wine-glass, upon which John had left his initials of finger and thumb. On Sunday I expect to meet these Methusalem Gemini at the Scandinavian Feast of old Woronzow, whom I met yesterday at Lord Guilford's, where we sate down twenty-five at dinner, with the noble Earl at the top of the table, whose new Ionian star and tri-coloured riband "streamed like a meteor to the troubled air."

It will require stronger evidence than I have yet received to convince me that the poor Duke of Richmond's[1] hydrophobia arose from the bite of any rabid animal. I admit that such a disorder exists in man, but not from such a cause. I did mean to rusticate with the boys as far as Holland House to-morrow and stay there till Monday, which, in honour of St. Luke and in defiance of Mr. Carlyle, is religiously kept as a holiday at Westminster; but Holland House is in much anxiety and distress. The youngest girl is in a very dangerous state of illness.

My poor Lady Ellenborough has reached Geneva on her course to Florence. A courier arrived at five in the morning, while she was in the inn at Frankfort, to say the Prince and Princess of Hesse Homburg would come and breakfast with her. It was kindly

---

[1] Charles, fourth Duke, Governor-General of Canada. He died there on August 28th, 1819, and, as is generally believed, from hydrophobia, resulting from the bite of a pet dog.

done, but an invalid could have dispensed with such a visit.

The Whigs are rubbing their hands and whetting their teeth for the 23rd of November, and it is believed that an illustrious lady [1] will arrive by that time to throw some of her magical ingredients into the cauldron, and give *petits soupers* at Kensington to Mr. Hunt.[2]

SPRING GARDENS, *November 17th*, 1819.

MUCH as I always delight in seeing you, it would be most unreasonable to expect that when you were making so momentary a transit through the metropolis you should be running after a fellow who is difficult to be met with at home in a morning. So I absolve you cordially on the principle of taking the will for the deed.

I have a cold, and as it was a miserable night sent an excuse to the Duke and Duchess of York yesterday, though they are in town only for three days, and I really wished to see them. Mr. Sloane would have been carried to dinner in blankets, but the Court of Chancery is as conspicuous for its prudence as its wisdom.

Think of me as a source of Newmarket news to William. Your own Lothario, Sir Thomas Charles Bunbury,[3] has lost his famous horse Thunderbolt,

---

[1] Queen Caroline.

[2] Henry Hunt, the Radical agitator. He was chairman of the meeting at Manchester in 1819, the dispersal of which resulted in what is known as the Peterloo massacre.

[3] The sixth Baronet, the famous sportsman, the divorced husband of the beautiful Lady Sarah Lennox. He died in 1821, aged over eighty.

brother to Smolensko, valued at one thousand five hundred guineas. The poor animal broke his leg in the stable, and was consequently shot. As I do not take in the "Racing Calendar" you will guess Birdy furnishes me with this intelligence. She is with me for a few days, and will recommence her Southampton routs and waltzes next week. I gently broke to her that in her absence there had been a blow of marigolds in the front of Mrs. Hamlyn, which had dazzled all who danced at her celebrated *fêtes* and *seguidillas*.

Extraordinary felony! The boys tell me a thief lately broke into Westminster Abbey and meant to pass the night there in depredation. Being disturbed in his purpose he fled, leaving behind him his hat full of cold beef and biscuits, but contrived to carry off the waxen effigy and royal robes of good Queen Elizabeth.

Surely you will come to town if there is a revolution, as such sights do not occur every day. Sidmouth has ordered all the cannon[1] which serve as posts in London to be sent to the Tower, lest they fall into Radical hands; and they have taken root so long that they are suspected to be Radicals themselves. The funds are to be annihilated at Christmas, and landed estates to be divided by Mr. Hunt in the spring. Your ladyship can set up a seminary for young *demoiselles*. I mean to have a theatre and write comedies and farces. Joseph and Edward[2] may tumble between the acts; and if they have already no engagement I am willing to take Gertrude and Freddy to

[1] An allusion to the Arms Bill.   [2] Mr. Jekyll's sons.

dance in my ballets. As I probably shall want Cupids to swing on ropes in the air, you may depend upon my taking also your smaller fry. The Game Laws will of course be abolished, and William's "occupation will be gone," like Othello's. He has therefore no gamekeeper's place. However, I think I can stick him in my orchestra; and if he has any gratitude he will give me continual obligatos on his violoncello. I am sorry for your friends among the clergy, but they may still get comfortable livings by writing and selling blasphemy, which seems the most profitable trade going.

P.S.—We had a jollification on Mrs. Coutt's birthday last Friday, near Highgate, graced by the Dowager Lansdowne. She had been to Paris to meet her daughter and Count Luzi. They have lost the little child at whose baptism, with a name longer than its life, the Duke of York, Lord and Lady Anglesea, myself, and other pious persons assisted in the summer. The Regent eats only fish and vegetables, abandons wine, and drinks punch.

SPRING GARDENS, *December 7th*, 1819

THE boys bring home from Westminster a shilling libel entitled "The Political House that Jack Built."[1] It has gone through twenty editions, and keeps four presses constantly at work. I am sorry to say it is formidable in point of seditious humour, and its cari-

[1] By W. Hone, illustrated by G. Cruikshank. It went through nearly forty editions. It is an incisive, if scurrilous, parody of the nursery rhyme.

catures on wooden plates are but too well executed, among them a severe one of the Regent. Heartily indeed, when I read ineffectual arguments, overwhelming majorities, and late hours of division,[1] do I rejoice that I am no longer a sharer in the purity of the House of Commons, where, as Mr. Pitt said when he was a Radical, "without reform no man of honesty could be a minister." It seems admitted by Government that there is no remedy for the distress of the lower classes as things are, so we must control them as they do at Algiers as long as the power lasts to do so. Lord Grenville, you see, takes a long date for disaffection of nearly thirty years back—a high compliment to his own and Mr. Pitt's conduct of public affairs, under which it took root and flourished into the fruit of to-day. What a senseless coalition was that of the Whigs and Grenvilles!

But I will cease to bore about politics, which is every way a frightful and disgusting topic. Thank God I have taken leave of them in public, and must now only suffer their evil consequences as a private man and a father.

*Je vois des deux cotés la fourbe et la fureur.*

VOLTAIRE.

We have Indian scandal. Don Moira[2] has forbid

---

[1] On the Arms Bill, the Training Bill, Libel Bill, etc. There was much anxiety at this time, as to the disturbed and discontented state of the country.

[2] The first Marquess of Hastings, at this time Governor-General of India.

Lady East, the Chief Justice's wife, to approach his court, for having connived at an intrigue of her daughter, who had made reprisals on her husband Mr. Croft's infamous seduction of a young lady during the voyage to Calcutta, and for which a jury gave enormous damages against him. To avoid the payment, it is added, the Chief Justice contrived to facilitate his worthless son-in-law's escape to Europe, and thereby so deeply incurred the censure of his learned brothers on the bench, that they refuse all private communication with him. I hope all this is not true; for I always respected the Chief Justice, but believe he was under the dominion of an unworthy wife. Probably you saw the trial in the papers; more ingenious villainy and hypocrisy never appeared.

Dowager Cork[1] writes to me for advice on a quarrel with her coachmaker, and steals an opinion because she is too far off to steal anything else. She has been quartering herself upon that lively person the Earl of Winchilsea, who has passed her to some parish in Yorkshire, and whose parson I hope will exhort her to say her prayers and pay Gunter, instead of chalking her floors and liveries for *fêtes* to all the fools in town. In the language of the Windsor doctors, the old creature's "bodily health is little impaired by age, but her disorder is unabated."[2]

May Heaven long preserve your intellect, my dear

---

[1] The eccentric Lady Cork, second wife of the seventh Earl.
[2] The bulletin of George III., issued during many years with little variation.

Lady Gertrude, though you live so much in the country. Several able anatomists assure me that on dissecting the brains of squires and rusticated beauties they have been found covered with moss and ivy, and which a few periodical alteratives of opera and Almacks would have extirpated.

SPRING GARDENS, *January 5th*, 1820.

THE *on dits* of the streets are amusing—that Lady Conyngham has superseded Lady Hertford,[1] that the Lord Chancellor will resign if a certain divorce be attempted, and that Lord Manners is to succeed him. In short, every sort of nonsense is talked and believed.

The poor Hollands have been again miserable about the illness of their only surviving daughter. However, she is out of danger.

The Mother-Bankes has manœuvred well for her parson,[2] and the Chancellor[3] gives him £30,000 with his daughter, and hereafter a prebend or deanery probably. Mr. Sloane met the old Bankes at the Staffords last week, Mrs. Bankes in all the vociferation of delight on the nuptials.

I have read "Don Juan." It is unequal, but abounding with most brilliant flights. They have printed Byron's entire works at Paris, comprising his suppressed poems.

I have also read amusing travels of poor Kotzebue's son in Persia.

[1] In the good graces of George IV.
[2] The Rev. E. Bankes, Prebendary of Gloucester and Bristol.
[3] Lord Eldon.

*January 7th*, 1820.

I DINED in company with Brougham[1] and wife. She has a good person, manners, eyes, and teeth, but is not handsome like her sister, Lady Graham Moore.

Peel has taken Lulworth Castle, and is advanced to £700 per annum rent. The Queen is treating with Prince Leopold for Marlborough House. Old D'Oyly well and merry. She showed the boys t'other day some drawings by her mother, a woman of extraordinary accomplishments, signed "S. Sloane, A.D. 1715."

Mrs. Coutts gave a Christmas dinner, as she called it, to the Duke of Sussex, Hat Vaughan, and other potentates. In the first course, a baron of beef, a baron of Glastonbury, and for side dishes two turkeys, two boars' heads, and a mince pie of the size of His Royal Highness, or J. T. Batt, Esq.

Belzoni's book[2] dull, but the plates interesting. Cleopatra's Needle is not to come from Egypt to Waterloo Place, as the portage would cost £10,000. That caitiff Chantrey has not yet washed your face, and Lady Pembroke is clean in comparison.

An invitation from old Coutts to celebrate the seventh anniversary of his marriage, and meet the Dukes of York, Clarence, and Sussex, the first and last well assorted.

The King well, but advantageously less bulky. Got into the Pavilion, and inviting people. God avert from

---

[1] Henry, afterwards Lord Brougham and Vaux. He married a widow, Mrs. Spalding, whose maiden name was Eden.

[2] "Operations and Recent Discoveries in Egypt and Nubia."

me a journey through snow to Brighton! for I am now shivering near a good fireside, and think every man whom cruelty asks out to dinner deserves part of the £10,000 given to Parry and his company for visiting the Polar circle.

I enclose some pretty verses of Anacreon Moore. The gallant Blessington writes this morning to request my name in a committee of Tories to erect an enormous monument at the Hyde Park turnpike to the fame and glory of George III., whose colossal figure is to be placed in a chariot drawn by four bronze horses on a pedestal supported by a vast rock of granite, surrounded with figures of fame, and Victory trampling on Discord; and emblems of his late Majesty's protection of education, agriculture, commerce, and the fine arts. Patrons: all the princes and princesses, above thirty ministerial and about five Radical peers, and concluding with John Julius Angerstein,[1] Sir J. Bland Burges,[2] Alderman Curtis, and Tegart the Apothecary. Though it may impeach my loyalty, I declined the proposed honour.

The Hollands have Lord Cornwallis' house in Burlington Street. I dined there yesterday, and *Miladi*

---

[1] The eminent merchant and patron of fine art. His exertions resulted in the establishment of *Lloyd's* on its present basis; and his collection of pictures formed the nucleus of the National Gallery.

[2] The politician, and colleague of Pitt, whose advice in matters of finance was of great service to the minister. A youthful attachment of Burges for Lady Margaret Lindsay inspired the poem of "Auld Robin Grey," written by her sister Lady Anne. Burges eventually married Lady Margaret as a third wife. He died 1824.

illuminated us with her presence almost till coffee appeared. A Tory Sunday paper called *John Bull* much circulated, said to be edited by Theodore Hook, full of broad anecdotes against the Queen and the Opposition, and, I think, displaying no great talent. By Canning's secession they have now not one debater left except Castlereagh on the Treasury Bench, for Peel seems to be disinclined to take office.

SPRING GARDENS, *February* 10*th*, 1820.

IT rejoiced me that the severe weather terminated before the dear little George braved the elements at school, as I feared cold and rheumatism for him on such a change.

Mr. Sloane is in his full cry of dinners, and the customary scramble of a lame horse and hackney coaches home on damp raw nights. He even dined with that pauper Lilyveld[1] on what was dignified with the title of a Dutch collation, consisting, as I learn, of raw herrings and stock fish as old as the Republic. The Methusalems had caught me so often that they began to consider me as property; but of late I have taught them by pretended engagements that I had rather dine with the waxwork than with automata who go so ill. Old Gilpin, the landscapist of Boldre, thought as fastidiously as I do. "I am," says he, "one of those odd fellows who prefer my own society to the generality of that I meet with."

There is much cant about the late King, but your

[1] The Dutch Ambassador.

French verses are aptly quoted. He had no abilities. It was well observed t'other day he would have made a very good and worthy gentleman farmer, though a little obstinate in parish affairs. What a disastrous reign! The loss of America, a public debt increased to a million of millions, and a people in beggary. To read his "history in a nation's eyes" (Gray). Two Sundays running lately I dined with his present Majesty at Lord Hertford's. Each time no other guest. On the last Sunday he told me of an incipient inflammation on his lungs, and the next day he was confined. Dr. Tierney[1] made the dash of much copious bleeding, and arrested the complaint.

I can tell you that I have seen the voluminous evidence of the conduct of a certain lady.[2] If the most fertile and depraved mind were to invent a tale of private and even public profligacy it could not equal the horrors now reduced to proof. For the honour of the nation and the security of the succession some mode must be, and will be, devised to repudiate the disgrace and the criminal. It should have been anticipated years ago on the then accusation and testimony.

The poor Duke of York's[3] £10,000 per annum! A story circulates too impudent to be true. Alvanley

---

[1] Sir Matthew Tierney. He gained great reputation by a successful operation on the King made against the advice of his colleagues.

[2] Queen Caroline.

[3] His allowance as custos of the person of his afflicted father, George III. He of course lost this on the King's death.

on coming into White's said, "How are you merry beggars?" Lord Foley replied, "Speak for yourself." There was a laugh. The anecdote got down to Oatlands before Alvanley arrived there, and the Duke quizzed him upon it at dinner. The Duchess inquired what the story was. "Oh, nothing, Madam," said Alvanley. "They talked of forming a new club, and wanted a name for it. I proposed calling it the 'Merry Beggars,' and we hope His Royal Highness will be our President."

We agree about "Ivanhoe." I think Athelstan's revival by the Humane Society useless and ill explained. The Jester fails in humour, and Ivanhoe and the King are too soon discoverable. But the tournament, the conflagration by Ulrica, Rebecca's character and the scene of her intended execution, are beyond all praise. My taste is not yet reconciled to this modern union of history and fiction. Each is injured by it.

To-morrow I dine with a rival queen, Lady Conyngham, who will not triumph. 'Tis *l'esprit faible contre l'esprit fort* of Lady H[ertford]. By the way, Lady C.'s daughter is a beauty.

We expect dissolution about April. Poor Dickinson! Lord Stewart starts a candidate at Durham to drain the scanty purse of the great Michael Angelo T.[1] By Ponsonby's Bill to continue office without fresh patents, the Chancellor loses almost all the £30,000 formerly gained on the demise of a king; and, to do him

[1] Michael Angelo Taylor, well known as a politician and man about town.

justice, he gave no opposition to the measure when proposed.

We venerable masters have tickets for the Coronation. On offering one to Joseph he said he would not give twopence to see it. I advised him to sell it to his grandfather for £50, as I am sure he will be in the Abbey by daybreak with Philly at his side, and her pockets laden with six months' provisions.

I have toiled through all the late Nubian, Abyssinian, and Albanian travellers, and am tired of sheiks, and camels, and stinking water. It seems that all these explorations of barbarous people have no sort of utility, and not much amusement.

Hatsell's nephew, now a lunatic, was rejected by Miss Yonge, and H. immediately gave her £5,000. This was before Sidmouth's son was dreamed of. What an odd old fellow! The miss is the very fool of Bedlam, had a mad lover, and then marries half an idiot. My poor friend, Sir V. Gibbs,[1] was finished by dropsy, the usual catastrophe of extreme debility, for the last few days delirious, perhaps partly the effect of the foxglove. They say the Queen styles Tommy Austin, Prince of Wales,[2] though in her old defence she took such pains to prove him the

---

[1] Sir Vicary Gibbs, Chief Baron of the Exchequer. He was known at the Bar as Vinegar Gibbs, his style of pleading being remarkable for its asperity.

[2] The boy whom the Queen claimed as her son in one of her rambling statements to Lady Douglas. The " delicate investigation " of 1806, conducted by Lords Grenville, Erskine, Spencer, and Ellenborough, entirely disproved the statement.

Deptford glazier's son. They say, too, she once had an interview with Hunt, and that he boasts of a paper she gave him, the suppression of which will ensure his pardon should he be found guilty on his approaching prosecution. Such are the *on dits* which circulate.

There is some figure dressed up to play butler in Harley Street, at the banquets, like the Dukes of Aquitaine and Normandy who walk in our coronations, so I suppose poor old Smith[1] is totally *hors de combat*. Mr. Sloane has probably read that odd book, "Fuller's Worthies," who, speaking of the dismissal of ancient domestics, quaintly observes, "It is not meet you should throw away their bones when you have sucked the marrow out of them."

The Mother Bankes affects not to have manœuvred her son's match with the Chancellor's daughter.

Heavens! what a volume I have written! God bless you great and small!

SPRING GARDENS, *Saturday, March* 18*th*, 1820.

YOUR epistles, my dear Lady Gertrude, are always delightful, but the last afforded me that immortal laughter, which Homer says belongs only to the gods, at the result of my manœuvres upon the Methusalems. The dear old souls have the octogenarian vanity to conclude that he who is desirous of escaping from their prosings is a melancholy, morbid hermit lost to all the

[1] Mr. Sloane's butler.

delights of society. Considering to whom my excuses were made, I anticipated such a conclusion, knew how it would be exaggerated, and how trumpeted to "all people that on earth do dwell," with the usual preface, "I'll tell you a very remarkable thing ; Jekyll has abjured the world."

But, old as I am, I am not old enough yet for such a circle, and I began to discover that they began to consider I must constantly fill a niche in their catacomb once or twice a week, and undergo the screech of Glastonbury and the torpidity of Grenville. Antrobus, Sir A. Clarke, the Dutch ambassador Lilyveld, now and then play the part of Don Juan at Lord Malmesbury's by feasting with a statue.

The evidence against the supposed traitors[1] is as yet secret, so we cannot judge how far it will support the charge of high treason for which eight or more are committed. If the project was to assassinate the whole Cabinet it was well imagined, as time for forms of new appointments would have created a delay which would have left the Empire without any Government to control the anarchy of the crisis. It is said that had the plan succeeded, the heads were to have been paraded, and, with the support of all who are destitute and ready for any change, London to be fired in various quarters. We are told, too, our menial servants are all secretly radical, and that such an explosion has been intimated to the Ministry for several months. As the organs of authority must have been paralysed by such an event

[1] The Cato Street conspirators.

as is supposed, military law must have governed solely, if the military, as in France, were not disaffected. I know nothing but from talk. *Sturgeon Brawn* knows more, as he examined the prisoners. No wonder he wags his chin gravely, as he would have been *pickled* with his *namesakes*.

A party of four dined with the Duke of York at old Coutts', two days ago. He said the dear little Duchess was so debilitated by illness and bloodletting that she could not walk five paces. Erskine made his pilgrimage to Scotland in a Leith smack, I thought from economy; but it seems his doctors advised lying in bed for a week, so he chose a vessel and a cheap voyage to comply with the prescription.

*The Queen of Great Britain* is going to Rome, which puts all the English ladies there in a pucker how to deal with her.

An English and Irish cobbler sate on the parapet of a quay on the Liffey at Dublin, each nearly drunk, and boasting the comparative excellence of beer and whisky. "Porter," said the former, "is meat drink and clothing to a man?" and at the same moment accidentally tipped over into the river. "Yes," said Pat, "and now you may say washing and lodging too."

Somebody asked old Barrington how long he had been in town. He said fifteen years next August. I shall have left London only six months during five years. I stayed here from March till the August of 1816, a period of seventeen months, and in each ensuing year was absent only six weeks. This, on reflection, is an odd state of things.

Stafford in the dumps, and the *Morning Chronicle* exulting on the defeat of rats and Highland oppressors, but with many civilities to Lord Gower for character and amiability. Think of Mr. Sloane paying them a visit of condolence—tastefully imagined. Thieves, say the papers, have robbed Sir A. Macdonald's house of plate and valuables, the latter probably including one thousand and one long stories.

An old usher has left Westminster after forty-nine years' slavery. Joseph, with about forty of his other pupils still left at school, have subscribed for, and inscribed a piece of plate to him—a pleasing trait of feeling and gratitude in boys. I once had a friend who was decidedly of opinion all men should be knocked on the head at sixty.

SPRING GARDENS, *April 20th*, 1820.

THE dangerous state of Dickinson's[1] nice boy really distresses me. The conduct at Harrow in detaining him so long under such alarming symptoms was unpardonable. Mr. Sloane is apt to pass the sentence of death, but he says Baillie has slender hopes.

I am very uncomfortable also on account of the dear little Duchess of York. Incessant bloodletting and that

---

[1] William Dickinson, author of "History of Southwell," and "History and Antiquities of Newark." He was a police magistrate, and died in 1822.

terrible foxglove have so debilitated her puny frame that she cannot walk five paces. Yet the Duke does not appear to think there is immediate danger; for my part, I fear the worst.

The Queen's intended invasion of us keeps all the gossips at work. They invented a mission of Lauderdale to her at Brussels by the King's command.

You will be in full time for the Metropolis on the 10th May, as the elections have extinguished all festivity for the last two months, and parliaments and coronations will keep people in town to a very late period. It is not settled whether the characters of the Dukes of Aquitaine and Normandy are to be sustained in the procession by Sir John Coxe Hippisley,[1] Michael Angelo Taylor, or Sir Stephen Claudius Hunter.

The King is well and looks well, but the Duke of Gloucester told me yesterday he cannot eat plain meat, and lives on Mulligatawny soup and combustibles, which, independent of the good sense of my informant, I have reason to disbelieve.

Poor old Coutts' two broken ribs are most successfully spliced; so his "third rib" informed me by a note yesterday. It seems to me that none but young people die. Yet Lilyveld has a sore foot, and Mr. Sloane describes Hatsell's legs to be wonderfully thinner than they ought to be; which is generally the case with a man's last legs.

[1] The able lawyer, diplomatist, and politician. He was a strong supporter of Catholic Emancipation in Parliament, and died in 1825.

Into the "Monastery" I could not get twenty pages. I think the fairy machinery of it is injudicious; and I grow tired of abbots, cowls, shrines, and chivalry.

The gallant Blessington[1] has bought Heathcote's house. He gave us a banquet last week composed of *beaux esprits*. *Miladi* is a beauty; leaves her card at my door in a morning; keeps an album, and desires all her literary friends to write in it to perpetuate their autographs. I am, of course, invited to immortalise myself in the record. There is no end of folly in this world, and for fear you should say there is no end of foolish letters I will conclude this; but not in the manner Sir A. Macdonald concludes a long story, by giving you another in five minutes afterwards.

Spring Gardens, *Sunday, October 8th,* 1820.

Such is the unfortunate unpopularity of Carlton House, the *ennui* of the Lords, and the clamour of Radicalism, that, as few things ever surprise me, I should not be astonished if the whole job[2] was abandoned; and as the evil either way must be encountered, it hardly signifies which way it terminates. As a lawyer, I cannot feel that Brougham's speech or his evidence as yet has overset the case against him; but the present crisis of disaffection, and something probably of pusillanimity in both Houses of Parliament, are much in his favour.

[1] Charles Gardiner, first Earl. His wife, the celebrated Lady Blessington, was a widow, Mrs. Farmer, whose maiden name was Power.

[2] The proceedings against Queen Caroline.

Lady C. Lindsay seems as prolific in "Non mi recordos" as Majocchi.[1]

William called on me the day after he came to town, and we paid a morning visit to Lady Grantham. She complained of His Majesty's prosing the whole evening on deck to the ladies the day they dined on board the yacht, and that they shivered with cold.

### ON DUTY AT THE HOUSE OF LORDS,
*October 17th, 1820.*

ON Sunday last I dined and slept at Holland House. *Miladi* from repletion *en petite santé* as usual. We had Brougham and Denman, and, of course, their Royal and persecuted client was the eternal topic. Lord Holland breakfasted with them in his first sleep on Monday, and off they bundled to the House of Lords together.

Brougham showed me two gold crosses worn by Bergami[2] and the other knights of the Holy Sepulchre and St. Caroline, of which I send you exact and beautiful representations. They are of the size drawn. That of St. Caroline has round the centre piece in a circle the motto *Honi soit qui mal y pense*. The centre and the four pieces forming the cross are made of red cornelian. You see they are good and cheap.

---

[1] An Italian witness at the trial of Queen Caroline. "Non mi ricordo" was so frequent an answer of Majocchi and his countrymen, that it passed into a cant phrase of the day. Lady C. Lindsay was a witness for the defence.

[2] The Queen's Italian courier, who was named as co-respondent in the Divorce Clause of the Bill.

It is whimsical to be behind the scenes of rival theatres. On Friday I dined with a circle of the Queen's foes.

To corroborate your idea of her insanity, one man said that he met her at some German Court, where a ball was given. I think it was Baden. On her appearing depressed and declining to dance, the Archduchess inquired if it was an amusement she disliked. She said no; but that she preferred dancing alone. She was accordingly accommodated with a private room and two fiddlers, where she danced for two hours, and then sank down, exhausted with fatigue and perspiration. To cool herself, she scooped out the moiety of a melon, and persisted in wearing it as a cap the rest of the evening. This latter species of toilette is also recorded in a trumpery book called "The Memoirs of Bergami."

Copley, the Solicitor-General, who had been much attacked for quitting his old political friends, in a cross-examination on Saturday, unfortunately brought out from the witness the name of a Milanese banker, Signor Ratti. You may imagine this has been a fertile source of epigrams.

The boys and I had Coutts' box last night. At all the revolutionary passages in the play of *Virginius* continual plaudits, particularly at one which glanced at subornation of perjury. The manager is democratic enough to announce a revival of *Cymbeline* to-morrow, where an Italian witness forges false evidence against a King of England's daughter. These are evil signs of the times we have to encounter, and remind me of the instrumentality of the French theatre in their Revolution.

God bless you, my dear Lady Gertrude! You live in peaceful shades, and read only the halcyon prospects of the *Courier*, and it is cruel in me to disturb your serenity.

*Tuesday, October* 24*th*, 1820.

TOPICS are so scarce that I write by snatches, and this will rather be a journal than a letter.

Yesterday I dined with the Duke of York, with Lords Lauderdale, Bathurst, and Huntly. W. Howard would have learned a very different story from the conversation there as to the result of this proceeding. By the way, it strikes me as a very awkward defect in the Queen's defence, that having in London at least five or six witnesses who were in the *polacca*, Brougham has not ventured to call them. I mean Oldi, Austin, etc., for Howman and Flyn did him mischief.

Mrs. Piozzi's "Retrospection," 2 vols., 4to, is a pleasant book for young people. It embraces the history of eighteen centuries in a lively style, though somewhat affected.

Hatsell is buried to-day with his brother benchers in the Temple Church. I hear nothing of his will. He died of water in the chest; they send me a mourning ring.

I have not a syllable more for you. So adieu.

*Friday, October* 31*st*, 1820.

POOR old Hatsell had not completed his eighty-seventh year, so died with less punctuality than he lived. He left £30,000 and all his goods and chattels to La Signora Bartona, and £5,000 additionally to the bride, Addingtona; so that with £40,000 settled on his nephew, the lunatic, and the gifts to his nieces, he must have been possessed of more than £100,000.

Yesterday I dined with the gallant Yarmouth, fourteen at table, and so mixed of Queenites and Anti-Queenites, that for the first time in my experience the name of that immaculate Princess was not even alluded to the whole day. It outdid Lord Holland's wish to live in Covent Garden, where the witnesses swore they never talked of her. It whimsically happened that the guests grouped themselves like partisans. On Yarmouth's left sate the Duke of York, Lauderdale, myself, Armstrong, Seymour, and Sir H. Turner, the King's equerry. On his right Duke of Argyll, Lords Foley, Alvanley, Erskine, Gwydir, and some others I forget, but of the same description; so we should have been beat on a division. On my way to dinner I met the Queen's processions, returning with banners and torches, to the no small alarm of my Tory nags, who I thought endangered my neck. They huzzaed at Carlton House, which the Radicals christen "Nero's Hotel."

The Boehms cannot liken my poor late Royal Master to a cruel Emperor. Since their misfortunes he has redoubled his kindness to them. They have visited the Windsor Cottage, and received such protection that they have taken a house at Brighton for the winter months.

The Solicitor-General yesterday commented on Denman's "Sin no more" exactly in the way that your observation anticipated. Party runs so high that I keep my opinion to myself; but, as a lawyer and a man, am satisfied that the evidence has proved the case. But such is the clamour out of doors by those "who" (as the Attorney-General said) "have the Queen in their mouths and revolution in their hearts," and such the attack within doors by those who only want to be ministers, that unless Government has stronger nerves than I suspect, some middle temporising course will be adopted.

Next week my labours re-commence, and I shall cease to be an idle gentleman tormenting you with the fruits of my leisure. As Dogberry says, "For mine own part, if I were as tedious as a king, I could find it in my heart to bestow it all on your ladyship."

*Wednesday, November 1st, 1820.*

LORD ORFORD[1] and Mr. Sloane dined with me yesterday. Mr. Sloane leaves town on Friday next, visits Mrs. D'Oyly again, and reaches Paultons on Sunday next. He said he had called on Mrs. Leigh. I told him that Colonel Leigh had given the little folks at Paultons, for their amusement, a monkey of the Duchess of York's. Mr. Sloane's countenance immediately fell with as much dismay as if I had told him

---

[1] The first Earl of the third creation. His father, Lord Walpole of Wolterton, was first cousin to Horace Walpole, whom he succeeded in the barony of Walpole in 1797. He was created Earl of Orford in 1806.

Paultons was burnt. An hour after he suddenly exclaimed, "I cannot help thinking about this monkey." An hour after that he again said, "I cannot help thinking of this cursed monkey." As he departed, I asked him whether he had anything to say to you, as I should write to-day. He replied, "Nothing but this; that it is my express direction that Lady G. should prevent the arrival of this monkey."

My old friend Harry Howard, the Duke of N.'s brother, I hear has been struck with apoplexy and palsy. Denman,[1] you see, castigated that sage personage of Clarence, who, with his accustomed wisdom, had detailed fifty anecdotes of the Queen's profligacy in the common mess-room of the officers on guard last week, when he graciously partook of their dinner.

Alvanley has all sorts of illness, and looks like what

[1] In his speech closing the defence of Queen Caroline, speaking of the Duke of Clarence's conversations respecting the Queen, Denman said: "I would fain say, my lords, that it is utterly impossible that this can be true, but I cannot say it, because the fact stares me in the face. I read it in the public papers; and had I not known of its existence in the dignity of human nature, I should have held it impossible that any one with the heart of a man, or with the honour of a peer, should so debase his heart and degrade his honour. I would charge him as a judge, I would impeach him as a judge; and if it were possible for one of the blood royal to descend to a course so disgraceful, I should fearlessly assert that it was far more just that such conduct should deprive him of the right of his succession, than that all the facts alleged against Her Majesty, even if true to the letter of the charge, should warrant your lordships in passing this bill of degradation and divorce." The reporter adds, "Mr. Denman, during this part of his address, looked steadfastly at the part of the gallery in which the Duke of Clarence was seated."

is elegantly styled "a Devil new hunted." But it does not force him to a *regimen*, and he has a singular mode of cooking his champagne by shaking the bottle vehemently with both hands till it seems to be a body of froth. As it appears to be his only medicine, I inquired if this process was by the direction of his apothecary, having read such advice on the label of a decoction, and which George Colman has immortalised in his poetical vagaries—

> "This bottle, first shaken,
> The draught to be taken."

God bless you and yours is our triple wish.

P.S.—It is believed that the Attorney-General sent a serious letter to Denman on an expression he used. Denman made a very gentlemanlike explanation, and the matter ended without the hostility of a meeting.

SPRING GARDENS, *December 5th*, 1820.

LONDON is again a blank, and I only scribble now to show you I am alive, though perhaps the scrawl may end without exhibiting one symptom of animation.

"The mob-led Queen," as Hamlet's player calls Hecuba, made but a sorry thing of St. Paul's,[1] as the congregation consisted of constables only, and Bergami was not seated in the Whispering Gallery. Sir Robert Wilson (like Prince Prettyman in the rehearsal) commanded "an army in disguise at Knightsbridge," but

[1] Queen Caroline went to the Cathedral to return thanks for her escape from "the conspiracy against her life and honour."

Falstaff's regiment eclipsed it. Upon the whole, the day ended without effect or advantage to any but the pickpockets; and I should think even an alderman may have taste enough not to repeat the mummery.

The Duke of York, it is said, has given the elephant of the poor Duchess' menagerie to Exeter 'change. I wish I had asked it for Freddy, as its known sagacity deserves a philosophical title. The officers on guard showed Edward—not the beasts, but the armoury of the Tower on his last holiday; and he reports the incredible total, as they told him, of eight hundred thousand muskets stored now in an additional building.

No wonder Sturgeon Brawn's jaw wags mysteriously. Gossip says the Queen has old *billets doux* of Canning's quizzing her husband.

The old King in his fits used to say he could bring any dead people to converse with him except those who had died under Baillie's[1] care, for that the doctor always dissected them into so many morsels that they had not a leg to walk to Windsor with.

[1820.]

THE feudal towers of Belvoir ought to possess so many bards and minstrels of their own, that you are very unconscionable in expecting verses out of the Court of Chancery. If every master in it had a muse for his mistress I would employ mine in an elegy on your poor old inamorato, Sir C. Bunbury. Though with

---

[1] Dr. Matthew Baillie, the famous morbid anatomist, and George III.'s Physician-Extraordinary. He was brother to Joanna Baillie, the poetess.

no disease that threatens life, he is reduced to a state of total apathy and stupor, from debility never leaves his bed, and the other day they found loose in his pocket draughts on bankers, dated last June, to a considerable amount, one among them of the Duke of Rutland's in payment for a horse.

The Duke of Marlborough's affairs are in my office, and on Monday last I sanctioned an agreement of the creditors with the Queen for the purchase of the remaining term in Marlborough House. She is to pay £28,000. Prince Leopold has four years to come in it, and would have bought the remainder at £25,000, but she outbid him. If he does not surrender his lease to her I do not see how it answers her Pall Mall intentions. It is said that three days before it came under my consideration she bought the lease of the Duke of Cambridge's house. Query, whence *now* comes the money?

The butler, I hear, tumbled down in a fit at Cashiobury on its being said by somebody at table that Howard and Gibbs, the moneylenders, were become bankrupts. These worthy gentlemen used to fleece rich old servants by dazzling them with 50 per cent., and now Alvanley has carried the long-hoarded board wages to Paris.

I dined with Peel last week, and saw his beautiful wife. Henry Baring tells him he may kill four thousand pheasants per annum at Lulworth Castle. I congratulated him upon having no neighbours but those he has a right to shoot.

Finding that accomplished artist Master Edward with his flute over a music book price sixpence, I ventured to inquire who composed such cheap jigs for him, and was answered with much importance and indignation, "Mozart."

It is said Harvey Aston stole two volumes of the "Harleian Miscellany." His father fought twice at the Cape of Good Hope, and was finally shot through the head. Captain O'Byrne, an Irishman we then had in London, said he never could make out whether his poor friend Harvey Aston was killed in the first or the second duel.

The late Mr. George Hardinge, a man of talents, was in Parliament, but grievously embarrassed by debts. Triphook, a bookseller, sent his bill enclosed in a letter directed "To the Honourable G. Hardinge, or, if he should be dead, to his executors."

The letter ran thus :—

"Having repeatedly sent the enclosed bill to Mr. Hardinge, of which no notice has been taken, I fear Mr. Hardinge may be dead. If that melancholy circumstance should be true, I beg you, gentlemen, as his executors will discharge it."

George wrote the following answer :—

> "Oh, Mr. Triphook, what is feared by you,
> The melancholy circumstance is true.
> True I am dead, and, more afflicting still,
> My legal ashes cannot pay your bill.
> For oh! to name it I am broken-hearted,
> This transient life, insolvent I departed.

And so for you there's not a single farthing.
For my Executors and self,
                    "GEORGE HARDINGE.

"P.S.—You'll pay the postage which these lines will cost,
    The dead their franking privilege have lost."

N.B.—Triphook was so amused by George's answer that he never dunned him again.

After the Bishop of London's declaration in the Queen's trial that "a King can neither think nor *do* wrong," this answer was given to a child who asked, "What's a Bishop, Mamma?"

"A Bishop's a thing
    That belongs to a King,
And that thinks the best way of succeeding
    Is to rail till he's hoarse
    At a Clause for Divorce,
And then vote for that clause on third reading.

"A Bishop's a thing
    So attached to a King,
Who 'by Law' we know cannot act wrongly,
    That by one Bishop's rule
    A King can't be a fool,
Which is thinking a little too strongly.

"When good Doctor Hooley[1]
    Reflects on this coolly
Such nonsense he'll never more dish up;
    For by stating a rule
    'That no King is a fool,'
He decrees the reverse of a Bishop."

---

[1] William Howley, Bishop of London, afterwards Archbishop of Canterbury. He was generally opposed to the popular side of the great questions with which he had to deal. He led the opposition to the Catholic Relief Bill in the House of Lords, and strenuously opposed the Reform Bill of 1832, the Jewish Civil Disabilities Relief, and Lord J. Russell's Education scheme. He died, aged 84, in 1848.

# CHAPTER IV.

*MR. JEKYLL TO LADY G. SLOANE STANLEY*
*(Continued).*

SPRING GARDENS, *Tuesday, July* 24*th*, 1821.

IN the midst of our insanities I snatch the first lucid interval to scribble to you. The town has been mad these ten days, and we are to wear our strait waistcoats at *levées*, dinners, balls, and drawing-rooms for a week to come.

It has been said "that everything went off properly at the Coronation, the Queen not excepted."

The day before it Yarmouth gave us an aquatic *fête* at Richmond in "old Q.'s" uninhabited villa; I enclose his lithographic bulletin. Mr. Sloane will tell you how the Queen scoffed at our Royal Duke and Royal Standard with her arms akimbo in defiance as we passed Brandenburg House,[1] so early in the day had *noyeau* inspired her with heroism.

Yesterday I went down with the aforesaid gallant Yarmouth to a *Fête Champêtre* at Lady Londonderry's in Kent, where we had the usual British fate of a rainy day, and waltzes went off swimmingly. I saw the Morpeths, *père, mère*, and *fils*.

[1] At Hammersmith; it stood on the right-hand side of the Fulham Road, and had gardens running down to the river.

Old Hertford has resigned.[1] I will bet the Marquis of Wellesley as his successor. I think Cholmondeley will soon be off, and then who knows but we may have the Lord of *Conyngham*? Sturgeon Brawn's head in his Privy Counsellor's ruff reminded me of the dish Herod's daughter got by her dancing.

*Ci devant* Sir W. Scott[2] in the costume of the Barony of Stowell was a fac- or rather a fat-simile of Falstaff.

Has Mr. Sloane given you the slander on Trentham? They say the Queen has taken a house at Pesaro. The King persists in his voyage from Brighton to Dublin, and Hanover is not given up. He looked like one expiring when he returned from the Abbey to the Hall, but has rallied.

Lady Morgan's "Italy" a contemptible specimen of book-making.

Alas! alas! we shall not see Paultons for ages. By Easter falling so late the Chancellor will sit a terrible time. I shall have the good fortune to escape from him as early as the 20th August. Last year I left him on the 9th. I deplore poor Edward, who will expend so much of his holidays in town, and even *I* shall begin to envy you the shade of green trees.

P.S.—Among other *incroyables* yesterday I saw at Lady Londonderry's three kangaroos, a tiger, a Peruvian llama, an Arctic dog, and five ostriches, which had been stripped of their tails by the Coronation.

---

[1] The Lord Chamberlain. He was succeeded by the Duke of Montrose.    [2] Brother of Lord Chancellor Eldon.

SPRING GARDENS, *August 7th*, 1821.

Under the necessary limitations of space and number Elliston has achieved a theatrical miracle in the Coronation at Drury Lane. The spectator almost sees the real spectacle, and Elliston contrives to personate the King like a portrait.

At the Drawing-Room Mrs. Lee and I shook hands for a moment. It was interesting to see His Majesty successively and tenderly salute the left cheeks of Ladies Hertford, Conyngham, and Jersey. The latter has made the *amende honorable*, and is everywhere gallanted by that withered inamorato the Duke of Wellington.

We dined at Lord Gwydir's t'other day with the Duke of York, and the plateau was garnished with the superb perquisites of the Coronation in gilt plate, of very classical execution and form.

Your bulletin of Castle Howard is excellent. What you say of poor Lady Cawdor is affecting; her whole life has been an example, and God Almighty wrote a legible hand when He made her like an angel.

Howard's "Pæstum"[1] is printed in the *Gentleman's Magazine* of this month. Parry's "North Pole" is a dull sea journal. Hughes' "Voyage through Greece and Albania," 2 vols.,[2] 4to, very interesting—too full perhaps of Greek criticism for general readers; but his long residence at Janina has enabled him to give a

---

[1] The Newdigate Prize Poem, by the Hon. G. W. F. Howard.

[2] "Travels in Sicily, Greece, and Albania," by the Rev. T. S. Hughes, the author of the continuation of Hume and Smollett's "History of England."

more minute history of the extraordinary Ali Pacha than even Dr. Holland's.

An Opposition member has just now exultingly told me Lady Conyngham means to rout out the whole Ministry and bring his friends in. He added that she went with the King from the Windsor Cottage to visit Lady Harcourt, who was not at home. The King said to the porter, "Tell Lady Harcourt that I called, and give my love to her."

The porter, being a person of accuracy, entered in his visiting-book—

"The King and his love."

A Bologna sausage has the discredit of the Queen's indigestion, but the bulletin of to-day prognosticates the defeat of this Italian assassin, who I suppose was instigated by the Milan Commission.[1]

P.S.—Lady Jersey loud and furious on behalf of the Duke and the Tory Ministers.

I hear S. Bourne is confined at Testwood by the gout, and that he wants to sell his London house. Mrs. Burn, an excellent old lady whom I used to meet at the late Archbishop of York's, and who lived next door but one to me, died this morning of injury from her fireside yesterday. Female drapery gives frequent employ to the coroner, and her very name was inauspicious. They apply flour to the wounds in these cases.

[1] A secret commission sent to Italy to collect evidence against Queen Caroline.

This reminds me of the conflagration of *Sal Petre*. I called yesterday on the Lady mother in vain, as they seemed to be repairing her house. However inattentive I was before Christmas, this is the third card I have left. So I sigh (like the dying Lovelace), "Let this expiate." Ellis says the King said lately to the Duke of Devonshire at Windsor, "Well, I suppose there are to be no more Kings, Dukes, or Knights of the Garter; I hope at least they will permit me to be Prince of Wales."

Mrs. Sheridan has written a tragical novel, "Carwell."

Palmerston makes good speeches, but the people want bread, and don't care about Portugal. Huskisson got damaged, and Althorp deserted the debate, though now named as the leader of a large Opposition party.

SPRING GARDENS, *November 22nd*, 1821.

IT is said the gallant Sir Coxley Hips of Quarantotte Cottage, Cowes, lost a large sum by the lead mine, the ruin of which led Moore the counsel to abscond, after involving Lord Grosvenor.

The last *John Bull* quizzes Alderman Claud [Hunter]. It seems the fool in a speech at some Bible Meeting said he never had read that valuable book attentively till he was Lord Mayor. Old Mrs. Heywood told the Duke of Gloucester lately at Southampton she hoped His Royal Highness would marry, and then asked how the good old King did?

Old Rose Fuller, a relation of Mr. Sloane, is dead leaving £100,000, which he has divided between his two illegitimate children.

The King will probably make a long stay at Brighton as usual, much to the annoyance of his Ministers, who always grumble at it.

At Brighton resides Mustapha the Turk, who bathes gouty gentlemen in the Mahometan, and shampoos them in the Indian style. *A propos* of Oriental matters, why is one's father in a sack like a town in Arabia? Because he is a *Bag-dad*. This is Westminster wit, and perhaps not of the newest.

Lady Grantham re-established. London still dreary enough; but I have dinners with judges and lawyers— nay, yesterday with the divine bit of blue, Lady Blessington and her comical Earl. I made love, and Mathews[1] was invited to make faces.

A new ballet among Ministers is always talked of at this time of year, and if you re-pass early through London it is not yet impossible but you may be appointed Master of the Horse. Canning is said not to display King Richard's "wonted alacrity of spirit," and desired, I hear, to dine last week at Holland House. But it is not of much importance who compose a Cabinet, for an Essex squire has just told me the farmers there are throwing up their leases and ready for revolution.

---

[1] Charles Mathews the elder. He was at this time giving entertainments founded on his experiences in France, Italy, and the United States.

SPRING GARDENS, *December 25th*, 1821.

I MADE Mr. Sloane buy Lady Hervey's[1] Letters just published, as she speaks much of Mr. Hans Stanley, Paultons, and the vivacity and accomplishments of the two young Miss Stanleys, whom she meets at Lord Cadogan's, before they espoused Mr. Welbore Ellis and Mr. D'Oyly. "Rome in the Nineteenth Century," 3 vols. of letters said to be by a lady, is a pretty book, lively and full of information, just come out, and the Journal as recent as 1818. I do not hear any praise of Byron's new work.[2]

London is never without the society of lawyers, and at this season learned hospitality abounds. I do not think of quitting it for Bowood, though under promise; and we shall hardly be more excursive than to Lord Clifden's at Roehampton, who, as some birds sing, may soon be your Ladyship's relation by his son's manœuvres

George Colman tells me an Irish strolling actor, about to play Othello in a barn, peeped through a slit in the curtain, and could count only eight persons composing the audience, to whom he exclaimed: "I will be hanged if I black my face for eight people. I will play white to-night."

Dickinson wrote to me from Cheltenham that the Antinous, George Isted offered his person in marriage

---

[1] Mary Lepel, the wife of John, Lord Hervey, author of the famous "Memoirs of the Reign of George II."

[2] *Marino Faliero, Sardanapalus, The Two Foscari*, and "*Don Juan*," Cantos III., IV., and V., were all published in 1821.

two years ago to one of Lord Arden's sisters. She broke her own corsets and her lover's heart with peals of laughter. It was unfeeling in him never to think of proposing through Mr. Sloane to Philly, as Poet Sotheby might have shone in an "Epithalamium," and you would have been kind enough to choose her lace veil and milk-white robes for her sacrifice.

My sleep has been broken for many nights with doubts whether Philly will hoard Mrs. D'Oyly's legacy for the gentleman's children, whom Mr. Sloane styles "Lannoy," or whether to regale Birdy. She will abandon conger eel, and substitute some more relishing and costly fish.

P.S.—Dent, the banker, tells me the Jerseys will in time be richer than ever. Jersey is accursedly bored with his Paris exile. What a season! Roses blowing in my room!

Spring Gardens, *Monday, January 14th*, 1822.

By the death of old Rose Fuller, William and Mr. Bond became the surviving trustees of my marriage settlement, and accordingly the bank stopped the payment of my dividends at Christmas till fresh powers were executed by them. I have waited till the King's licence appeared in the *Gazette* for Mr. Sloane and his heirs to take the name of Stanley, that William might be properly named in the new instruments.

Lord Clifden is going to Lord Spencer's at Althorpe, and fears, from something George said, the Morpeths might come to town in his absence, though it will be short.

The Staffords, I hear, are coming, perhaps to see after Buckingham and Chandos, or whether there be any other stray dukedom to be picked up.

I don't admire the " Pirate." I think it too long, full of improbability, and of plagiarism from former characters in the other novels of the author.

Never did the Opera present such a bill of fare of singers and dancers, though all have not yet arrived. There is a machine at Covent Garden of Cleopatra's Galley most wonderfully constructed. The undulation of the artificial water incredible. To correspond with the vicious taste of the public, the managers now get up one of Shakespeare's worst dramas, and stick it full of songs and spectacles. Miss Tree's [1] leg is so beautiful, that were I as rich as old Coutts I also would send her £50.

By the way, he gave us a dinner to the Duke of York on Thursday last, and it was doubly attentive to His Royal Highness, for he appeared to have been dead for some time. There was every other symptom of it but putrefaction.

"Mémoires du Duc de Lauzun," a new French book of lies. Stories of Sir C. and Lady Sarah Bunbury and Lord Carlisle at Paris. I wish you joy of the Duke of Rutland's intended publication. Murray gave Lord Byron two thousand guineas for his Life [2] when written.

---

[1] Miss Ellen Tree. She married Charles John Kean in 1842.
[2] The famous "Memoirs of Lord Byron," the MS. of which

Byron gave it to little Moore the poet. Lord Lansdowne also gave him £1,000, which he repaid in a month.

I wish some peer of the realm would give his hand and name to Miss Tree, as it makes her leg sound like a wooden one.

Now did I begin this letter seriously on a piece of business, and lo! it ends in a piece of nonsense.

P.S.—London is by no means yet a desert. Lately we had a grand dinner at Lord Blessington's, who has transmogrified Sir T. Heathcote's ground floor into one vast apartment, and bedizened it with black and gold like an enormous coffin. We had the Speaker, Lord Thanet, Rogers, Sir T. Lawrence, and the Duke of Hamilton grumbling at a summons from Paris to attend His Majesty at Edinburgh, as hereditary keeper of Holyrood House.

*Monday, February* 12*th*, 1822.

IF it were possible to detail in a lady's ear the proceedings of Lord and Lady Erskine in Doctors

he gave to Moore in Venice. On his return to London Moore offered them to Longmans for two thousand guineas, but they declined the offer. Murray then accepted a similar proposal, subject to the condition, however, that the work should not be published in Lord Byron's lifetime, and that during that period Moore should have a right of re-purchase at the same price. Byron's death in 1824 made the MS. Murray's absolute property; and though he then declined to re-sell it to Moore, on hearing that Lord Byron's representatives desired the Memoirs to be destroyed, he, in the presence of certain selected witnesses, burnt them in his drawing-room fire at 50, Albemarle Street.

Commons, I know not whether the ridicule or disgust they would excite must be the strongest sensation. Suffice it to say, that both the charge and defence present scenes of the most crapulous character, and that insanity as a motive is the only charitable construction.

The King, with his usual kindness, has given my poor friend, the widow of General Gwyn, a pension of £400 per annum. You know she was a sister of the late Mrs. Bunbury, and equally a favourite of the Duchess of York.

The sister Muses of painting and music grace my family. I laughed a full hour last night on being told by Joseph that Edward had learned from a schoolfellow to perform on the German flute! And he produced two books of two hundred popular airs most accurately noted by the aforesaid artist. The instrument had never been introduced at home for fear of horrifying me with the discords of "Rule Britannia." You see Providence does not bestow thick lips in vain, and nothing is more ludicrous than the gravity of Master Edward's features when accomplishing his melodies, of which I insisted on an immediate rehearsal.

At last Chantrey has applied his cosmetics to your ghost, and you look as white as if you had invited a vampire to supper.

SPRING GARDENS, *February 28th*, 1822.

YOU must put up with the gossip of my *levée*, as they now permit me to hold one (of intimates only) on my return from a daily dowagering in the Parks.

Lord Clifden was a few days at Chiswick last week, and delighted with the Morpeths; no very singular taste. Ellis, I believe, has taken the late Lord Stair's house in Spring Gardens. I remember it in old Lord Malmesbury's time, and it was a terrible tumble-down concern then. My neighbour Ellice, M.P., is within five doors of it, so there will be as much confusion as with your brace of birds at Southampton.

When Kean played *Hamlet* last the ghost was seized with such a fit of sneezing that he could not get on with his speech. The audience, who had never before had a specimen of a cold caught in the other world, encored it.

Old Coutts left all to the widow, not a single legacy to daughter or grandchildren who surrounded his death-bed. They talk of six hundred thousand pounds and half the property of the bank also, which amounts to as much more. So she may have an annual income of sixty thousand.

Lord Holland tells me Burdett (who was no favourite) desired to see him, and was received. Coutts could no longer articulate, but he took Burdett's hand and kissed it.

Canning has made an excellent joke on Coke's marriage. I wish it was tellable to a lady.

Yesterday we had a solemn meeting of Mrs. D'Oyly's executors at my house. *Entre nous*, the share of each of us will turn out nearly a third more than was expected.

My recovery has proceeded without interruption, and

as a proof of the horrible life we lead in this good town, I find my general health, from *regimen* and no wine, better than it has been for years. So that I can say of myself what has been so often said of your Ladyship for a month together, "I am as well as can be expected."

Adieu!

SPRING GARDENS, *November* 19*th*, 1822.

THE Ministry, they say, is changing partners, and that Canning is to be placed somewhere in the new dance. Perhaps, like country bumpkin, alone, in the middle and with his hat on. It is ungrateful if he does not make Sturgeon Brawn Lord Mayor and get him knighted, as the title would be so savoury among the aldermen at Christmas.

SPRING GARDENS, *Friday, November* 29*th*, 1822.

WE shall mutually meet our male brats about the same period, and I rejoice to think that at the expiration of the holidays you think London may be no bad remedy for the *ennui* of Paultons.

An enemy of Mrs. Coutt's, *ci-devant* Melon, advertises a libel in *John Bull*, entitled "Memoirs of Harriet *Pumpkin* before she married *Crœsus*," and adds a caustic motto from Shakespeare about a *will*.

Lord Byron sends me *Werner*, his new tragedy. He is grown a good boy, and there is none of *Cain's* wickedness in it. The story, he owns, is taken from one of Miss Lee's "Canterbury Tales." Of course it abounds with many brilliant passages, but the dialogue is frequently so prosaic, that if it were not printed in the form of verse it would scarcely resemble it.

My brother benchers expect a satire from Poet Sotheby. He has a house of ill fame at the Temple Gate, which he lets to a fellow who harbours a nest of gamblers. He refused to sell it to us at a fair price, and we are taking the whimsical revenge of blocking up all his back windows, which will leave his tenant in utter darkness. The remonstrance he wrote to us was, without exception, the most ludicrous attempt at the pathetic I ever read. Quotations from Milton, etc., and altogether such a Galimatias of poetry and prose that manifestly Byron did not christen him "Botherby" without good reason.

*Thursday, December 13th*, 1822.

COMING on business at an early hour before dinner last week at Harley Street, I was present at a consultation of Sir D. Dundas, *ci-devant* apothecary, Tegart, and the patient.[1] In vain did the doctor advise abstinence and two glasses of claret. Good feeding and Oporto were persisted in. Going away John ejaculated, "Alas, sir! by long fasting my master eats too much at dinner;" and E. N. Lee told me when dining *tête-à-tête* with him, he did not only devour an immense dinner, but drank above half a bottle of strong port wine. As all this tends to a determination of blood to the head, one cannot but be uneasy about vertigo.

[1] Mr. Hans Sloane Stanley, Lady Gertrude's father-in-law.

So much for tragedy. Now I shall proceed to split the new sides of the Lady G. Stanley with comedy.

It is a literal fact, that two months before the whitlow burst, George Isted at the age of sixty-eight, after being a cripple for ten years, desired a noble friend of mine to propose marriage for him to a lady neither young nor handsome, said he would willingly accept £3,000, and settle £1,000 a year. He was then a beggar in debt. My noble friend, to amuse himself, carried the embassy, and the woman fainted with laughter.

Lord Spencer seized his miserable furniture for rent the moment he died. He inhabited a hovel of the noble Earl's in St. James's Place.

The Hollands are come early to town. I dined there on Sunday. My lady more Madagascari than ever.

Poet Rogers playing Petrarca in Italy. I understood Philly played Laura at Paultons to the Melesina Trench.

Spring Gardens, *December* 15*th*, 1822.

I AM very well, and drive out daily, yet prudently refrain from the fogs, which form the dessert of dining out, and let Joseph perform as my proxy. He says Fanny Kemble's Belvidera surpasses her Juliet.

Your little niece of Cadlands seems a delicate structure, and frequent confinements have not fortified it.

The town is so barren of topics that lies multiply upon us hourly. A boy was brought before the magistrates yesterday as a vagrant, and questioned how his father maintained him. He replied, "An't please your worships, my father is murder maker to the newspapers."

William[1] met at my house in full vigour Mr. Tucker, the Surveyor-General of Cornwall, a great and lucrative office of which an effort was making to deprive him. Yesterday he died of palsy, produced, I have no doubt, by anxiety and nervous agitation. The fat Viscount Sidney has rallied. Lord Essex has bought a pretty picture of Joseph's friend Newton. "The Abbot" is one of Scott's novels.

How happy are you in rural innocence and ditch-water entrenched by the moral society of Bethell and Beddome, and Jones and Parson Penton to preach to you. But beware of the Chief Commissioner of Woods and Forests, who is as false as he is fair, and very pretty. Scandal, like Brougham's schoolmaster, is abroad, and mummies, like Andrew and Lady Mary, are hardly safe in these slanderous times.

Sidmouth and Clifden press me to villas, forgetting that my own bed, my own fireside, and twenty French books are better things in December.

P.S.—*Ne vaut il pas mieux écrire des riens, que ne rien écrire?*

Bowood, *The last day of old* 1822.

A copy, not very correct, of my "Advertisement Extraordinary," I saw last week in two London papers, The *Sun* and the *Morning Post*. My name was not published, but the squib was ascribed to a "Gentleman well known in legal and literary circles."

Mr. Stanley had seen Lord Morpeth on a morning

[1] Mr. W. Sloane Stanley, Lady Gertrude's husband.

visit made rapidly after his arrival, but knew nothing of poor Lady Carlisle's illness. It must console you much to feel that Lady Cawdor is with her, and I wish you could be with her also. Alluding thus to domestic subjects, and feeling, as I ever shall, a deep interest in all that concerns your dear children, I will preach a little on the text of education.

In my opinion all the public schools are equal as to the means of instruction, and the proficiency in learning must always depend upon the disposition and industry of the individual boy. With the exception of Winchester, I think the habits and manners of the world may also be equally attained at all of them. There is a vulgar rusticity about the *élèves* of Winchester which continues to be their characteristic at the University, and the mass is chiefly composed of boys in the middling classes of society. It never happened to me to weigh the respective merits of schools. My predilection for Westminster naturally arose from the recollection of my own successful education there, and the same predilection from the same recollection extended itself to Christ Church. I had trodden the path myself, and knew all its turnings and windings. I was of course anxious that my boys should make a similar pilgrimage, and I hoped with similar benefits.

In William's letter he hinted at Eton for George. I have already stated my opinion as to the equality of instruction at all public schools, and I confess that the separation of brothers appears to me very impolitic. It weakens by estrangement that union of attachment which through life should subsist between them. It checks a species of emulation, and it often throws an unpopularity about the boy when the masters discover that a different school is preferred by the parents for his brother.

These principles I carry still further. It would have vexed me to send Edward to Cambridge, which I once apprehended from necessity.

This subject is so important that I do not apologise for the length of my preachment, founded, as it is, on much thought and experience, and the production of a snowy morning.

This place[1] has been much improved during my long truancy. Lord Lansdowne has *Fonthillized*[2] (a new verb) the interior with a due proportion of pictures, antiques, library, etc., and Smirke has tastefully decorated the exterior with architectural terraces and fountains, so as to give it the air of the Italian palaces one sees in drawings.

The owners are a most exemplary pair of young people, the establishment has a proper proportion of magnificence, and they bring round them a society of talent and conversation. We have a succession of guests, and hear no nonsense; so that I am content to endure a country house till the end of the fortnight.

Yesterday Lord Lansdowne gave the corporation of

[1] Bowood.
[2] Fonthill Abbey, near Bath, was the seat of Alderman Beckford, a vast building by Wyatt, in the Gothic style. It was sold with the furniture in 1822 for a large sum, by his son William Beckford, the author of "Vathek."

Calne a civic feast, at which I assisted, with my present members, in the character of Alderman Sir Claud Hunter's "feu Lord Maire," and returned thanks to my health being drunk in "a most appropriate and eloquent speech."

We have Miss Fox and Miss Vernon, and we have poets too,—Bowles, the little Anacreon Moore,—and politicians in plenty.

The Lansdownes desire to return your kind remembrance of them. Mr. Stanley finds the Glastonbury revived, but the poor General in a sad state of suffering.

London I left in no state of desertion. The Hollands were domiciled in Burlington Street, and we dined at Rogers' the day before my departure with William Ward, Luttrell, and Armstrong.

The *Dives* Hertford[1] swears he will never live at Ragley, will keep Sudborne for his shooting friends, and laments that from a dread of the imputation of parsimony he must quit his residence in Seymour Place.

We were calculating the other day what the Wellesley family now draws from the expenditure of Great Britain. With pensions to ladies and all it amounts to one hundred and eleven thousand pounds.

I have just read the famous new French tragedy *Sylla*, which I do not admire, though it may be well calculated to display Talma's powers of declamation. Nor do I like de Souza's new novel, "La Comtesse de Fargy."

---

[1] Francis, third Marquess. He married Maria Fagniani, the adopted daughter and heiress of George Selwyn.

The men skate, and invent a skating boat for the little Kerry, so I expect they will drown the heir-apparent. It is whimsical enough, but, counting the little boy, we are seven Westminsters now at Bowood.

SPRING GARDENS, *March 14th*, 1823.

LORD CLIFDEN inquires of me whether from the accession of income, the mansion of Harley Street is likely to be any cleaner? I told him not till Normanby moved to abolish the old mad housemaid, who held a sinecure more notorious than the Postmasters-General, or the two Junior Lords of the Admiralty.

It is believed that Mrs. Coutts is to do munificent things by the daughter's dependants, and that her late *sposo*, who was not called Canny Coutts for nothing, made her the depository of his intentions to chouse Vansittart of the Legacy Tax, thinking, perhaps, that the Probate Duty on more than a million was a sufficient sop for the said Van's appetite.

*A propos* of executorships, I believe our respective shares of Mrs. D'Oyly's residue will be nearer fifteen than ten thousand apiece. To me, who want nothing, it is immaterial, but to the boys no bad thing. Joseph visits me at the end of the month for a short vacation of a fortnight.

Mr. Stanley calls frequently in his round of morning visits, complains of his head, but dines out and gives repasts *à l'ordinaire*. Memory much impaired. He read me for the third time yesterday a tattered letter from the Dowager of Malmesbury, with the history of old Louis XVIII.'s new love affair.

I proceed prosperously. My general health much improved by regular hours and quiet living, which I am not only reconciled to, but delighted with. My *regimen* does not extend to the circulating library, so I devour new publications voraciously. But Horace Walpole's huge memoirs stand like cold meat on the side table, and will only be resorted to in case of bad dinner.

Sir H. Bunbury gives me an oil painting of a Welsh landscape after Nature, and a drawing, never engraved nor published, by his celebrated father.[1] The drawing is a caricature group of the turf men of Newmarket thirty or forty years ago. I make out easily those I remember, the Duke of Grafton, Lords Orford, Clermont, Spencer Hamilton, Colonel O'Kelly, the proprietor of Eclipse, old Vernon, Dowager Lady Warwick's father. There is also an outline of the late Sir Charles. I wish it were a miniature, as I know our *tendresse* would like to wear it, unless Tom Smith has obliterated all your former attachments. What a volatile thing is woman!

SPRING GARDENS, *November 5th*, 1823.

"THE Miseries of Life" in the country have never been fairly classed by themselves—as, blowing weather; no fish at the market; newspaper not arriving; window broke in bed-chamber, glazier five miles off; leg broke, surgeon eight miles off or gone a-hunting; family circle; opera eighty miles off; bores on a fortnight's visit, with

[1] Henry William Bunbury, the caricaturist, died 1811.

a desire to be shown the lions in your neighbourhood; a rainy day, and the last volume of your favourite new novel in the paws of an old lady checkmated by words of five syllables.

On the vicissitudes of weather I felicitate your Ladyship, as a new topic occurs now daily in a country house, and it is inexhaustible. A French writer says when two Englishmen meet in the rain they always inform one another that it is wet weather.

*Monday, November* 11*th*, 1823.

ON Saturday last I dined with neighbour Ellis and wife, a very pleasant *partie quarrée*, for we had only neighbour John William Ward, in high and humorous eccentricity, which with him is only *journalier*. He abused the vulgarity of his family name, said that half the thieves carried to Bow Street were Wards, and that his name was larcenous, felonious, and burglarious.

To-morrow the Ellises depart for Castle Howard, and Lord Clifden the day after. Read " Letters from Spain," by Don Leucadio Doblado, a new publication by Colburn,[1] very entertaining, the author, in fact, an Englishman, but long resident there.

I lately read the life of Brown, the American novelist, which led me to peruse his novels published about ten years ago, " Wieland," " Ormond," and " Arthur Mervyn." They repaid me well, as they are most singular, and

[1] Henry Colburn, the publisher. Among his successful ventures were *Evelyn's Diary, Pepys' Diary* and the *New Monthly Magazine.*

quite out of the ordinary sphere of that species of composition. Think of weaving a most tragical story out of Ventriloquism!

The Ellises did not like their steamboat voyage from London to Calais; a smoking hot dinner as they got out of the Thames into a rough sea, which was not likely to obviate the qualms of the stomach, though it economised the viands which the proprietors were bound to supply.

The new Lady Liverpool[1] as ugly and smoke-dried as the mermaid in St. James's Street. The secession of my young companions having rendered me solitary, I dine continually with my brother benchers in the Temple Hall, an early dinner in a collegiate style, a small party, and some of the cleverest men in our profession,—no bad resource at this season, and especially to a gentleman of *regimen*. It suits me, for I never felt myself in better health.

The life of Ali Pacha, just printed, will amuse you. Among the *on dits* of the day they have conjured up a party among the Ministerialists against Canning, and the Duke of York at its head. To this they also ascribe the new Lord Hertford's rage for buying seats in Parliament.

Spring Gardens, *December 12th*, 1823.

THE postponement of the Hertford Trial[2] was not necessary, but perhaps it was politic to sacrifice a little month to popular clamour.

---

[1] Miss Bagot Chester.

[2] The trial of Thurtell and others for the murder of Mr. Weare near Elstree. This murder, from the horrible circumstances created a great sensation.

Bankes makes progress, but I should think parliament would now be a dangerous attendance. On the paralytic seizure Mrs. Bankes was found by her servant out of bed, and lying on the floor. She was a good mother, and her children are much afflicted.

Playhouses in their zenith. Kean, Young, and Macready[1] in nightly rivalry. Braham, Sinclair, and Miss Stephens encored three times three, and ten pair of piebald horses clattering on the boards. Widow Coutts still absent, so I have not graced the boxes nor put the managers to the trouble of carrying candles before me.

George Colman called here to-day, and when I complained that the paviours had obstructed my coal-house door, he said, " Blockheads love blockading ; and as you are a poet they persecute your *mews.*"

They talk of a statue to Erskine, but it seems to languish under *la crapule* of his latter life. His son David is a good fellow, but will be a pauper peer. The miserable Sussex domains do not produce £500 a year. He has a diplomatic pension of £1,500, but there are a wife and twelve children, and 'tis said the pension is mortgaged.

There was a story lately in the papers of a northern peer who has been haunted by a spectre. Sitting in his study, a female in white appeared sitting in an opposite chair. He addressed her frequently, but in vain ; and after regarding him half an hour with a melancholy aspect she vanished. He pondered this

[1] Kean as Othello, Shylock, etc.; Young as Brutus, Cato, and Leare ; Macready as Caius Gracchus, etc.

singular appearance, and next day mentioned it at breakfast to his family. His second daughter trembled, grew pale, and declared that a similar spectre had appeared at her bedside the last night, and had remained about the same period of time, that she rung for her maid, and the spectre vanished. Query, was it the ghost of Opposition? for Lord Shaftesbury said at dinner yesterday that this story is told of Lord Grey and his daughter.

Now as a ghost story is the very climax of all gossips I shall conclude, only wondering that after the cataract of nonsense I have lately sent you my stock at all holds out.

SPRING GARDENS, *December* 23*rd*, 1823.

THE boys—I ask pardon, the Oxford men as they style themselves—are in high feather, and amuse one with their theatrical accounts of Kean and Young and the extraordinary acting of a little girl named Fisher.[1] But the new Juliet is over puffed, I find. Edward was much gratified by Gertrude's music, and he has possessed himself of a most elaborate flute, with a thousand new keys to do it justice.

Mr. Wetherell, the King's Counsel, having made a most bitter and personal attack on the Vice-Chancellor in his Court, it has been said Wetherell was to be chosen President of the Society for the Suppression of Vice. The said little old coxcomical Vice, it is reported or invented, made an offer of marriage to Lady Glengall, which she scornfully repelled.

[1] Clara Fisher, as "Little Pickle" in the *Spoilt Child* at Drury Lane.

Our Opposition friends are busy in slanders of Canning already, and the *Edinburgh Review* leads the attack rather coarsely. They add that the Duke of Wellington insisted on Canning's writing a letter of censure to Lord Strangford for his diplomatic errors at Constantinople, which Canning did, but accompanied it with a private note to say the letter was to go for nothing, but in compliance with the Duke's absurdity he was forced to send it. But duplicity is not the only ground of attack. They swear that out of hatred to Londonderry's memory he meditates the subversion of many of the dead Secretary's late measures, among the rest that he means to extinguish the Embassy to Switzerland, for which Londonderry fought so strenuously as to declare he would resign if it was not carried.

But a truce to politics and its odious *tracasseries*. Mr. Stanley says you think of Harrow for William. I placed my ward and nephew there (Lockwood), because at Westminster I thought he would be always running to three uncles in London. His health was then slight, and I was alarmed at learning that Harrow, though elevated on a hill, was very damp from a soil of clay, and the dame desired he might have the thickest shoes and the warmest stockings. However, he remained there till he went into the Guards and in perfect health. Dickinson's poor boy was of a consumptive habit, and fell a victim to neglect; but he should not have been placed in so high and cold a position.

The *men* and I send our best loves to all.

SPRING GARDENS, *December 24th*, 1823.

WE had the Duncannons, Lord Ellenborough, and Luttrell at Lord Clifden's, from whence we returned yesterday. Lady Jersey has been very ill, but is recovered.

Your niece I like more and more—sensible, chatty, good humoured, and I think very pretty. We shall meet them all again on Saturday next at Lord Ellenborough's, where we are going to pass two or three days. They talked, I think, of a visit to Althorpe, but I believe she wrote to you on Monday last.

Lady Aberdeen visits Lady Holland at Brighton, and Lady King starves her—for the Kings are so stingy that Lady Holland complains she rose fasting from their dinners. Her daughter, the little Fox,[1] has had a serious and strange complaint. One evening after a dance her knee was so weak and swelled that she could not stand. Leeches were applied, but the part is still extremely debilitated, though recovering, and they are coming to town.

Lawrence has made a drawing of Madame de Lieven,[2] which has been beautifully engraved. Strange to say, and in spite of teeth, I admire her. I have never known her intimately enough to object to the effects said to be produced from her economy of clean linen.

---

[1] Miss Mary Fox, afterwards Lady Lilford.
[2] The wife of Prince de Lieven, the Russian Ambassador. She was a great figure in London Society, and a patroness of Almack's. Her famous *salon* in London was the rendezvous of the distinguished politicians of both parties. She died in 1857, at Paris.

From his *pensoroso* visage and manner they call Lord Auckland "George Barnwell." Luttrell told us of a strolling player acting Lear who called his daughter Cordelia "Butchess of Durgundy."

Joseph you made such an adept of at *écarté*, that I saw him sweep a pool of four guineas into his pocket on Monday evening at Roehampton.

Lord Holland has dined at the Pavilion. They speak well of "The Spae-wife," and I have just got it. It is written by the author[1] of "The Annals of the Parish," and that secondary class of Scottish novels which really tread hard upon the heels of Walter Scott.

It is well that the Hippopotamus decamped to foreign parts. It seems he had sworn falsely in the Court of Chancery, and might have been prosecuted, if any pillory could have been found to fit the head and shoulders of that amphibious animal.

The new Lord Dudley[2] returns from Italy in May, and has ordered for his *début* the finest service of plate ever heard of. Giving his wife to Dr. Jones at Paultons was the heaviest fee ever bestowed upon a medical man for his attendance. You know she is a poetess, but I cannot think where the Doctor can buy *blue stockings* big enough for her.

[1] John Galt.
[2] John William, the first Earl of the first creation. He died unmarried in 1833.

# CHAPTER V.

### MR. JEKYLL TO LADY G. SLOANE STANLEY

*(Continued).*

BOWOOD, *Tuesday, January* 10*th*, 1824.

TO-MORROW we conclude our fortnight's visit to Bowood, and return to London. The time has passed very pleasantly and much to my taste, and the boys have had fine weather for exercise. They return to college on Saturday, the 18th, so will have another week in town.

We have had a continual supply of agreeable people in the house, and it is impossible to live more sensibly and creditably than our host and hostess. As you say, "They are of the right sort." On New Year's Day Lady Lansdowne had a long table set out in the conservatory, and gave a dinner to seventy-two poor children whom she clothes and educates. It was difficult to decide whether she or the little creatures seemed happiest.

Little Moore the poet has amused us inexhaustibly with humour all the day, and his tasteful singing of an evening. He has a cottage in the neighbourhood for his little wife and his two little children, and is a great resource of amusement to Bowood. It is a good little fellow, with as much sense as talent, and a most independent spirit. His new poem, "The Loves of the Angels," I have read here. It is in the rich flowery style of his "Lalla Rookh," and, though glittering with beautiful passages, does not delight me. It is like dining on sweetmeats.

You know my habits in a château, and I have devoured all the new French and English brochures on the tables. "The Entail"[1] is not a bad imitation of Walter Scott's Scotch novels, but I think we have had Scotch enough.

We have a Mr. Stanley here (Lord Derby's grandson), who reports well of Lancashire as to the manufactures. The rents there have been reduced, but are now well paid.

Wiltshire in a bad state. Lord Lansdowne has lowered his rental forty per cent. I really believe our papa-in-law[2] has suffered less than anybody.

SPRING GARDENS, *July 17th*, 1824.

JOSEPH and I are going to play a prank of some novelty.

In about a week or ten days we mean to scramble away to Switzerland. Geneva will be our first place of residence, from whence we shall make some further deviations. Whither I know not. But that will be determined when there. Perhaps run over the Alps for a short peep into Italy; but that is by no means decided, and must be determined by events, for on a pilgrimage I do not like a positive plan.

[1] By J. Galt.     [2] Mr. Sloane Stanley.

Our return will be through Paris, where of course we must make some short stay. But we expect to be in the land of beef and pudding again by the end of October.

Edward seems to expect that about the time of our return he will have leave from his regiment for an absence of three or four months, so will join us in London.

Now, I am so bad a felicity hunter, that having formed all this Quixotism I feel a regret that I am not to sit under an orange tree with you at Paultons. Tom Onslow confessed to me he was never at the Play without wishing to be at the Opera, and *vice versâ*. Such is the restlessness of knights errant.

We dined at A. Ellis's last week with the Poodle who has buried his measled Majesties.[1] Thank God Freddy was not a queen!

The Ellises are on the wing for Ireland, and then for Rome. I wish you joy of your divine's union with his divinity, which is perfectly *en règle*. They talk of four-and-twenty marriages all in a row, but I do not know who compose the six matrimonial quadrilles. Don't be surprised if I espouse and bring home a Swiss giantess. Grievances are useless topics, but I feel a sad loss of poor dear Mr. Stanley.

---

[1] The King and Queen of the Sandwich Isles, on a visit to England, died of measles within a few days of each other, at a hotel in the Adelphi. Mr. Byng, nicknamed Poodle, a well-known man of fashion, had been deputed to show them about London.

SPRING GARDENS, *July 27th*, 1824.

TO-DAY brought a merry letter from the Ensign who is up to his ears in Irish festivities, going a cruise in a yacht to the Giant's Causeway, his regiment soon marching to Belfast, and finally to Dublin. He has been engaged in quelling an Orange riot at Newry by opposing bayonets to brickbats, and seems as happy as fighting and fluting can make a man. Next October he expects some leave of absence, and on our return at the end of that month I have some hopes of seeing him. During his stay in England I wish we may be able to contrive a visit to Paultons. But we lead such a gipsy life for some time to come that nothing can be decided.

I called on poor Lilyveld t'other day in Cadogan Place. You cannot think what a pretty quiet house he has, and a right of promenade in a large and beautiful Botanical Garden. The din of London kept his noddle in the state of a watermill.

Almack's is dead. Lady Jersey's last rout expired; but Joseph says Semiramide was crowded on Saturday. There is a certain class of *vauriens* that never seem to quit London. Lady Ellenborough gave us a dinner yesterday, and the misses looked as misses do after another campaign without matrimony. Yet if one may calculate from favours in coachmen's hats celibacy is not universal.

I saw Lord Morpeth yesterday, looking well, and on horseback; last week, at Miss Berry's[1] blue stocking,

[1] Mary Berry, the elder of the two sisters so well known as the

I met Lady Stafford. As Sir C. Bunbury's executor, I signed a deed last week, by which Miss Fox settles something on Charles Fox's marriage, and Miss Vernon gives him £1,000.

Lord Clifden's, Roehampton Lodge,<br>
*Thursday, November 4th,* 1824.

After fasting three months, you may guess with what voracity I devoured your letter this morning. The handwriting was positively a refreshment to me.

The Hollands have been in town a few days on their way to Brighton. Joseph went two or three times to the play with them. Lady Holland seems in sad health, and looks wretchedly. I marvel she escaped Captain Medwin's book,[1] as all Byron's world has been scratched in it.

The Bedfords are also going to Brighton, and as the Windsor Cottage streams with water and the Castle is torn to pieces, I think His Majesty will also be driven to the Pavilion.

Lord Ellenborough and his bride[2] are absent from this place, so I have not seen her attractions, though I hear she is very pretty. If you want a palace the

---

friends and correspondents of Horace Walpole in his old age. When he succeeded to the Earldom of Orford in 1791, it is believed that he was prepared to go through the ceremony of marriage with either, in order to give her the rank of Countess. Miss Berry died in 1852, in her ninetieth year.

[1] "Journal of the Conversations with Lord Byron at Pisa, in 1821-2," by Thomas Medwin.

[2] Miss Elizabeth Digby, second wife of the Earl. They were divorced in 1830.

dowager Ellenborough is desirous of letting Cambridge House.

The public appetite for hell and the devil has been much gratified by the new German Opera[1] at Covent Garden. Don Giovanni's infernal regions are nothing to it. To "sup full of horrors" is a taste not confined to our countrymen, for at Paris we were regaled on the stage with the perdition and torments of Danaus' fifty daughters for the slight impropriety of murdering their fifty husbands. I think, with due gratitude to the revolution, they have a livelier conception of what fiends really appear to be than ourselves, and their fire and brimstone are infinitely more brilliant.

We see many people here daily, but London and its villas are equally barren of gossip; and unless I transcribe from the newspapers anecdotes of Mr. Fauntleroy, it is utterly impossible to make out a decent epistle to a lady so much nearer the North Pole than we are.

Spring Gardens, *December 16th,* 1824.

I DON'T envy you the amusement of selling a house, or repairing a house, or rummaging papers. I too am bored with removing plate, and books, and pictures from Wargrave Hill, and preparing the place for the purpose of letting it, as you know my detestation of the country, and my opinion that every day spent there is a day given to the grave before one's decease. When

[1] *Der Freischütz.* At the first representation, when there were calls for the composer, Weber failed to recognise his name in the English accent of the pit and gallery, until it was explained to him what "Weeber" meant.

you dismantle Harley Street give me my wife's portrait, which Mr. Stanley often promised he would leave me by his will.

I saw the Hollands yesterday. They have got old Bouverie's house in Burlington Street. *Miladi* is by no means recovered from her state of illness, though the air of Brighton was adopted. The *fricandeaus* tell. The Duke of Bedford[1] was there, and I thought looked well.

Among other refinements of rural life I see the Duchess of Rutland gets[2] prizes at Smithfield for the delicate and feminine accomplishments of improving rams and bulls—a branch of natural philosophy that has hitherto, from the prejudice of education, been left to the other sex. It has made a good laugh in London, and produced some epigrams that you would not read unless you were a candidate at a cattle show.

The Parisians have hissed *Der Freischütz*, and three months ago they scouted Rossini's best opera. Well did Rousseau say they had no taste for the best music, and no music of their own. As to our own opera, it seems likely to be performed only in the Court of Chancery.

I dined and slept lately at Roehampton, to be presented by Lord Ellenborough to his bride. Very pretty, but quite a girl, twenty years younger than himself. We had two Dowagers Londonderry, the

---

[1] John, sixth Duke. Died 1839.
[2] The Dowager Duchess. Lady Gertrude's sister was at this time Duchess of Rutland.

*ci-devant* Castlereagh, and my old friend of Boldrewood.

I rejoice to hear all Stewart Rose's *riches* were not swept into the sea, though a poet seldom abounds in that commodity.

SPRING GARDENS, *March 25th*, 1825.

We had Rogers all the time at Lord Clifden's, and one day the Bessboroughs and Duncannons. If you love gossip read the new quarto of Lord Orford's letters, and if you love admirable nonsense read a "Six Weeks' Tour in Switzerland," by two romantic daughters of Mrs. Wollstonecraft.[1]

Scandal! Scandal! Scandal! W. Spencer's daughter, in spite of the *moral example* of her parents, has produced a baby, and has not yet selected its father. I pity the poor girl's puzzle. Botherby[2] has left a card with me, which he has not done these seven years. It has no black edges, so it is probably to show he has not hanged himself.

Lord Holland has printed, though not published, a pretty *morceau* enough, entitled "A Dream." He supposes the King introduces him to talk with some great men of former ages—Lord Burleigh, Milton, Cowley, Addison, etc.

Drury Lane, they say, is so near total ruin that

---

[1] Married to William Godwin. The two daughters were Fanny, daughter of Mrs. Wollstonecraft by Finlay, an American, and Mary by Godwin, afterwards married to Shelley the poet.

[2] William Sotheby, the poet.

Vansittart[1] means to buy it for a parish church, and Kean is to preach.

I rejoice to hear you found your nursery in confirmed health. Disease was formerly only calamitous, but since Canning's epigrams on palsy, dropsy, apoplexy, and consumption, it is now understood to be ridiculous also. It is very condescending in you to correspond with any being so ludicrous and contemptible as a gouty man.

Spring Gardens, *October 6th*, 1825.

I can predict nothing at present of encountering the Zephyrs of Paultons in November. But if I emigrate anywhere it will certainly be to you. Change of air is the jargon of physicians when they can do nothing. Change of place is the disease of the healthy, and never was so epidemic as in these our days. You remember the Italian's epitaph, " I was well, I tried to be better, and I lie here." The confessor of Francis I. was scolded by a Cardinal for preaching that the King went directly to heaven, as it seemed to deny the doctrine of purgatory. The poor priest defended himself by saying His Majesty never stayed in a place.

I dowager daily in the carriage, read all a circulating library pours out, and never fail of the delights of some morning visitor; for this Metropolis, as Cobbett[2] calls it, is never totally deserted.

---

[1] Nicholas Vansittart, Lord Bexley. He was Chancellor of the Exchequer in the Liverpool Administration until 1823, when he was elevated to the peerage. He died 1851.

[2] William Cobbett, whose famous "Rural Rides" were at this time appearing in his newspaper, the *Political Register*.

Tom Moore's "Life of Sheridan" is out, and what I have seen of so difficult a job I like. My friend Mrs. Opie (and the title is appropriate, as she has relapsed into Quakerism) has published "Illustrations of Lying," of which the morality is so austere that I dare not tell a servant to say I am not at home, nor subscribe a letter with "Your obedient humble servant."

You know what a bookworm I have always been, but I did not know till yesterday that my feelings had the honour of resembling those of Mr. Pope on the subject.

He writes thus to Spence : "At this day, as much company as I have kept, and as much as I love it, I love reading better. I would rather be employed in reading than in the most agreeable conversation."

Joseph is "a chip of the old block," and pores upon books incessantly. When he does condescend to dissipation he reports to me five theatres brimful, but chemistry is his rage for the moment.

SPRING GARDENS, *October* 31*st*, 1825.

*Pour égayer votre veuvage* it delights me to hear of your trips to Wilton and Broadlands, and that the echoes of Hants have been enlivened by dowager screech-owls. I think I was once a favourite of that tuneful bird, but lost her affection by neglecting her invitation to a morning visit during her bivouac at Lord Palmerston's ; for on dining with her at Lord Pembroke's last spring she seemed cold and coy. However, I bore it like a man long experienced in the caprices of your sex and never once thought of suicide.

News I have none of the London manufacture. From Staffordshire I got yesterday some scandal, that the second son of a gallant military Marquis had eloped with the married daughter of a Piccadilly Earl. There is no degeneracy in the proceeding, as the noble families on each side are celebrated for morality.

George Cholmondeley married in the style of Petruchio, and painted up his old chariot for the nuptials. There was nothing new in the whole set out, except the bride's consent to make a part of it.

Paris is London at present—Lansdownes, Hollands, Ellenboroughs, Rogers, Poets, etc. The Bedfords are going through it for Nice. The Abercrombys just returned to frank this epistle for me. The Granvilles got into their Ambassadorial Hotel, and have public *soirées* once a week.

For lack of more intelligence I must now tell you a story which at least is *ben trovato*.

Some years ago an Englishman long resident at Paris was in the habit of visiting several evenings every week La Marquise de —— at her villa two miles out of town, where the best society met. She put this question to him, "Why do you come here with one livery servant behind your carriage and return with two?" He denied the fact, and added that he had but one *laquais* in this world. Next day he ordered his servant to explain this mystery, and menaced him with the police. The fellow confessed as follows, "that he had long been employed by some surgeons to procure dead bodies for dissection, and that he was frequently supplied by some resurrection men from a cemetery close to the villa of La Marquise, and that to elude all questions at the *barrière* on re-entering Paris at midnight he always dressed the corpse in one of his old liveries, and upheld it behind the carriage."

ROEHAMPTON LODGE, *Christmas Day* [1825].

THE Knight Templar and I came here on Saturday last, and your kind letter, which breathed the true spirit of a merry Christmas, was the first thing that greeted me.

Lady Georgiana's present state becomes her. I never saw her looking better. Her boy is really a nice fellow.

Your query on hobgoblins places me like the boy in Shakespeare's *Henry V.*, who tells Pistol he does not know what is French for "Fer, and Ferrett and Firk." I don't believe they possess in France our true species of British hobgoblin. Ours is neither *mauvais fée*, nor *loup garou*, nor, as old Boyer stupidly has it, *esprit spectre fantôme*. Our true hobgoblin is ugly, tragic, mischievous; but I should not know how to dress the character for a fancy ball at a county member's. It would be Dalmation difficult.

Country neighbours are a species of hobgoblin. What a comfort it would be to possess the French secret of bottling them, and then I would throw away the corkscrew.

It will be the same thing to John Bull whether the Guards shoot woodcocks or guerillas. A long bill is the result either way.

Nobody breaks the King of Spain's bones, and you see the poor King of Prussia breaks his own. How unjustly are fractures distributed in this world.

We have here Lord Duncannon, William Lamb, Luttrell, and the Poodle Byng.

The poor Duke of York's case grows so gloomy that I hate to revert to it. Daily attendance of Sir Astley Cooper on the legs, and we have nothing left but to hope for improbabilities.

We return to town on Wednesday, when Joseph takes wing again to Mr. Grenfell's, near Windsor. He has been so long domiciled with me that his residence elsewhere as yet seems strange to me. However, he dines with me as often as he can.

Lady Caroline[1] is kept alone at Brocket Hall (Lord Melbourne's), and well watched.

Yesterday we had pretty Lady Gower, who sends her love, with Lady Georgiana's, to you. I hear the King has given Mrs. Boehm a pension, and promise of apartments at Hampton Court.

The writing machinery here is so out of order, that my epistle looks as black as an elegy.

With a complication of loves and compliments.

Spring Gardens, *December* 29*th*, 1825.

PEOPLE from Paris amuse me much with Lady Holland's manœuvres there. In one of the five carriages which formed her ladyship's *cortège* was exported a certain poor Mrs. Somebody skilled in the

[1] Lady Caroline Lamb.

art of shampooing. This operation is daily performed at her *levée* on her ladyship's feet, divested of shoes and stockings, and which are so whitened and beautifully formed as to *extasier* every French or English dandy present. Mirabeau once said to me *Le monde est un charge de théâtre.* Things are done every day which would be hissed as *outré* in a farce. It is said Henry Fox[1] is in *la belle passion* with my pretty friend Lady Blessington at Naples. Perhaps Lady Holland will extend her tour to extricate her Telemachus from this Calypso, recollecting, too, that Italy is the region of love, and that at Florence she first fascinated his father.

You may suppose I have devoured an entire circulating library, but I have nothing to recommend. People admire "Granby,"[2] a new novel, and another called "The English in Italy." I can only say they are certainly above mediocrity. But I languish for the Margravine's Memoirs of her life, and hope I am not in her *dramatis personæ.* If she will tell all and fairly they will be amusing; but perhaps, like Madame de Genlis, she will endeavour to prove herself a very good sort of a woman, and then the work will be as dull as incredible.

The Dickinsons in passing through London to Mr. Smith's in Hertfordshire called here yesterday to learn the state of our legs and arms. Joseph has been perfectly re-established for a long time. They came

[1] The fourth and last Lord Holland. He married Lady Augusta Coventry in 1833, and died in 1859 at Naples.
[2] By T. H. Lister.

to town thus early on an alarm that their Westminster boy had a serious cough, but he has perfectly recovered, I believe. Batt at his advanced age has been successfully operated upon for a cataract.

Mrs. Coutts is still an enigma. Warrender told me that at his table she called his grace[1] "My dear," but this is far from decisive. No more is Lauderdale's reply when asked in Scotland whether he was to give her away. He answered, "I shall neither give nor throw her away."

Greenwood tells me one half of the people who overwhelmed his *fête* were unknown to him, and with the *nonchalance* of modern times sent to desire invitations. He painted his house lately, and I sent him this:—

On a green door in South Audley Square—

"To tell a man's door by inscribing his name
　Was a practice established of yore,
But my friend has contrived, with his green and his wood,
　How to tell a man's name by his door."

Lord Clifden is now here, but I am determined you shall pay for so much prose and poetry; and if you are not too angry at the postage to send me an answer, pray tell me that your delightful sister Lady Cawdor is well. I believe the sun is gone into Wales to visit her, for he has left town this morning, and I am writing at two o'clock by candle light. I admire his good taste, but I wish he would leave us his younger sun Phaethon as a deputy during his absence.

[1] The Duke of St. Albans.

SPRING GARDENS, *January 5th*, 1826.

IT was evident from the dandling of the Strathaven[1] at Windsor that some *cunning game* was to be played. It has been observed that in all the newspaper bulletins of royal airings to Virginia Water *Le vieux papa* is never named but as the Lord Steward, and *John Bull* does not know who he is, or why he is so constantly *L'ami de la maison.*

Lord Clifden and Rogers gone to Cashiobury, I believe, to meet the Ellises. I am not bold enough for the exploit.

It is delightful to hear a long married wife still describe her spouse as the God of Love, and give him the characteristic attribute of a pair of wings. If he had found the Romsey bankers possessed of an equal ability of flying I think he would have hardly guaranteed their stability.

Poets are nominal friends, but they do not spare each other. When Stewart Rose heard that there had been no run upon Rogers, poet and banker, he observed, " A run I should have deplored, but a little trot would not have been objectionable."

Joseph dined yesterday with Sir C. Flint, the Irish Secretary, who has been paying a long royal visit to the Duc de Bourbon, and describes Chantilly as having

[1] Afterwards tenth Marquess of Huntly. The allusion is difficult to explain, but Lady Conyngham's influence with George IV. is well known. Her daughter, Mary Elizabeth, married Lord Strathaven two months later, and the Lord Steward was the Marquess of Anglesey, Lady Conyngham's father.

recovered its ancient magnificence. Such an establishment of horses and servants as is indescribable.

Dickinson is with his papa-in-law for the holidays, where, I take it, a merry Christmas is always out of the question. I have seen lively blacksmiths, gay whitesmiths, and comical locksmiths, but a pair of more solemn Smiths I never encountered.

Tom Moore has had a dreadful diatribe poured out upon him by the *European Magazine* for the "Life of Sheridan," which was a perilous task, and sure to incense Whigs and Tories.

I met Canning yesterday. He looks shockingly, and twenty years older than last year. The campaign of fatigue and anxiety, too, will soon open upon him.

SPRING GARDENS, *February* 11*th*, 1826.

TOWN has been comparatively filled by Parliament, and politics are in high bustle. As I have long bid adieu to them, corn trade, Catholics, currency, and country banks molest me very little; but every hour brings a new anecdote of quarrels among Ministers, that one half of the Cabinet wants to throw t'other overboard. In short, the day is not long enough for the botheration it teems with.

Sir Walter Scott is ruined by the bankruptcy of the Scotch booksellers[1] who published his works, and with whom he had embarked all his money. The day after

---

[1] Constable & Co. of Edinburgh.

this blow up an anonymous friend offered to lend him £30,000.

Old Antrobus[1] has left £40,000 to one nephew and £200,000 to another, besides large estates. Doing the honours of Mother Coutts' dinners wore him out, though he had shaken off the palsy, and died of inflammation of the chest, which has been universal of late. Lady Cowper nearly carried off by it.

Madame de Genlis[2] describes some sentimental hours she passed with the two old ladies[3] in the Vale of Llangollen, who both declare they never saw her face in all their born days. For veracity *la Comtesse* beats *la Margravine*.

Joseph does not give a very splendid account of the opera. Edward writes of great festivities among Irish balls and belles, and of his victories over snipes and smugglers.

They talk of Lord Granville going to Ireland, and say Lord Wellesley would return to India if he were invited. The King says Lady Wellesley[4] is one of the most sensible and highly bred women he ever

---

[1] Sir Edward Antrobus, Bart.
[2] In "Souvenirs de Félicé."
[3] Lady Eleanor Butler, sister of the seventeenth Earl of Ormonde, and Miss Sarah Ponsonby, related to the Earls of Bessborough. They lived in seclusion at Plasnewydd, in the Vale of Llangollen, and became celebrated as the "Ladies of Llangollen." They died within a short time of each other—viz., June 1829 and December 1831 respectively.
[4] She was the daughter of Mr. Richard Caton, of Philadelphia, and married a Mr. Robert Paterson, by whom she was left a widow.

conversed with. It seems she went to Ireland on the avowed project of fascinating His Excellency, and that for some time she made no impression.

The Duke of York's Palace[1] begins to present a magnificent front to the Park. The *façade* seems double the extent of Lord Spencer's, and reduces Lord Stafford's to a Lilliput villa.

The Duke recovered of a late indisposition, and could I hobble more gracefully I should have dined with him yesterday, though still I feel from so long a domestication a decent horror of late dinners and cold evening voyages, an amusement which Joseph is my proxy for. So I shall wait to come out with the lilacs.

Our Lady of Holland still detains *Milord* at Paris on the luxurious *entremets* of Talleyrand's cook, though he had probably passed his time more agreeably in the House of Peers.

Spring Gardens, *Tuesday, July 18th,* 1826.

The eternal dry weather brings frogs out everywhere, and the croaking is universal. Blighted cauliflowers, shrivelled pease, Yorkshire rebellions, starving manufacturers, and Catholic disaffection. Plenty of evils for the new M.P.'s to discuss as an amusement.

Lord Manners was in hopes to have resigned the Seal this summer, and has taken a place in Suffolk, but His Majesty's Ministers are at such a puzzle about the choice of his successor that he must return to

[1] The present Stafford House.

Ireland for another year. The Lord-Lieutenant [1] has taken a singular turn for economy, and the Castle is devoted to conjugal love and saving money. His Excellency's protection of Papists does not tend to render Lord Manners' political position more palatable.

London is of course depopulated. A few are left to eat whitebait at Greenwich, and yawn under Lord Hertford's marquee in the Regent's Park.

My babies are paddling on the Thames to Richmond, and stewing themselves at night with " Paul Pry."

Lord Clifden meditating his annual visitation to Ireland unaccompanied by the Ellises, who have no taste for whisky, priests, and Paddies, but disport themselves at Cashiobury, the Priory, and Worthing.

The Duke of York better, but terribly *ennuyé* by Halford's imprisonment of him, and I dread his first attempt to escape from it.

Lady Holland has transported her Telemachus to some place abroad, where medicinal springs cure the sweet passion. The Calypso is said to be very talented, and *Miladi* declares there shall be no *bel esprit* but herself in the family.

Piccadilly is animated now and then by Napoleon's niece [2] looking out of Mother Coutts' window, and poor Rogers does not dare peep out of his into the Green Park, as *John Bull* advertises that he is the person who lay dead under an avalanche for a century and a half.

[1] The Marquess Wellesley.
[2] Lady Dudley Stuart.

Don't read Lady C. Campbell's "Alla Giornata," don't read Lord Blessington's "Reginald de Vavasour," both duller than death.

Poet Sotheby invites the boys to a *Fête Champêtre* at a hovel he has built in a bog on Epping Forest, where his brother the Admiral is to waltz, but they have no stilts, so decline it.

SPRING GARDENS, *Saturday, October 7th*, 1826.

LAWYER LEE, who saw me yesterday on business, has found benefit from the necromancer of Cowes. He reports that Dr. L'Afan married a widow worth £4,000 a year near Canterbury, a place famous for tales of all sorts, and consequently practises physic rather as an amusement. He has above thirty patients in the island, mounts them on donkeys daily and early, and, I believe, graces the squadron by riding at the head of it. He gives very gentle medicines, but inculcates severe *regimen*, and bullied Lord Anglesey most peremptorily out of his yacht and Lord Galloway out of two cooks. In a fortnight he cured the Duchess of Sussex of an abscess, blistered Lady L. Cadogan with success, and has defeated Lord Anglesey's tic doleureux for many months, though he declares he will never attend another patient in that inscrutable disorder. The doctor makes those who consult him keep a journal of their most minute feelings, which Joseph applauds as the system of his new idol professor, Hahnemann[1] of Leipzig.

[1] Samuel Hahnemann, the founder of Homœopathy. He died in 1843.

That luminous and interesting Cabinet minister, the Earl of Westmorland, nearly closed his valuable life at Cowes very recently.

A fantastic letter yesterday from the Honourable Elizabeth Law,[1] who desires me to admire the motto of her seal composed by herself—

> "Blest be that hand which letters first designed,
> And thus gave wings and language to the mind."

To which I replied—

> "Blest be that silly goose who first
> Gave belles her quills to taper,
> And blest that dirty beggar too
> Whose rags first gave them paper."

Yesterday I called at the Duke of York's, and received the usual account. He was out airing. I have too much authority to believe he underwent the operation, but only to relieve him from a very moderate accumulation of fluid, the removal of which, it was supposed, would facilitate the effects of medicine. There is, however, a very general despair as to total recovery. Rumour has even added an ulcer on the leg, which threatened mortification for some hours, and Lord Huntly has been named for the Grenadier Guards.

Among other exaggerations of gossip is the Chancellor's intended resignation at Christmas, and Copley's succession to the seals.

Mr. Shields has vomited another tirade in Ireland against the poor Duke of York, more brutal and

[1] Afterwards Lady Colchester.

malignant than the first, and the *Morning Chronicle* is proud to give it at full length. The Duke's letters to Mrs. Clarke, are raked up, and to each of the Duke's declarations of fidelity to her is added from his Catholic Speech, "So help me God!"

That little coxcomb, the Vice-Chancellor, gone to bore Lord Granville at Paris. He struggled in vain to succeed Lord Gifford in the House of Lords, but must content himself with dowagers and *écarté*. *Les ennuyées* begin to muster at Brighton; Lady Holland as usual the *prima donna* of the corps till Mother Coutts arrives with the *rouleaux* from the Strand, and a majority of side dishes.

We have no news except of a clever plan of Colonel Trench to supply the new palace with fish, by salting the Serpentine river to breed tame turbot, and making lobster sauce by the treadmill. A meeting of fish-mongers and other sea-holders is advertised to oppose it; and as it is to be held at Billingsgate the language of the debate will probably be less polite than at Andover.

Spring Gardens, *October 28th*, 1826.

JOHN PEARSE, who sees the Duke of York frequently, gave me an excellent account of him yesterday, and has sanguine hopes of recovery. The Duke slept seven hours the preceding night, a length of continued sleep he has not enjoyed for twenty years. In an adjoining room, with the door open, a daily dinner is served for his medical and military intimates—Halford, Taylor,

Torrens, Greenwood. The Duke of course dines alone, but by these means he hears their talk, and pleasantly and cheerfully sees them by turns. There has been an erysipelas on the leg, and Sir Astley Cooper was called in.

When that strange man Lord Wycombe was dying of liver and dropsy he wrote his own epitaph: "Here lies William, Marquess of Lansdowne,[1] who was drowned in his armchair." There is a newspaper story of a young peer ruined by noble gamblers. Lord Clanricarde is named, but whether as dupe or duper I cannot learn. They say it has brought Canning, his father-in-law, from Paris.

Your album makes me believe you are a Latin scholar, so I venture to send a Latin epigram, and what is more, composed by a lady. The various *équivoque* on the verb *solvo* is excellent and untranslatable.

### ON A DEBTOR WHITEWASHED UNDER THE INSOLVENT ACT.

> Qui niger et captivus eram, candore nivali,
>     Splendidus egredior carcere, liber homo—
> Solvuntur curæ—solventur vincula ferri
>     Solvitur attonitus creditor—in lachrymis.
> Solvor ego—solum non solvitur æs alienum—
>     A non solvendo rite solutus ero.

Henry Fox vacates the Duke of Norfolk's seat in Parliament, stays abroad, cured of love, and exemplifies

---

[1] The first Marquess, better known as the Earl of Shelburne, who succeeded Lord Rockingham as Prime Minister in 1782. He introduced Mr. Jekyll to political life.

the couplet in the puppet show which so exasperated Don Quixote—

> "Don Gayferos at tables playing
> Of Melissandra thinks no more."

Walter Scott going to Paris for six volumes of Napoleon anecdotes. Mademoiselle Las Casas[1] offers him a deluge of them to gratify the modern rage of disfiguring history in a novel.

*Monday Evening, December 18th,* 1826.

LORD COLCHESTER has defeated Agar Ellis in a lawsuit about a chimney the latter had built to keep saddles warm, and, strange to say, Edward's dry nurse, my old Mary, was called as a witness to prove the little Colchester's house had stood where it still stands for the last twenty years. The smoking of a new peer will be a costly amusement to George. But we must pay for our pleasures.

The "Memoirs of Mrs. Siddons"[2] are amusing; but there is too much of the green room, and too little of her, in the book. The "Memoirs" and "Journal" of la Princesse de Lamballe are interesting.

No one seems to entertain a hope of the permanent recovery of our poor Duke. The King very well, and I should guess in good spirits; for the other day when Edward was on guard he gave "Calne"[3] as the parole to the regiment.

---

[1] The daughter of the Marquis de Las Casas, the companion and biographer of Napoleon at St. Helena.

[2] By James Boaden.

[3] The borough which Mr. Jekyll represented in Parliament for many years.

# CHAPTER VI.

## MR. JEKYLL TO LADY G. SLOANE STANLEY
### (*Continued*).

SPRING GARDENS, *January* 15*th*, 1827.

IT was unfortunately too certain in June last that a disease so desperate, at the Duke's time of life, would terminate fatally at no distant period, and I never entertained a hope of recovery.[1] He had a heart of feeling, sincerity, and attachment, and for a long series of years manifested towards me the most disinterested kindness. Yet miscreants were to be found whose malignity could asperse him while scarcely cold in his coffin. Hard is the lot of princes. The errors or follies of other men are smiled at, but theirs are magnified into crimes. The world, however, has done justice to his memory by an unfeigned and universal sorrow. On Friday Edward marches with the Grenadier Guards to Windsor to escort the last remains of one who had voluntarily promised to protect him when I ceased to exist.

It is the common misfortune of those who attain an age like mine to outlive many they loved. Yet I am thankful for a prolongation of life which has enabled me to see my sons fairly launched in the world, and fixed in professions which will not force them to desert me.

[1] The Duke died on January 5th, 1827.

Joseph has become the pupil, for a year, of an eminent special pleader in the Temple, and his mornings are now devoted to that difficult branch of the law. They both dine with me continually, indeed, whenever they are disengaged. Positive happiness I never enjoyed since I lost their mother, to whom my attachment bordered on enthusiasm; but their own conduct, my extraordinary spirits, and the return of health I now enjoy, render my existence as satisfactory as I have any right to desire.

I found Lord Stafford as well in health, nay, better, I think, than when I last saw him two years ago. I passed two very pleasant days there, and Lady Stafford hoped I would repeat my visit with Joseph, who had gone to Mr. Grenfell's, near Windsor, and could not accompany me. We had the Gowers, the little Vice-Chancellor and his unremitting *écarté*, and the very agreeable Mr. Hay, Lord Bathurst's secretary. Sir Humphry Davy gone abroad for health.

Lady Cawdor has produced, and Lady Georgiana has produced, and both most propitiously. Not so my friend Sir J. Stanley's daughter, the recent bride of Captain Parry.

Lord Orford's sister [1] asked Wolff, a converted Jew and a beggar, to marry her. Lee is framing the settlements. The couple set off for Syria and the Holy Land directly on his pilgrimage as a missionary to convert Jews.

[1] Georgiana Mary, daughter of the second Earl of Orford. She married the Rev. Joseph Wolff, D.D., vicar of Isle Brewers.

Another religious union is taking place, that of Lord Rocksavage[1] with a daughter of Sir George Gray, the sainted Commissioner of Portsmouth.

London will begin to fill in February. Sir J. Stanley has let his moderate house in St. Audley Square for three months at £700.

Yesterday, at the request of my old friend, Smith, M.P. for Norwich, I seconded the nomination of his son-in-law, your neighbouring nightingale, as a candidate for our Athenæum. I hope Cobbett will spare our club. On Saturday last in his paper he called Boodles "Noodles."

We suppose the Duke of Wellington will be Commander-in-Chief, and the Duke of Cambridge have the Grenadier Guards, Lord Huntly probably the vacant regiment of Guards. The King much depressed in health and spirits.

SPRING GARDENS, *March 20th*, 1827.

LET me congratulate you on your nephew Morpeth's *début*[2] in the House of Commons, which is highly spoken of. A host of young gentlemen have appeared there with more effrontery than talents; and as Parliament no longer possesses the supereminent characters of ancient days, the *débutants* are fearless of eclipse, and spout without control. Lord Morpeth and Villiers Stuart are the only exceptions *dont on parle*.

---

[1] The second Marquess of Cholmondeley. This marriage did not take place.

[2] On a motion for the relief of Catholic disabilities.

Politics I have long bid adieu to, or the present moment would not supply me with very comfortable speculations on the state of public affairs.

Poor Lord Liverpool[1] is still without speech, and almost without consciousness. Yet the machine of government moves on. On the introduction of the guillotine in France, I remember a young Englishman wrote a treatise to prove that a man's existence might be continued by art, though his head was wanting. He did not extend this reasoning to an Administration, but merely applied it to the ordinary class of mankind, such as Justices of the Peace, county gentlemen, and dandies.

Huskisson, too, is in a precarious state, such an affection of the trachea, and such nightly perspirations, as in an earlier stage of life would indicate consumption.

Under the pretext of resorting for health to the waters of Leamington, the Lady-Lieutenant[2] of Ireland is said to be separating herself from her Lord. These waters, like those of Lethe, probably teach wives to forget their husbands, and resemble those Lady Holland sent her son to drink in Italy as a cure for the tender passion.

The Lord-Lieutenant, though by no means in despair at this Catholic emancipation from wedlock, shuts himself up in total seclusion. Whenever he does deign to appear in public he presents a singular spectacle — a hoary head with eyebrows artificially blackened,

---

[1] He died on December 4th, 1828.   [2] Lady Wellesley.

checks highly rouged, and a forehead painted white. Grimaldi in a pantomime is a less picturesque Viceroy. It is said Lady Glengall some time ago forced her way to his toilette, and caught him in the very fact of repairing himself.

Somebody said to-day the gallant Hertford was to carry the Garter to the Emperor of Russia. Near the aforesaid Marquess' Villa in the Regent's Park the Zoological Society[1] is about to create a menagerie of wild beasts and birds similar to that in the Jardin des Plantes at Paris, much to the terror of Sir Herbert Taylor's old nuns of St. Catharine's, who have just built their new monastery hard by. The poor old bodies expect tigers at their tea tables and hyænas as chaperons in their evening walks. The wolf who devoured Lord Orford's Little Red Riding Hood is to be chaplain to the menagerie.

My friend Luttrell, who is too good-natured for a satirist, has published a poem on the modern Greeks of Crockford's Gambling Club, and another on the modern Romans, *Il écrit les vers de société assez joliment*; but neither of these is so good as his "Letters to Julia." Dr. Parr's life is about to be published, and they have written to me for my correspondence with him. So ends this budget on nonsense.

I sat two hours yesterday with my old friend Mrs. Siddons, a majestic ruin; but her powerful eyes reminded me of Constance, Isabella, and Lady Randolph. She promises me a *tête-à-tête*, and to read

[1] The Zoological Gardens were opened in April 1827.

*Macbeth* to me. She describes Mrs. Fitzhugh's nervous irritability as almost amounting to craziness.

The late Lord Guilford left a good estate to his poor nephew, Lord Sheffield; but for want of the legal number of witnesses the will is waste paper, so superior is the talent of an attorney's clerk to that of the founder of an university in the Ionian Islands. As St. Paul says, "This is to the Greeks foolishness."

P.S. the second.—When old Baxter, the fanatic, died, a man sold so profitably a pamphlet entitled "The Last Words of Mr. Baxter," that he published a second, entitled "More Last Words of Mr. Baxter." And I am following his example.

Edward has just paid me a visit from Kew. He dined there yesterday with the Duke of Cumberland, who had been at Windsor in the morning, and said the King never was in better health. On his telling the King that Edward was to dine with him that day at Kew the King said, "Jekyll is coming down here when I get into the Castle."

I remember one day at the Lodge he said generally, "You must visit me in the winter." If a command came at present I should certainly plead the gout (though it has left me), as a convalescent would not relish a castle.

However, he cannot get into the Castle for some days; and if even then I felt stout enough, between ourselves, I had rather avoid the honour, and prefer home to magnificence and a cold excursion in the snow.

The Duke said the King had ordered that the uniform of the three regiments of Guards and the Blues should be changed in April, each officer to have three coats with embroidery, at the cost of a hundred and twenty pounds, though they had new uniforms last year. Now this really seems a wanton expense; and there is no reason why it should not recur in six months if a new fancy took place. However, as a Lieutenant's pay, after regimental deductions, is only ten pounds a year, it is presumed a young gentleman ought always to be in debt to his tailor.

The last piece of nonsense I have heard is that Lord Hill will resign the command of the Army, as he thinks the King communicates more with Sir Herbert Taylor than with himself, and that Sir George Murray will leave the Colonial Office to succeed him. It was not said where Wellington could get a new Secretary of State.

But I will have done, for the daily *on dits* would fill a quire.

*January 14th*, 1828.

YESTERDAY we had a pleasant dinner with Poet Rogers, Lord and Lady Holland, their pretty dimpled girl, and Tom Grenville, whom I amused with the following family anecdotes :—

A volume entitled the "Interior of Foreign Courts," and translated from the French, is now in circulation.

Mistaking Greville and Grenville, it gravely asserts among the anecdotes of Naples that the present correct Lord Grenville kept Lady Hamilton several years, but falling into poverty handed her over to his uncle Sir William Hamilton, who married her, imputing thereby to his sedate and opulent lordship both penury and profligacy. Lord Nugent told me this morning that they contrived to hoist the Duke of Buckingham to the top of Mount Etna. What a compliment to the mechanical powers this age of intellect has arrived at! If they had thrown the corpulent cratur in they would have blocked up the crater of Etna for ever, and, as the servant says in the *Clandestine Marriage*, got rid of two confounded things together.

They said at Rogers' Sir Astley Cooper the surgeon was to marry the widowed Lady Bridgewater.[1] I venture to hope he had not trepanned her into the match.

Miguel[2] has been feasted and ducked at a stag hunt and a review, has visited St. Paul's and the waxworks, paid for seeing outlandish beasts at the Tower. As they also saw him, it was disgraceful to take his money. He mistook the pantomime at Covent Garden for *Hamlet*. Lady Morley will make a good sketch of him on his visit at Saltram. They wisely marry him

---

[1] He did not.
[2] Don Miguel, brother to Pedro IV., King of Portugal and Emperor of Brazil. Miguel usurped the Crown of Portugal from his niece Queen Maria II., in whose favour Pedro had abdicated in July of this year, and retained it until 1833, when Maria was restored.

to a miss of nine years of age, as no miss of ten would have consented.

Lord Carlisle called here last Saturday. The King far from well when they were at Windsor, and the botheration of the present moment will not relieve gout.

> SPRING GARDENS, *January 24th*, 1828.

THE day before yesterday in the Park I met the late Privy Seal[1] riding with full as much complacency as if he was still in office. At least the merit of philosophy cannot be denied to the late Administration,[2] for I never saw a set of gentlemen who seemed to care so little about their catastrophe. But I think it may be fairly added that they manifested as little avidity to get into their late eminence. Nay, they went further, for many of them seemed to accept with reluctance. Twenty years ago I was a hot politician, and the passing events would have excited me. At present I feel no interest about them, except that with such a fluctuation of men and measures it may become more and more difficult to keep the country on its legs; and that is a general concern.

The King is convalescent at last, but he has been well bothered as an invalid, and it retarded his recovery. Lord Byron's shabby friend Hunt[3] has published a large volume of rather abusive anecdotes of his Lord-

---

[1] George, sixth Earl of Carlisle, Lady Gertrude's brother.
[2] Lord Goderich's.
[3] Leigh Hunt. This book, "Lord Byron and Some of His Contemporaries," was the great mistake of Hunt's life. "The only book that Hunt ever regretted he had written . . . its

ship. London, you may be sure, has not been deserted during all this *tracasserie*, and I have been heroic enough to dine out frequently.

Lady Holland is the only dissatisfied minister out of office. She counted upon sailing down daily with her long-tailed blacks and ancient crane-necked chariot to sit with Holland at the Secretary's office, to administer the affairs of Europe, and make Sidney Smith a bishop. As for him, he never cared twopence about the whole job, and the delightful fellow was very wise in so treating it. To say the truth, I never augured well of the permanency of the whole concern, even if Canning's death and Goderich's impotency had not blown it up.

Talking of the Hollands, Joseph said this morning they resembled the different ends of a magnet, attractive one and repulsive the other. This was very good; but don't circulate it, for she is really kind to him, and it would seem ungrateful.

I live in hopes of your arrival.

P.S.—If anybody had asked me I should have said I had no lady correspondent but yourself, yet to-day I received a letter from Elizabeth Law to express to so very old a member of the family their satisfaction at Lord Ellenborough's[1] admission to a Cabinet office, and

manifold faults of taste and temper were severely criticised, the book having especially hurt the feelings of many literary gentlemen, who envied Hunt his opportunities of receiving ill-treatment at the hands of a lord."—*Athenæum*, March 25th, 1893, p. 377.

[1] Lord, afterwards Earl of Ellenborough, Privy Seal in Wellington's Administration.

the prospect, within three or four weeks, of Lady Ellenborough presenting him with a heir or a heiress.

She writes she could be present at the first interview between His Majesty and her brother, but that the former is so good a performer that probably it would not be discoverable that the latter had ever been in disgrace, and she trusts now that the unfortunate rest of the family will no longer be cut by their sovereign.

She adds that Lord Wharncliffe and his friends at Brighton declare that the admission of her brother into administration is a positive insult to the memory of Canning, and that she hears Lady Holland is so furious that she nearly killed old Allen for telling her that, like an aloe, she must be content to have blossomed for three months, and now make up her mind to be shut up for the ninety-nine years of the future hundred.

Such are the Miss's communications of political feeling, and which I have confided as a matter of amusement to you. The exultation on the event must be considerable, as she volunteers so unexpected an epistle to convey it to me.

Spring Gardens, *March 22nd*, 1828.

Edward chronicles the gaieties of Dublin, the balls, the drawing-rooms, and the popularity of the Lord-Lieutenant.[1] Poor Lady Anglesey, I hear, wished much to have gone over in the present spring, but it was overruled.

Joseph is very well, and a great resource to me. He

[1] The Marquess of Anglesey.

went last night to Lady Lansdowne, who had *Pasta Caradori*, and all the thrushes and blackbirds who whistle in the present season of London.

"Columbus" bored me before I got half across the Atlantic with him, and I kicked him out to read "The History of George Godfrey," which is a comical lie from one end to the other, and therefore ten times more edifying than four volumes of truth.

The crash of the Goderich Theatre maimed and bruised many of my friends, but it murdered Tierney and Abercromby.[1] The ruin of the latter I am really and sincerely hurt at. He abandons London and an income of three thousand a year, cannot return to his profession, and unwisely thinks he can find resources in a Derbyshire rustication.

A penurious father with a large income forces Spring Rice[2] to exile himself to the East Indies. His rising talents and virtues deserve a better fate, and the event is universally deplored. Such are his popularity and importance, to the interests of Ireland in particular, that I have heard of many who were willing, if delicacy would permit, to subscribe a magnificent free gift to him with a view to keep him here.

---

[1] James Abercromby, afterwards Lord Dunfermline, who certainly survived the shock. He was Judge-Advocate-General in Canning's Administration, and Speaker of the House 1835-9, and retired on a pension of £4,000.

[2] Thomas, first Lord Monteagle, the friend of O'Connell, and an active Liberal. He was Chancellor of the Exchequer 1835-9, in the Melbourne Government, but was not a success in that office. He died in 1866.

Miguel is a splendid performer. When he caused the murder of the unfortunate gentleman[1] who made such successful love to his sister, they were so puzzled about hiding the corpse from the King in his apartments, where the deed was done, that Miguel contrived to put it under the King's dining-table, and during the repast kicked it near him, that his royal father's foot might not discover it.

The murdered man's son took a singular revenge. He made equally successful love to Miguel's next sister, married her, and scampered to England. They were very near meeting here when Miguel was sent to stare at Greenwich Hospital.

The King has really no complaint but lameness. I saw a letter yesterday from Jelf,[2] the tutor of the Duke of Cumberland's[3] boy,[4] enclosing the following essay by his pupil at eight years old.

"A good king should love his subjects, and particularly locksmiths and clockmakers, as they make the cleverest things I ever saw." This young Telemachns does not degenerate from George the Third and his love of pendulums.

The Dissenters have exchanged a bitter pill for a sweetmeat. I wish our poor Catholics had also some

---

[1] The Marquis de Loulé, suffocated by Miguel or his orders in the royal palace of Salvaterra.

[2] Richard William Jelf, afterwards Principal of King's College, a noted theologian, and the friend of Pusey and Newman.

[3] Ernest, King of Hanover, died 1851.

[4] George Augustus, King of Hanover, died 1878.

candied orange-peel for their desserts, but I despair even of the House of Commons.

SPRING GARDENS, *Friday, March* 28*th*, 1828.

AN invitation from the Archipelago, I am sorry to say, was generally more successful than in the present instance has been that from Belvoir.

On Thursday next I am engaged to dine with our new Privy Seal Lord Ellenborough, to meet Lord Eldon and some of that ancient school. But Trojans and Tyrians when mixed form no bad society, because that bore called politics is necessarily excluded.

On Monday last I dined with the King; and though too lame to stand, I never saw him in better health and spirits; a small party. We had only the Duke of Leeds and Lord Ravensworth. On Wednesday last I dined with him again, and he was able to use his crutches. We had only the Conynghams and their pretty daughter, and two or three men of the Household.

The King goes to Windsor for the holidays, and on his return to town *levées* and Drawing-rooms are expected. If he determines to sit, there would be no difficulty in all this.

Edward writes that the Paddies are delighted to see their Lord-Lieutenant ride about Dublin with no attendant but his groom; "Because," says Paddy, "it's for all the world as if he was a raal gintleman."

A poor young Prussian artist is under Joseph's patronage, and has drawn in pencil a very good likeness of him for a guinea. I believe Sir Thomas Lawrence asks more, as Lady G. Ellis and her boy will cost an additional four hundred and ninety-nine.

The papers announce nothing but balls and suppers. Gunter and Weippart[1] more talked of than Nicholas and the Grand Turk. On Sunday last I dined with the Chancellor. Let Dudley beware, for Sir. F. Burdett dined there, and is become a rival.

Remember me most kindly to Lady Cawdor.

NORMAN COURT, *Friday, September* 19*th*, 1828.

WE leave Norman Court next Monday, having, at the hospitable instance of Wall, prolonged our visit beyond its intended limits.

Our host has an admirable establishment, luxury, comfort, good taste, and not a syllable of ostentation. A succession of pleasant society, plenty of books for the lame, and plenty of game for the active. We have pretty women, too—Lady Caroline Calcraft and Mrs. Vernon Smith. Marsh passed a day with us, and we talked of you.

The weather has been propitious for my daily drives, as I have been amused with the Memoirs of Le Comte de Tilly[2] just published, who gives rather a profligate account of himself in the true style of a French *fanfaron's* veracity. It seems like an appendix to the rascally anecdotes of the Duc de Lauzun. Tilly, however, does justice to the unfortunate Queen, and

[1] A fashionable bandmaster and composer of dance music.
[2] "Mémoirs pour servir à l'histoire des mœurs de la fin du dix-huitième siècle," 3 vols.

confines her attachments to Coigny and Fersen, which I know to be true from authentic information, though the Jacobins gave her a hundred lovers.

The book came awkwardly here for Mrs. Wall, for Tilly recounts his elopement and marriage with Miss Bingham in America, and his receiving a large sum from the family to consent to a divorce on account of some legal defect in the ceremony. The lady, you know, is now the wife of Alexander Baring.[1]

The Speaker says the first time old Lord Stowell dined at Holland House *Miladi*, in her usual style, addressed him as follows :—

"Sir William Scott, to speak honestly, the first time I knew you I hated you extremely."

"To speak honestly," replied Lord Stowell, "is an admirable principle in your ladyship, and I am bound to adopt it in declaring that the aversion was reciprocal."

We shall lounge along the coast to Worthing, and if we tire of it proceed to Brighton. A line to the Post Office, Worthing, will either find me there or be forwarded.

YORK HOTEL, BRIGHTON, *Monday, October 6th*, 1828.

BRIGHTON is very pleasant and comfortable, a good hotel, a fine sea view at my windows, my morning drive, my lounge at a library, a late dinner, and an early bed. So I have paid no visits for fear of repay-

---

[1] First Lord Ashburton. The lady was Anne Louisa, eldest daughter of Mr. William Bingham of Philadelphia, a senator of the United States. They were married in 1798.

ment; but Sir A. Legge[1] and I consolidated our meals yesterday, as we are under the same roof. Here are people I know, if I choose to look for them; but Brighton is so like London decanted upon the sea shore, that I will not complete the resemblance by morning visits and dinners.

Here are the Argylls, old Lord Harrington, Lord Camden, and I believe the Hollands and Tierney, but I am quiet and sulky. Not so the Guardsman, who improves his mind with dandies of the Tenth and their valuable occupations.

The harridan Countess of Cork and Orrery is hunting for me all over the place. I have told the master of the hotel to inform the Countess' servant that while bathing yesterday I was unfortunately drowned.

Chantrey is coming down to place the King's statue on the Steyne, which we subscribed for years ago. The Brighton democrats pelted the former to pieces in gratitude for creating their town.

SPRING GARDENS, *November 3rd*, 1828.

WE left Paultons, as we always do, with regret, and I think more so this time than ever; we were so comfortable and snug. I must repeat the greatest compliment I know, in saying I never once felt I was a mere visitor.

I have been already among my lawyers, Joseph among his philosophers, and Edward among his redcoats, but I have gleaned little more gossip than the

[1] The Admiral.

gossiping *Morning Post* I send you. Lord Stowell was one of the three peers to adjourn Parliament, and tells me the King's signature to the Commission was quite illegible. He says the gout fled from the arm to the bowels, and occasioned alarming inflammation for many hours. This has been confirmed to me by Lord Farnborough. But certainly at present there is convalescence, however precarious as to duration.

Nothing transpires as to Ministerial intentions towards Ireland when Parliament meets after Christmas. It is said somebody tried to pump the Duke of Wellington on the subject, who replied, "No pumping! It won't do! If the hairs of my head knew what my brain had decided I would cut them off and wear a wig."

I see my friend Will Smith has not learned soothing notes among the nightingales, for he announces, as Chairman, a public dinner in honour of Mr. Shiel, to manifest a total union between Catholics and Dissenters, and bother the Brunswickers. This is not gratitude for the repeal of the Test Act. As far as I can form an opinion on this horrible dilemma, I fear Government will be compelled to violent measures. But a truce to the odious topic of politics.

P.S.—As a frank has dropped in I enclose the Minerva Seal of our Athenæum Club, engraved by Wyon of the Mint from a drawing by Sir T. Lawrence.

*Thursday, November 19th,* 1828.

JOSEPH and I met Tom Moore t'other day at dinner,

and he amused us with stories which manifest how sincerely the poets love one another, so I must send you a brace of them.

A friend of Rogers' observed that viper broth was very nutritious for persons of weakly and decaying habit, and that Rogers lived upon it. Somebody said it must be an expensive diet. "No," replied the friend, "Rogers finds his own venom."

Rogers dined last summer where the Duke of Wellington came the very last to dinner. In the evening the Duke apologised to the master of the house, and said, "The real fact is, I was detained in the House of Lords on the Anatomy Bill,[1] but I did not like to mention it, as Mr. Rogers was present."

We were abusing the drama of *Don Juan*, which has been popular in all countries, and agreed it was a disgusting tissue of fire, murder, violation, and concluded with sending a human being into eternal perdition. Tom said it was a moral spectacle, because it taught people to take care whom they invited to supper.

I called on your delightful sister. She had left town, and was to return for a single day, and then proceed northwards. I told our friend the Attorney-General (Scarlett), who was fortunate enough to find her at home on that single day. He tells me she had a bad cold—the customary tribute of coming to town in November—but it did not prevent her journey.

Rogers was here yesterday from the Splügen. He

---

[1] An allusion to Samuel Rogers' personal appearance, which was a standing subject for the jokes of his contemporaries.

was "beat bootless home and weather beaten back," but he contrived afterwards to scale St. Gothard at Mayence. Like the Devil of old, he took himself up to an exceeding high tower to view the landscape of the Rhine, and who should come up, to his surprise, while there, but the Arch-Duke Constantine. His Imperial Highness, with that talent of questioning which is not confined to the family of the Czars, inquired rapidly to whom two châteaus in view appertained, and, without waiting for answer, said, "I suppose nothing more is to be seen?" and descended.

His plea on visiting Germany is to escort a sick wife to some baths, but I suspect Nicholas has sent him on a sort of honourable exile, as his craziness and tyranny at Warsaw had almost disaffected the Polish army.

George IV. is very well, though the newspapers give him a mortal disease once a week. I had a letter yesterday from Lord Conyngham.

Lady Holland is beating up for recruits at Brighton, Rogers, Whishaw, Luttrell, Moore, and Mackintosh, but they seem lax in their obedience. "I can call spirits," says Shakespeare's Mortimer, "from the vasty deep." "But will they come when you do call for them?" is the reply of Hotspur. *Miladi* calls her *beaux esprits* to the vasty deep as unsuccessfully.

Lord Lansdowne called just now on his way through London, and seems much amused at being elected,

Lord Rector of the U-
-Niversity of Glasgow.

SPRING GARDENS, *November 24th*, 1828.

A SLIGHT attack of gout confined me some days; but I am well again, though it has left me very lame for the present.

Lord Blessington told me just now his lady's pretty sister, Mrs. Purves, is to marry the Speaker[1] next week.

Miss Pinney's nuptial day was announced to me by a despatch from Mr. Gunter, in the form of a huge cake, which looked so much blacker and sweeter than an ordinary honeymoon, that we left it for the indigestion of the servants. The newly married couple went immediately to Paris, whither the parents followed them on their progress to Nice and Italy for the winter.

The Ellises are returned from Venice and Florence. To avoid the heat of the Italian journey they left their boy at Geneva, and took him up on their rebound.

Yesterday I saw a letter from Lord Anglesey, who reports himself in perfect health; and so is the King, in spite of newspapers.

Torrents of scandal afloat. They call Schwartzenberg Cadlands, as he has beat the Colonel (Anson) out of Lady Ellenborough's good graces. It is added that she talks publicly of her loves, and, moreover, is turned Catholic, and never misses her Sunday Mass at a chapel.

I saw to-day a letter from Navarin describing Ibrahim Pacha, a jolly Mussulman who swills champagne. He

[1] Mr. Manners Sutton, afterwards Lord Canterbury.

asked a French officer if he had served in Spain to restore Ferdinand? He was answered, "Yes." "You are odd fellows in France," replied Ibrahim. "You go to Spain to destroy liberty, you come to Greece to revive it."

I should think Lord Morpeth would rather have excused O'Connell's public dinner.

If George is to begin residence at Oxford in October he should be entered there in the preceding term in June, as the term of entering is counted without residence. Till this is decided I do not write to the Dean of Christ Church.

P.S.—Will you have the two Rutland prints when you come to Town?

At the hotel at Paris her Grace of St. Albans ordered a *Bif Stake*, a *Maître d'Hôtel*, and a *Diable*.

The poor *Maître d'Hôtel* was alarmed at hearing what she ate for dinner.

SPRING GARDENS, *December* 13*th*, 1828.

LAST Saturday I was to have dined with the Carlisles and half the Cabinet at Lansdowne House, but sent excuses from prudence. Lady Goderich is half mad. She makes my apothecary drive out with her daily in an open carriage; she lies at length. He feels her pulse the whole way, and two maids sit opposite with brandy and water. Your sister, Lady Cawdor, will be very sorry to hear Lady Scarlett has undergone the operation of tapping, but it is a species of dropsy which frequently admits of a cure, being of a local nature.

Edward writes that Dublin is very gay, and that an Irishman declared he was the youngest child that ever came into the world, as he was born on the very day after his mother was married.

Your *ci-devant* butler came to ask me a bit of law, brought a cargo of papers, and bored me about nothing for more than an hour.

An antiquated piece of furniture, who played footman to Mr. Stanley at his death, came to-day to desire I would speak to Lord Stowell to get him a place in the British Museum, which he said Mr. Stanley had promised to obtain for him. But he could not describe what sort of place he wanted, nor whether any place was vacant by the departure of any porter, trustee, mummy, or crocodile.

Joseph gives a good account of Mrs. Feason Glossop the singer, who has been *prima donna* at Naples and Milan.

A. Ellis gives Lawrence five hundred guineas for a portrait of Lady G. and child. I have a picture he painted for half-a-guinea.

They say His Majesty detests his London palace. Walter Scott's "Chronicles of the Canongate" fall off.

Sturges Bourne is preparing to inhabit his official house. The Grand Turk and Don Miguel keep the Ministers in London. Miguel either stays four days or eight, and dinners will be arranged accordingly. George paid me a visit, but I was not visible.

*Monday, December* 15*th,* 1828.

DICKINSON tells a marvellous story of the two young men, Anson and Strangeways, who were said to have died of the plague on their Eastern tour. He says they were discovered in a Seraglio, and the Turks gave them the choice of poison or mutilation. Anson preferred the former, and Strangeways chose to have his nose and ears cut off and his tongue torn out. Tastes differ. The papers said yesterday Strangeways was returned to London; and as a dandy in Bond Street without nose and ears is an awkward personage, I doubt Dickinson's history. As to the loss of a tongue, considering the usual conversation of dandies, the grievance seems unimportant.

Half the plum-cake Gunter manufactures finds its way to Spring Gardens—a huge slice a week ago from the Speaker and his bride, who are honeymooning at Hastings. It had a novel accompaniment of white kid gloves, which my Grenadier pounced upon for ball-cartridges.

Agar Ellis is ambitious of being enrolled in the new edition of noble authors. He advertises two octavo volumes of State papers[1] of some Ellis during the Revolution. An ancestor probably. Lord Morpeth's speech was temperate and judicious, and it was a difficult position to deal with. One of the Brunswick Irish papers says of him that "he is certainly a clever young man, not of age till two years hence, and little

[1] The Ellis Correspondence.

known but as the brother-in-law of Agar Ellis." So much for the Anti-Catholics. Brighton has been literally crammed. Of nobility and mobility they count three thousand visitors, but the aristocrats are retreating from it.

Joseph says Lady Flint passed a month at the Duc de Bourbon's Chantilly, and met there Lady Steele, Tom Steele's daughter-in-law. *John Bull* said the collision of two such ladies must have supplied them with sparks enough.

Poor Miss Macdonald devoted herself to the ravings of Irving the preacher, whom all the fine ladies flocked to hear in the City some years ago. Her brother paralytic.

London not empty, people always fluctuating to and from it. Daily political fables: Ellenborough squabbling with Wellington and retiring; Aberdeen going out, and fifty other absurdities; the potato in O'Connell's brain leading him to quarrel with the English Catholics; that Scandinavian gander Nicholas, as if his old namesake were at his heels, running away from the Turks;[1] the Balkan Mountains are well named. I was always a Turk in my heart, and could sit for ever on a divan with iced sherbet and a pipe, and surrounded by pretty women. Their only defect is they never subscribe to a circulating library, and it is my daily bread.

[1] The retreat of the Russians from Shumla in the autumn of this year.

# CHAPTER VII.

*MR. JEKYLL TO LADY G. SLOANE STANLEY*
(*Continued*).

*Thursday, January 8th*, 1829.

WE had three pleasant days with Lord Clifden, and we had postponed our visit till Ellis and Lady G. returned from Royalty at Windsor. We had Lord Melbourne, Lord Clanwilliam and Sharpe, and Parson Bouverie with us.

On Sunday last Rogers gave Edward and me a *dilettante* dinner, Sir T. Lawrence, and three other Royal Academicians, Wilkie, Callcott, and Newton— and last, not least, Callcott's wife, the *ci-devant* clever Mrs. Graham,[1] who wrote that excellent account of her travels in South America. The Emperor had persuaded her to return to the Brazils to educate his four infant children, but she found it so uncomfortable a job that she stayed only ten months.

The Emperor,[2] only twenty-seven years old, good-looking, and of course unlike brother Miguel, but an unpleasant character, and behaved so ill to his late

[1] The widow of Captain Graham, R.N. She was a daughter of Admiral G. Dundas, and wrote much. Her most successful work was "Little Arthur's History of England."

[2] Pedro I. of Brazil, the IV. of Portugal.

Empress,[1] an amiable woman, that he has in vain asked half the European Princesses to fill her place. Among other comforts, she was never allowed to quit the Palace, not even for an airing. She says thirty years will not civilise the manners of the country.

The King very joyous with his numerous guests at the Castle. He rises from his chair without assistance, and walks very well, but is grown much thinner.

On his visits to Lord Clifden Luttrell comes down in the Roehampton Stage, and has twice had the misfortune of travelling with the fattest man alive, who has a cottage in the neighbourhood; and, as Luttrell learned from the coachman, is really a Colonel Dudgeon.

The Princess Lieven said yesterday Miguel is still in a most dangerous state.

The times are most prolific in gossip—the Scotch murder,[2] the runaway banker, and the abdicating Anglesey in succession. The political cauldron was boiling pretty highly without the last ingredient.

Will Cobbett accept the Lord-Lieutenancy?

P.S.—They say Lord Ashburnham is to have one of the Blue Ribbons.

Lord F. Leveson remains in his office of Secretary. The King delighted with the little Queen of Portugal, and talks much of her.

"The Sorrows of Rosalie"—pretty verses dedicated

---

[1] Leopoldine Caroline Josèphe, Archduchess of Austria.
[2] By the notorious Burke. He was executed at Edinburgh on January 28th.

to Lord Holland by Mrs. Norton,[1] a daughter of the late Tom Sheridan.

*Monday, March 16th*, 1829.

THE system of Burking I hope will proceed, as it really ascertains the true value of one's acquaintance. I know a great many of those one calls friends in London whom the surgeons, when dead, will think worth ten pounds, and for whom, when alive, nobody would give half the money.

Lord Morpeth comes to see me. He is a delightful personage, so clever and pleasant, "one of the hopes of Rome," as an ancient writer said when the Republic, like Great Britain at this day, was overrun by dunderpates.

Yet never let it be said again that soldiers are unfit for political debate. In the late speech of Sir George Murray there was a passage of as much beauty and eloquence as ever was pronounced by man. At Sir L. Cole's I once passed three days with him, and a mind better informed I never met with.

For a sketch of roguery Garth[2] beats Hogarth out and out; but it is said that the letters in no way

---

[1] The Honourable Caroline Elizabeth Sarah Norton.

[2] Captain Garth, son of General Garth, delivered up some papers to the bankers of Sir Herbert Taylor on condition of his debts being paid and £3,000 a year settled on him. The terms of this alleged agreement were not fulfilled, and he commenced an action for its performance. The papers were said to contain damaging evidence against certain members of the Royal family.

support the slander on the Duke, and others say the reverse.

A son of Sir J. Stanley, now at Valparaiso in South America, begged of a farmer there a glass of water when shooting on a hot day. The farmer learned his name, and asked if he was of the Derby family. "If you are," continued he, "be so good as to desire the Earl, who has the best game cocks in the world, to send me a brace, and in return I will send him the finest horse of our celebrated Valparaiso breed." Cock-fighting is the rage of South America, and seems particularly appropriate to what was once called "The Spanish Main."

The King, sympathising with half his subjects, has had a cold. I wish he would attend to his diet as his brother monarch of Poland used to do; but he has now a favourite beverage, called his beer cup, to assist gout and other bilious amusements.

They are playing theatricals at Lord Harrington's, and, they say, so well, that I regret I have not gone there. Coughing and sneezing and the Catholic Bill are all one hears in London, and the opera *donne* are as hoarse as if they had been marched with their dead compatriots by Napoleon to Moscow. The wheels of the doctors catch fire in the streets, and there is a subscription to convert the Serpentine River into lemonade and barley water and gargles.

P.S.—Palmer, M.P. for Surrey, says he became a convert against the Catholics by reading the 17th verse of the 17th chapter of the Revelation, and would now die on the field or scaffold rather than vote as formerly. "Mark," says Shakespeare, "how the devil can quote Scripture for his purpose!" Joseph was dancing at a ball last week with one of Anglesey's misses, and when the father came in there was a sort of respectful silence, as if Royalty had arrived,—a tribute to honest conduct, which speaks a great deal.

*Saturday, March* 21*st*, 1829.

I REJOICE that you are so surrounded *par les impies* (whom I remember Madame de Flahault once mistook *les M.P.'s* for), and that you continue to worship my correspondence as our friends the Popery folks do their saints with frankincense.

It is impossible to describe the credit Palmerston's speech has universally obtained. Everybody was dazzled by it. Sturges Bourne said to me to-day (and whatever may be his nature, he is a most competent critic of such a display) that he thought eloquence in the House of Commons had expired with Canning, but that it had actually and positively revived in Palmerston. He always, when in office, spoke well and sensibly, but this burst was in the highest style of oratory and argument; and I am free to confess I did not think he possessed powers of such a superior cast. We had a banquet with Lord Dudley on Wednesday, and you will not wonder at a sort of gloom coming over me when I reflected that in the room where we assembled the poor Duke of York expired.

The remembrance of all his kindness to me and his *bonhomie* to the whole world was painfully excited.

Joseph was gallanting last night at Mrs. Hope's. Tom turned me off as an acquaintance because, unfortunately, I was counsel for the painter who drew Tom and wife as *la belle* and *la bête*, and Tom called his best friends to prove it could mean nobody else; though I of course termed it a mere fancy picture, wantonly destroyed by a foolish parson, Beresford, her brother.

Our Catholic tide flows merrily. Neither the dykes of Holland nor the banks of the Commons can obstruct it; and as for the attempt at a breakwater by the wisdom or piety of the Lords, I trust, without profane swearing, it is not worth a dam.

But as the delicacy of my style seems now fairly on the decline it may show some sense of shame to conclude this despatch.

More last words.

Edward came off guard just now to tell me the Duke of Wellington and Lord Winchilsea fought this morning. The Duke fired first, and missed. Lord Winchilsea fired in the air, so probably was the person challenged. The cause was not mentioned.[1] Precise details are not yet given so accurately as in the *School for Scandal's*

---

[1] George William, ninth Earl. Lord Winchilsea wrote to the Secretary of King's College: "The Duke, under the cloak of some coloured show of zeal for the Protestant religion, carried on an insidious design for the infringement of our liberties and the introduction of popery into every department of the State." The Duke replied with a challenge, and at the meeting fired first. Lord Winchilsea apologised, after firing in the air.

account of Sir Peter Teazle's wound in the thorax. I guess it arises out of Winchilsea's letter about the college which you alluded to. The duel was said by Edward to have taken place at Chelsea. How comes a saint to fight?

Spring Gardens, *October* 24*th*, 1829.

LONDON of course is a desert—pavements broken up; and the nearest way from Pall Mall to Berkeley Square is through the Regent's Park, I believe. Nor will the population increase to maintain Mr. Malthus' system, as, for want of a railing round it, good folks are fished up every morning in the Green Park Basin[1] stone dead.

But I have my judges and lawyers in town, and dinners and Temple repasts, so I care nothing for barometers and thermometers, and have but one tree to tell me of the fall of the leaf.

Gertrude and I had conversations about new literary works, so tell her I am not much delighted with Mr. Cooper's[2] American tale of the Borderers.

Edward surprised me by a short visit yesterday. He was sent, a single officer with sixty men, from Windsor to Kew, where he stays a fortnight, to protect the old palace and the Duke and Duchess of Cumberland, who have an ordinary dwelling on Kew Green. Edward had dined the day before with Sir George Quintin, of the

---

[1] The reservoir of the Chelsea Water Company, made in this year, and filled up in 1855. It occupied the northern side of the Park, facing Piccadilly.

[2] J. Fenimore Cooper.

10th Dragoons, who lives with his family there, and met the young Prince George,[1] whom he represents as a fine, active, pleasant boy, very like George III., but an odd cast about his eyes, talks English pretty well, and fills up his leisure moments with rattling castanets. He wears a sort of Hussar uniform, and it is his daily amusement to walk to the palace and barracks, at each of which the whole guard is obliged to turn out to salute him. Ladies came at night to Sir G. Quintin's, and among them the widow of my old friend General Gwyn, who retains her beauty at near eighty. She told Edward the mosaic on my snuffbox was brought many years ago from Italy by her husband, and presented by him to the King, whose equerry he then was. Jelf, Prince George's parson tutor, is about to marry a Polish countess attendant on the Duchess of Cumberland, with a name which defies spelling or writing.

My lieutenant speaks with wonder of the Botanical Gardens, four hundred acres, with glazed conservatories lofty enough for palms and other gigantic exotic trees. For lies and gossip I refer you to the *Morning Herald*, which are more plentiful commodities than franks at this season, as you will know to your cost for this scrawl. In return pray give me an early bulletin of Willie. I saw the Stafford carriage yesterday at the Ellises.

*Tuesday, October 27th,* 1829.

As A. Ellis offered a frank, I may as well contradict, on the authority of the *Morning Chronicle*, the surmises

[1] The present Duke of Cambridge.

of the *Morning Herald* on Huskisson's visit to Sudbourn, which is said to have taken place merely on Wellington's liberality as to meeting foes or friends indiscriminately.

Wellington's system is to get as many clever heads as he can from any party, and so far Huskisson would be an advantage. But the Duke has not room for what the Scotchmen call his tail, though, as Huskisson is a soldier of fortune, perhaps he would not be very scrupulous as to the abandonment of his adherents, and be willing, at any rate, to resume a seat in the Cabinet.[1] Yet, on the whole, I give no credit to this guess work.

Lady Conyngham has had a bad illness, but is recovered. She does not like Brighton, from some ill treatment there formerly from the populace. It is said Halford played a *ruse de guerre* in advising the King to go there, where he uniformly shuts himself up. Halford fears that at the Castle he will occasionally drive out, and so incur the risk of colds and habitual inflammations.

Edward called again this morning, but returns to Kew to dine with the Duke of Cumberland, who sent him an invitation yesterday, and an inquiry after me. As Edward is not known to him, this is very civil.

A. Ellis says Lord Grosvenor's palace[2] is detestable in point of taste, though it cost £700,000! I admired the drawings of it.

---

[1] Mr. Huskisson entered the Duke's Cabinet as Colonial Secretary.
[2] Eaton Hall.

Lord Kerry,[1] Lord Lansdowne's son, is six feet two inches high, and has been ill. It is feared his uncommon growth is injurious to health, as he has always been weakly.

Codrington[2] is at Sir H. Bunbury's, and I hear in high spirits, and meditating a public retort on the Admiralty, which perhaps he had better decline.

I must go and congratulate Mrs. Siddons on Fanny Kemble's[3] triumph. Was not Mrs. F[itzhugh] in additional frenzy upon it when she gratified you with her visit?

Lady Quintin has musical evenings, and Edward pipes. A new uniform for the Guards is ordered to rob their pockets. No lace, but covered with embroidery. What folly!

*November 6th*, 1829.

JOSEPH last night saw Fanny Kemble in *Juliet* a second time. He says she is excellent, but, with his usual fastidiousness, declares she is no miracle.

Lady Ellenborough had Prince Leopold's[4] box yesterday, and gave Joseph and three dandies a supper

---

[1] He died in 1836, aged twenty-five, before succeeding to the Marquisate.

[2] Admiral Sir Edward Codrington, who commanded the allied fleets at Navarino. He had been recalled from the command in the Mediterranean after an inquiry as to the circumstances of that action. He eventually completely justified himself.

[3] This lady, afterwards Mrs. Butler, made her *début* with great success as Juliet, at Covent Garden, on October 5th. Her father and mother, Mr. and Mrs. C. Kemble, were both acting (as Mercutio and Lady Capulet). She died in 1892.

[4] Prince Leopold of Saxe-Coburg, husband of Princess Charlotte of Wales.

after the play, till two in the morning. A fine dissipated dowager!

As it was only a drive, I visited Edward at his earnest request one morning at Kew, and found him in an extremely pretty cottage and garden, which is given to the single officer on the detachment from Windsor. The Lieutenant was anxious I should enter his residence, and there I found a most dandy set-out. A table with inkstands of Sevres china, cut-glass bottles of Eau-de-Rose and Cologne, six snuffboxes, a doll of elastic rubber given by an Irish flirt, and a great half-grown Newfoundland dog, which he called a "Retriever." I laughed excessively at the furniture, and almost forgot a German pipe set in silver, with an ivory head of Punch.

The Duke of Cumberland asked him continually to dinner, a family party, the Duchess only and her *suivantes*. Plain service of soup, fish, roast mutton, and game; sherry, port, and claret. Edward returned to Windsor on Tuesday, so was not made entirely a Brunswicker.

To-day I have had a letter from Lord Conyngham in answer to my inquiry about Lady Conyngham as to her late serious illness, for I have known them both intimately thirty-two years. He says it was a bad bilious fever, and that she is still low and weak; and he adds that the King's eyes are exactly in the same state as when I left him, which seemed by no means formidable.

Poor Birdy left all, as she told me, to a Miss Emery, her god-daughter. I take it she died of the disease of eighty years of age; a very good and religious woman, and I daresay gone to heaven, but latterly grown peevish, morose, and very intolerable. To me, I may add, ungrateful, for I offered to receive an apology for her language, which she was absurd and obstinate enough to refuse, and it was language not to be overlooked. Dowager Lady Carnarvon recommended her as a *gouvernante* to Mr. Sloane, for my wife, at her very early age on the loss of her mother, as a sedate person, though without any means of instruction as to any accomplishments in music, languages, etc., for she possessed none. She had lived many years with Mrs. Damer, and parted in a quarrel. Strange to say, though I often spoke of Mrs. Damer as a friend, she remained silent.

Lewis Way, a mad sort of fellow, and I, visited Miss Sloane from Southampton when we were both riotous on the circuit. On our way back in the evening from Stoneham, Lewis made verses on poor Birdy, who had been as grumpy as if we wished to carry off her *protégée*.

> "The Father is gone to Vienna,
> And leaves behind a Duenna,
> Whom I heartily wish at Gehenna."

I count nothing for her rumpus with Philly, whom the devil could not live with, for she has neither brains nor good temper.

L'Abbé Morellet, of high talent in literature, and ruined by the French Revolution, desired me to negotiate the sale of his Library at Brussels for £3,000. He had a *catalogue raisonnée*, and it was well worth the money;

but it failed with Lord Spencer and others. He had made a singularly ingenious and novel arrangement of his books under the three operations of the human mind, "Memory, Judgment, and Imagination." Under Memory he classed history, etc.; under Judgment works on science, morals, etc.; under Imagination poetry and works of fiction, etc.

At dinner with Fox one day Fitzpatrick and I had a long contest where to class Addison's "Spectator"—whether under Judgment, as morals, or under Imagination, as a work of invention? It remained undecided.

Heavens what a volume is this! so I will have done.

More last words.

Miss Fox shocked me yesterday with an account of the death of my intimate and interesting friend, M. Dumont,[1] of Geneva, one of the most learned men in Europe, and the most engaging. The Duke of Cumberland told Edward to invite me to meet him at dinner at Kew, but Edward wisely said I was out of town.

*November 6th*, 1829.

THE Guards are to have their dress changed—no lace, but embroidery on the collars and cuffs, and gold instead of silk sashes. A shame and folly! for half of them had just got new coats at the expense of near £80, and must now dress like French marshals. His Royal

---

[1] Pierre Louis Dumont. Mr. Jekyll probably made his acquaintance at Bowood, where he at one time was tutor to Lord Shelburne's children. He was a friend of Sheridan, and Fox, and Romilly, and a fellow-worker with Jeremy Bentham.

Highness told Edward that if he was Commander-in-Chief the whole army should wear moustaches, and no officer appear out of regimentals. This would increase popularity.

The summer has been postponed to November. Tom Moore says an Irish woman was charged before the Cheltenham justices with being a street-walker.

"Plase your Worships," she said, "must I be walking on the tops of the houses?"

*November* 12*th*, 1829.

I DON'T remember whether I ever sent you these verses or gave you the anecdote :—

> Though years have spread around my head
>   The sober veil of reason
> To close in night, sweet fancy's light
>   My heart rejects as treason.
> A spark then lies—still fann'd by sighs
>   Ordained by beauty's maker,
> And fixed by Fate, burns yet, though late,
>   For lovely Molly Dacre.
>
> Oh! while I miss the days of bliss
>   I passed in raptured gazing,
> The dream impressed still charms my breast
>   Which fancy's ever raising.
> Though much I meet in life is sweet,
>   My soul can ne'er forsake her;
> And all I feel still bears the seal
>   Of lovely Molly Dacre.
>
> Whene'er her course by chaise or horse
>   Conveyed her to our City,[1]
> How did I gaze in blest amaze
>   To catch her smile of pity!

[1] Carlisle.

> Around the door the night I wore,
>   Still mute as any Quaker
> With hope-fed zeal, one glance to steal
>   From lovely Molly Dacre.
>
> When rumour dear proclaimed her near,
>   Her charms a crowd amassing,
> How would I start with fainting heart
>   To catch her eye while passing.
> When home she turned I ran and burned
>   O'er many a distant acre,
> To hope by chance one parting glance
>   From lovely Molly Dacre.
>
> I've often thought that happy lot
>   Of health and spirits lent me,
> Is deem'd as due to faith so true,
>   And thus by Fate is sent me.
> While here she be there's life for me;
>   But when high Heav'n shall take her,
> A like last breath I'll ask of death
>   To follow Molly Dacre.
>
> *From* CAPTAIN MORRIS.

These very pretty verses of the celebrated Captain Morris should be accompanied with an anecdote.

Molly Dacre was the beauty of Carlisle. She married, and is now living at the age of eighty-four. Lord Stowell, at the age of eighty-six, and Captain Morris, at the age of eighty-one, declare they adored her, and though both widowers, declare they never loved any woman so ardently. Nay, they go farther, and say they still love her. In the year 1745, at the moment of her birth, the Scottish rebels entered Carlisle, and an officer of the Prince Pretender, with his soldiers, quartered themselves in her mother's house.

At such a crisis a remonstrance was made on the disturbance of the household and the mother.

The Prince Pretender immediately ordered the soldiers to be withdrawn, and the officer requested that the white cockade he wore in his hat should be pinned on the newly born infant's cap. This was done, and Molly Dacre has preserved it religiously.

All this came out last June at a dinner I had with Lord Stowell and Captain Morris at John Pearse's, and the very next day the old bard sent us the verses.

The joint ages of the three lovers amount to 253 years. I am sure the song deserves a place in Gertrude's book or yours, and perhaps the explanation also.

*Saturday, November 19th, 1829.*

THE Lieutenant is under orders to send me all the scandal of Brighton. While my lord is dispensing justice in London, Lady Lyndhurst is dispensing smiles on the Steyne, and I trust with the same equitable principle between her ancient idolaters Dudley and Burdett. I do not hear that the tide rises there, so presume that your friends the Petres do not bathe, as, philosophically speaking, the displacing so large a mass of the ocean would naturally produce that effect.

Joseph dined yesterday with that crazy metaphysician Lady Mary Sheppard, who swore to me that she read and mastered Mr. Locke's profound treatise at eight years old. The best of it is that Joseph will not admit that she is insane, as she gives him *fricandeau*.

To-day our Dowager Donegal gives him and me a dinner and a constellation of wits and poets, Rogers,

Tom Moore, and Washington Irving, whose "Bracebridge Hall" Joseph purloined from George when we stole away from Paultons.

George Colman advertises his Memoirs under the title of "Random Records," and I fear very much the comical dog will put me into them.

They kill the King once a week, though the dying man drives his phaeton daily. "To catch the flying Cynthia of the minute," I will see to-day if your fair sister has flown northwards.

I must ask Miss Fox for a lithographic print of her pretty niece. I heard that the Duke of Somerset's eldest son was an admirer whom *Miladi* would probably not reject as a son-in-law. I heard he had a rival, but forget who.

In visiting from Castle Howard to Testwood, I rejoice that the gout has not dropped a card at my door on his way, and my spirits are better than Sultan Mahmoud's[1] at the present moment, so I could not read the "Borderers."

Spring Gardens, *Monday, December 7th,* 1829.

EDWARD and his four comrades have marched back their three hundred fur caps to Windsor in deep dismay at quitting the delights of Brighton, where they were *fêted* and dandled from morning till night. Dinners, balls, assemblies, and suppers incessant, and invitations whether acquainted or not. They were

---

[1] Mahmoud II. of Turkey. He had recently been forced by the Russians to acknowledge the independence of Greece.

hailed as the harbingers of Royalty, and hopes did not vanish till they were recalled. Lady Holland gave the Lieutenant *fricandeaux*, lots of old women playing loo at the routs, and cheating the dandies, who called them "the forty Thieves." The Guards stayed nearly three weeks.

Glengall has made what he calls a comedy[1] by stealing ideas from Sheridan, Cumberland, and the elder Colman; and Alvanley has made what he calls an epilogue to manifest that the best joker of White's bow window cannot string two lines together.

I meant to write a memoir of my poor friend Dumont, but Sir James Mackintosh has done it in the *Foreign Quarterly Review*, and butters the *élite* of Holland House by saying: "No such assemblage can ever again be found till another house can find such a master." Will *Miladi* be pleased to hear that Holland is the master there?

I have no patience at seeing Morpeth's excellent verses mixed up in the trash of the annuals, and Lady Ann Becket engraved among the beauties, "The Exclusives," miserable stuff, and poor Lady Jersey the heroine; Ministers visiting their enemies and hunting and shooting with friends. H. Baring sends me pheasants killed by Wellington and the Cabinet. They had better bag Charles X., who seems playing away his crown. Think of Poet Sotheby translating Homer after Pope.

[1] *The Irish Tutor*, acted at Covent Garden October 28th, 1822, and never afterwards repeated. Published in 1829. "A poor piece."—GENEST.

Poor M. Angelo Taylor undergoing a sad surgical operation.

Playhouses crammed, and many people in town. Lord Sydney[1] said to be dying, so his son-in-law Cholmondeley will survive him. Lady Conyngham not yet quite well, but getting better.

P.S.—You are no stranger to my inveterate cockneyism. Petersham, who I hope has not lost his wit with his title, by becoming Earl of Hair-in-town, always said, "London is the best place for nine months in the year; and there is no place so good for the other three."

*December 9th,* 1829.

THOUGH I despatched a volume on Monday, a frank has occurred, and I may as well scribble to say I remain quite well without a *soupçon* of gout. A. Ellis says Lady Lyndhurst endeavours to captivate the obdurate heart of the Duke of Devonshire at Brighton. The Ellises are going to Prince Leopold for a few days.

Tierney, I am sorry to hear from Brighton friends, looks ill, and has a serious cough. The Duke of Cumberland's inflammation was at one time alarming, and resembled the Duke of Kent's.

A fable has been circulated, probably by herself, that Miss Chester, the handsome actress, who lived long with Calcraft, reads comedies to the King. Three years ago it was rumoured, with equal truth, that he had beautified a cottage for her near Windsor. As Lady Conyngham

[1] Thomas Townshend, first Viscount Sydney.

remains an invalid it is said the King dines in his chamber with her and her family, and not with his suite.

Chantrey's bronze statue of Canning is to be placed in Palace Yard, and Westmacott's statue of Pitt in Hanover Square.

Joseph reports last night from the playhouse that *Black-eyed Susan*[1] is the most interesting and pathetic thing ever played. The audience in tears. The scenery of a man-of-war, the court martial, the preparation for the execution, and the unparalleled acting of T. P. Cooke, surpass anything ever seen. Miss E. Tree's[2] eyes are unluckily blue, but the audience kindly accepts them as black for the beautiful use she makes of them in Susan.

Don't you long to see a waltz by the Siamese Boys?[3] By the way, what a misfortune it might be to be so attached for better or worse to such an inseparable companion! Imagine yourself linked for life to Mr. Timpson, or me tied to a fox hunter. Almack's would be ruined for want of single men at Siam. Edward's new friend, the Duke of Cumberland, will soon leave Kew for Windsor, when he is to have apartments in the Castle for himself and Duchess. I did not expect this.

Edward's journal of Brighton is very amusing. The

[1] By Douglas Jerrold, produced at the Surrey Theatre by Elliston on June 8th, 1829. It ran for three hundred nights.
[2] Mrs. Charles Kean.
[3] The Siamese Twins, exhibited this year at Bullock's Museum, Piccadilly, now the Egyptian Hall. They lived till 1874.

Petres very kind to him, asked him twice to dinner, and carried him to Mrs. Fitzherbert, and other places, both Popish and Protestant. He dined often with the Hollands. Much civility from *Lannoy* Hunter, and from my friend Tierney.

Mother Coutts has two houses, one to breakfast in with a view of the ocean, as she says she cannot eat prawns except when looking at the sea. Time was when she had none to eat. After her ball she gave a grand supper, and drank soda-water the whole evening to alleviate the thirst brought on by Madeira. The bulk decreases, not so that of Edward's friends, the Misses Petre, the eldest of whom was compared to a "fillet of veal on casters."

Two Jewish misses, daughters of the rich Rothschild,[1] with enormous fortunes, and whose vulgar phrases were the joke of the day, but I hear of no beauties. At two o'clock a string of carriages two miles in length.

They say the pedestal of the King's statue looks like the box that brought it; people giving twenty-five guineas a week for a house, and hardly a bed to be had in an hotel; the women walking with the men from morning to night; for freedom of manners beyond what Bath was in old times; and for total dissipation beyond what London is in new times. Fifty-four years ago, when Osgood and I first embarked there for France, it was a fishing town, with one bad inn and a packet once a fortnight.

[1] Nathan Meyer Rothschild, Baron of the Austrian Empire. He died in 1836.

On the march near Kew Edward met the Duchess of Cumberland, and halted his army to salute her.

Arthur Upton in bad health at Brighton; a handsome niece of his there. The pastry-cook's girl at Brighton, whom Ellenborough preferred to his bride, very pretty. I recollected to-day, with contrition, as the verses were prophetic, that at Lord Ellenborough's request I wrote some in his bride's album when I visited him at Roehampton in the honeymoon. The general subject was his lordship's lamentation at being called away so frequently from his beautiful wife by debates and politics. I forget the verses, but there was this line,—

"And peers in vain by *proxy* love."

*Miladi*, however, found it practicable, and I suppose *Milord* has now cancelled my poetry.

I asked Rogers to-day what he thought of Fanny Kemble? The cynic replied "Master Betty."[1]

*Christmas Day*, 1829.

WRITING to-day to Dickinson, I enclose for his perusal the enclosed curious account, which, according to my promise, he will frank to you.

"Upon my being taken, an order was sent to Havre to send to Paris *ce monstre qui brulait Toulon, etc.*, and I was for three months in close confinement in the

---

[1] A celebrated boy actor, William Henry West Betty, the "young Roscius," who made a large fortune between the years 1803 and 1808. He was quite a failure as a man, and Rogers' comparison was of course a sneering one. Betty died so late as 1874.

Abbaye, without anybody but my guard. I was then removed to the Temple, and had the apartment of the Royal Family, with orders to keep me a close prisoner, but I won over the sentinel to my interest. Some of the Royalists got among the guards who were to do duty at the Temple, and I had a letter given me by the sentinel from Wyndham. I got boots, walked in the garden with his leave, and several times he permitted me to go with him to the play, and once I went two posts off a-shooting. When I returned, after being out upon my parole with my guard, I used to say, 'Now lock me in, the agreement is over; you must lock me in, or I shall be through the keyhole.' At last there was an order issued for the transfer of the prisoners from some of the prisons to Fontainebleau. An order to this effect was forged, and a man dressed like an officer of police came to the jailer at the Temple about eight in the evening, showed him the forged order, and demanded me. The jailer came up as pale as death. I said, 'What is the matter?' He replied, 'I am very sorry,' etc., etc. I went down inquiring what accommodation I should have there, etc., etc., with great apparent anxiety. The pretended officer of police immediately carried me off. I walked through the gates, and then got into a carriage and went off. At two or three of the towns a party of a dozen or more walked out to meet me. One of them took my place in the chaise, and I took his place in the company, and walked back with them as one of the party, and was so passed on, and got safe to Havre. At one house where I stopped upon the road I found four or five who had escaped like myself. One said, 'I ought to be in the *conciergerie*,' another said, 'I should be at Cayenne. I escaped from the Abbaye, and no names were asked. The master of it, upon my entering, showed me a picture, saying, " In case of alarm, behind that picture you'll find a place of concealment."'"

The above account I had from Sir Sidney Smith in 1802, and made the above memorandum of it, which I have transcribed from my octogenarian reminiscence, if that term is not out of all repute. He did not mention the persons by whom all the arrangements had been made for obvious reasons. At the same time he told us that after the siege of Acre he took a boat containing from ten to twenty very emaciated French soldiers, who said that they, with many others, had been poisoned, but had survived it. Sir Sidney delivered them up to some French officers upon the coast, who admitted the fact, and afterwards Captain Wright, a very temperate, credible man, confirmed the account, saying he was with Sir Sidney at the time, and that he had heard it also from the physician whom Bonaparte applied to in the first instance to administer the opium, which he declined doing. Captain Wright added if Bonaparte should ever deny it he should publish the account. He was afterwards captured, and certainly murdered in the Temple. He imputed the act to Bonaparte being desirous of relieving himself from the embarrassment of removing them in his retreat, without the discredit of leaving them to the English.

Sir Walter Scott discredits the story, because he says if it had been true Sir Sidney must have known it, and that he never mentioned it.

P.S.—If Shakespeare had called *Romeo and Juliet* Tapps and Buggin after your two Hampshire Baronets, do you think anybody could have wept at the tragedy?

Imagine how an audience would be affected at hearing Fanny Kemble, as Miss Tapps, exclaim in the third Act:—

"Oh, Buggin! Buggin! Wherefore art thou Buggin?"

I once asked Dr. Goldsmith what he thought the meanest name in England? He said "Tibbs," and he was a great artist of the ridiculous. So I always felt a secret pang when I called a Hampshire friend "Knibbs." I could make Willy laugh in his bed with this nonsense.

# CHAPTER VIII.

*MR. JEKYLL TO LADY G. SLOANE STANLEY*
*(Continued).*

*January 8th,* 1830.

EDWARD called yesterday, and had again dined the day before with the Duke of Cambridge. The Lievens dined there, and they only. By the postponement of the Brighton trip, and no invitations being sent from Windsor Castle, so usual at this period, I should guess Lady Conyngham is still unwell.

Lord Holland has the gout, and *Miladi* the blue devils. Their son Henry and his sister went to Bowood at Christmas, and crossing Marlborough Downs imprudently at a late hour of the night, got completely bothered by the snow. A guide whom they had taken behind their carriage from the last inn had disappeared, and could not be heard of in any way.

The Lansdownes are uneasy about Lord Kerry, who outgrows his strength, lives on a *regimen*, dines at three, and requires much care and attention.

The newspapers have accused Palmerston, Wilmot Horton, and the Gally Knight of forming a Jacobin junta at Paris to depreciate Polignac as the puppet of Wellington. The lie is ridiculous, and I see Palmerston is come home.

The press is grown cruel as well as revolutionary. Three days ago the *Herald* made great merriment of the poor King's supposed cataract. Yet Scarlett is horribly abused by them for prosecutions. The Radical Alexander, who is convicted of the libel in the *Morning Journal*, for many years conducted a slanderous newspaper in Edinburgh.[1] My poor imprudent friend, Sir A. Boswell, lost his life in a duel for publishing some squibs in it.

A man said to me yesterday with a very grave face, "The Attorney-General admires Lady Cawdor extremely, and would probably like to marry her." I said, "So do I; and if her Ladyship chooses a lawyer, I am a much better match than Scarlett, as I should die much sooner."

Petrified sufficiently by the weather, I have not even visited Lady Petre. This is ungrateful after the caresses at Paultons, and their kindness to Edward at Brighton. I hope she thinks me out of town, and I am not supposed to know she is in it.

*Monday, January* 18*th*, 1830.

JOSEPH and I are just returned from Lord Clifden's, where we have spent four pleasant days in a warm

---

[1] The *Glasgow Sentinel*, of which Robert Alexander was a proprietor. There were law suits between him and his partners, and Boswell, (the son of James Boswell,) attacked a solicitor, James Stuart, who was engaged in the case, in the issue of October 20th, 1821. In the course of the action Stuart discovered who his assailant was, called him out on March 26th, 1822, and killed him.

house and good society, Lord Ashley, Lord Clanwilliam, Mr. William Howard, and Mr. Hay, the Under-Secretary of State. Lady Gower came one morning in high good looks and spirits. We had a corps of infantry, Ellis's nice children, two pretty girls of Lord Gower, and a brace of Lord Carlisle's boys.

Vesey Fitzgerald [1] must resign from ill health, which is a serious loss to the Cabinet, but the other rumoured changes are groundless.

I have seen the extraordinary correspondence between the Duke of Cumberland and the Lord Chancellor.[2] The Duke begins by indignation at a newspaper paragraph stating that Lady Lyndhurst had turned him out of her house for impropriety of conduct, of which he asserts the falsehood, and desires that her ladyship will confirm his assertion.

The Chancellor replies that Lady Lyndhurst has been of late assailed by similar falsehoods, but despises them.

The Duke rejoins, and repeats his desire that Lady Lyndhurst will support his denial of so scandalous an insinuation.

The Chancellor finally answers much to the same effect as before, so that the Duke does not ultimately obtain what he asks for.

Lord Albert Conyngham, indignant at some national

[1] William, first Lord Fitzgerald and Vesey. He was President of the Board of Control in the Wellington Administration.
[2] Lord Lyndhurst. The facts appear to have been exactly as stated in the newspaper paragraph which the Duke wished contradicted. See Greville's "Memoirs."

reflections cast on England by the Secretary of the French Embassy at Berlin, calls him out. They exchange a pistol shot, and then fall to with sabres. Lord Albert is slightly wounded in the hand, which terminates the matter. He is young and dashing, and I suppose they must both be withdrawn from Berlin.

Poor Sir T. Lawrence is the subject of universal regret, terribly in debt, £6,000 they say to Lord Dudley, and God knows how much to others. To Colnaghi they say £2,000, in short, to everybody who would lend. It is false that he ever played. The riches of his portfolios very great, for so he spent all he had. They talk of a value of £60,000 in sketches, studies, etc., of the great masters, an irreparable blow to the Academy. No such successor can be found. Beechy is old, Wilkie, Chantrey, and others talked of are vulgar men, and cannot represent as he did.[1]

Tatham called in my absence, and left word he had a daughter dangerously ill. The King has had a bad cold, but is recovering. His colds are so inflammatory that some bleeding becomes necessary.

SPRING GARDENS, *Tuesday, January 26th*, 1830.

REJOICE, my dear Lady Gertrude, that you are ploughing the snow, living with innocent country neighbours, and soothing yourself with the bagpipes of Mrs. Dugald Stewart, for this infamous town swarms with slander to such an excess that the most immaculate characters are unsafe.

[1] Sir Martin Shee succeeded Lawrence as P.R.A.

Even H.R.H. the Duke of Cumberland, with all his purity, cannot escape, and is charged with an unfortunate love for Lady Graves. It is added also that her Lord has adopted the language of Romeo's apothecary: "My poverty and not my will consents," and taken £30,000 to keep the secret. Edward dined with me yesterday from Kew, and declares the whole is an infamous falsehood, and merely a joke upon Ernest. If so 'tis a pity, and spoils a conundrum. "Why is the Duke like a resurrection man?" "Because he disturbs the Graves."

When Foote attempted a grave rebuke of the bass-viol in his orchestra for making love to the flute's wife, he ruined all its effect by saying, "Sir, you have been guilty of a base violation of this man's domestic happiness."

In the catalogue of slander next stands Mrs. Parnther, who is said to have played Calista to the Lothario of that wrinkled Adonis, the Earl of W. For some years she has attempted to become a beauty, is an exquisite, her husband a *nimini pimini* gentleman, who talks pretty in the matter of Lord John Fitzroy, and one fine morning had just sense enough to quit the law when he never would have got a guinea.

The King had a cold, and was bled, but is perfectly well. The Duke of Cumberland confined by illness to his bed. Poor Lord Lansdowne has been obliged to receive Gloucester's Duke at Bowood.

What a havoc has death recently made among my friends Redesdale, Lawrence, Lady Donegal, Miss

Vernon, and now poor Tierney. They said yesterday old Lady Cork had departed also.

Poor Tatham in sad tribulation. Waters, a son of the Opera Waters, after a courtship of seven years and a house taken for the marriage, has suddenly jilted his daughter. It has affected her health, and she is going to Sir A. Paget's for a change of scene.

Moore has crammed his book of " Byron" too much. As he was forced to slur Sheridan's treachery to his party, he is forced to slur Byron's treachery to his wife. But what can a man do who, like the Newgate calendar, selects only rogues for biography?

Read "Tales of a Curate," Colman, very good fun indeed. Lord King mortal heavy.[1] The Squires will come sulky to Parliament, and leave wives at grass, for the rents won't pay opera boxes. They deserve it, for they huzzaed Mr. Pitt and his wars into a debt which has ruined the country. Joseph and I unite in loves to sick and well.

P.S.—Miss Vernon was an excellent woman. She bought a seat in Parliament lately for her nephew Vernon Smith, the son of Bobus,[2] who, though rolling in riches, would not draw his purse-strings. I pity poor Miss Fox, who is now solitary. Lord Holland would delight to have her. But there is *Miladi*, and neither she nor Miss Fox would muster any delight

---

[1] "The Life of John Locke, with Extracts from his Correspondence" (London, 1829), by Peter, seventh Baron King.

[2] Brother of Sydney Smith.

between them. Two more opposite beings never existed.

I cease to grumble at the folly of my portrait, as it supplied me with a relic of poor Lawrence. It was impossible to find a successor with talents and manners like his. And when the country manager had no more white paper to make snow in his pantomime he exclaimed, " Curse you ! why don't you snow *brown* ? "

SPRING GARDENS, *February* 12*th*, 1830.

DON'T go into hysterics at a Radical frank of Burdett's, and expect a tirade on Parliamentary Reform ; but as I wanted to thank you speedily for a very newsy letter, I have put the rebel Baronet's hand in requisition.

Joseph and I had a comical dinner yesterday with Kenney, who wrote *Raising the Wind* and other excellent farces. We had all the wits, poets, and authors—Rogers, Tom Moore, Washington Irving (the Sketch Book), Barry Cornwall, and George Colman. They were quizzing Shee, the new President of the Royal Academy, for publishing his pedigree in the papers to prove he was a gentleman and a relation of Sir G. Shee and my idol Mrs. Shee. I said a man might be proud of his family from antiquity when the first *She* was Mrs. Eve.

Kenney said when last at Paris he was seduced by a placard in the Palace Royale signifying that within was to be seen a curious animal, the offspring of a duck and a rabbit. He paid his franc and went in.

The master of the show apologised to him for the

accidental absence of the prodigy by saying it had been sent that morning to the Jardin des Plantes, for the inspection of Cuvier. "Mais, Monsieur," said he, pointing at a cage which contained a duck and a rabbit, "Voila ses respectables parens."

Joseph condescended at last to assist at one of Lady Holland's *soirées*, and found there a round dozen of discontented peers—Devonshire, Lansdowne, Carnarvon, Clanwilliam, Normanby, Palmerston, etc. They did not seem to object to Wellington if he would sweep out his Cabinet and stick some of them into it. I heard yesterday that Lord Lansdowne brings in a Mr. Macaulay[1] at Calne in Abercrombie's room, perhaps to sit till Lord Kerry is of age.

Lady Belgrave wrote these lines on leaving the Staffords' House :—

> "'Mong the terrible punishments censured by Bentham
> He omitted to mention a fortnight at Trentham."

One of Edward's cronies in the Guards has had a tiger skin sent him, and cuts it into waistcoats among his friends, and Edward is fitted with one splendid enough to ornament the Zoological Menagerie or fascinate Mr. *Parnther*. He says it is for travelling in wet weather, and it is really too tremendous for general use, and exceeds the hat he brought to Paultons.

Byron was certainly half crazy, but he must have had lucid intervals, and in one of them admired your interesting friend, Lady Surrey. It would have been well if

---

[1] Lord Macaulay.

his admiration had always been as judicious. Edward saw in the new pantomime last night an ingenious clock-work spider, who weaves a web of twenty feet square round the clown. What things they rack their brains for!

Brougham has wisely shifted his flag to Knaresborough under the Duke of Devonshire. John Williams (Queen Caroline's counsel) supplied his seat at Winchilsea under the Marquess of Cleveland.

The Duke of Cumberland denies the whole story, and now they say Graves[1] killed himself merely on being hurt at the scandal. Is that likely, as it would tend to confirm it?

Poor Tierney seems entirely forgot. Byron says, of human life—

"Passion, ambition, dust, perhaps a name."

*Monday, March 15th, 1830.*

THE ministers, I am sure, ought to be as popular as they really seem to be in a great measure, for they appear to be bullied into all the wishes of their opponents. Peel civil and obsequious, and Reform becomes the watchword of Tories as well as Radicals. All my consolation in the crisis is that we have got some sunshine; but it comes with so much dust and east wind that one is little the better for a peep at a crocus or a violet. It is said Lord Colchester died at sea lately.

[1] Thomas, second Lord Graves. He was Comptroller of the Household to the Duke of Cumberland.

A courtier tells me that Lady Conyngham since her recovery is so *embellie* in point of beauty that she looks twenty years younger. That pious prop of our Protestant religion, Edward's friend, the Duke of Cumberland, has not yet regained any popularity, and it is said that the King declares if he stays in England, and subjects himself to any insult from popular indignation, he cannot protect him. They add also, that the Directors of the Ancient Music have abolished their dinners to avoid his intrusion.

Read two novels, "The Manners of the Day" and "Cloudesley," the first by some one who knows well the London world and paints it often, with wit and humour, the second a serious story by Godwin, the celebrated author of "Caleb Williams," and who at an advanced age still writes with vigour and talent.

Stapylton, a natural son of Lord Morley, and private secretary to poor Canning, advertises the life of his patron, of which it is said the Minister prohibited the publication. If he were a lord of the bedchamber the Duke would turn him out *sans façon*, but he can hardly divest him of his Commissionership of the Customs. To vindicate also Canning's politics, and attack the Duke, a strong pamphlet has appeared, and is said to be from the pen of Lady Canning. The young Frenchman who had a duel with Lord Conyngham at Berlin behaved well, seeing that his antagonist knew nothing of the use of the sabre, played with him, and ended the conflict by a slight cut on the wrist so as to disable him.

From Ellenborough's[1] foolish letter to Sir John Malcolm in India, he goes by no other name than the elephant. Rogers gave us one of his pleasant dinners yesterday, and mixed blue ladies with us—Morley and Lindsay and Davy. My boys report poorly of the opera. We are on tiptoe for the Budget to-night, and are dazzled by an expectation of an enormous sacrifice of taxes by the minister. God knows how it could be afforded; and as a property tax would only drive money into foreign funds, a scrape either way. Do not hunt for franks, for I have several ninepences left.

*Sunday, March* 28*th*, 1830.

YOUR account of Miss Petre's[2] rapid death really shocked me—poor, good-natured, amiable, young woman. In a gross habit like hers fever is a fatal antagonist; and little did I expect so sudden a termination of our acquaintance. But such is fate.

Tatham called yesterday to invite me to follow Tom Grenville's example, and give twenty-five guineas to a Mr. Pyne for a hole in his new *cimetière*[3] of four

---

[1] Lord Ellenborough was President of the Board of Control of the East India Company, and wrote to Sir John Malcolm, Governor of Bombay, describing one of the Judges of the Supreme Court as "a wild elephant led between two tame ones." There had been friction between the Government and the Court, and two new judges, to whom he alluded, had just been appointed. The matter was discussed in Parliament, but no motion was made.

[2] The third daughter of the tenth Lord Petre.

[3] Kensal Green Cemetery was opened two years later, in 1832, but consisted only of fifty-three acres.

hundred acres, on the model of Père la Chaise, in the centre of which will be a Trajan's Pillar and an Acropolis. As the work may take some years for completion, I inquired where I was to be lodged by Mr. Pyne in the meantime, as my corpse would naturally be impatient for the new landscape, and to lie among daffodils, jonquils, and rose trees; and as the gaiety of France had found out that funerals were only *vaudevilles*, I meant to have a pink-and-silver hearse, with Matthews and Liston as chief mourners.

But Tatham's friend has a rival, who proposes to let lodgings in a pyramid on Primrose Hill, which is to contain five millions of nervous defunct who are afraid of the surgeons. Now really there is foolery enough among us while we are alive without inventing projects to continue the foolery to parterres and pyramids hereafter.

Dining at Lord Camden's yesterday I met Lord Chatham,[1] cheerful but very feeble, observing to my youths that so much dissipation before Easter was unusual. They said the girls prophesied a short season after it, as Parliament would probably rise early, and they would be packed home by papas. It is not impossible that the misses may conjecture rightly, and so are glad to work double tides at present.

Her Grace of St. Coutts announced supper by the tolling of an immense bell, which shook the house and the nerves of fifty dowagers to a palsy.

I dined t'other day at the Morleys. The comical

[1] John, second Earl, brother of William Pitt. He died in 1835.

Countess is Hogarth in petticoats. She showed me a quarto of caricatures of her own—The History of the Families of Snuggins and Sucklethumb—from their own ancestors, who were aldermen in the reign of Henry VII., to the young cub of the two families entered at Christ Church, Oxford, last month, accompanied with biography written in the various English of the times, and the costume of the different periods admirably accurate.

*Monday, March 29th*, 1830.

THINK of my partaking yesterday of a really splendid dinner at Mr. and Mrs. FitzHugh's. We had Lady Pembroke and her very handsome daughter, Captain and Mrs. Bowles, Lord Sandon, Lord Palmerston, Mr. Temple, and Sir George Staunton, who went to China with Lord Macartney,[1] and with his Lordship refused to knock his head nine times at the Emperor's feet in the ceremony of Kotoo. Palmerston looked pale and jaded, and five years older since last summer, from his parliamentary anxieties and displays. Mrs. Bowles told me that house in Stanhope Street would have suited the Bournes, as she inspected it for them, but found that it had been suddenly sold for £6,000.

She said old Woronzow reads all night, remains in bed till six o'clock of the day, when he gets up to

[1] In 1793, on a mission to negotiate a commercial treaty to the Emperor of China. Lord Macartney evaded the ceremony by consenting only on condition that a Chinaman of equal rank to his own should make a similar obeisance to a picture of George III. This was refused, and the ambassador made the usual salute by dropping on one knee.

dinner, and then drives to Lady Pembroke. It is thought he is ninety years of age. There is a talk of a young Irish painter coming over, who is a second Sir T. Lawrence.

My youths say that a Miss Brandling of the north is the reigning beauty of London. I think last year it was a Miss Bailey, who is now of course "the unfortunate Miss Bailey" of Matthew's ballad. But I am as little read in the list of beauties as I am in the "Racing Calendar," so can only speak from dandy reports.

Spring Gardens, *May 1st,* 1830.

The King's health is certainly precarious, and the bulletins are so clumsily and cloudily worded, as to increase instead of quieting the public fears. Water is surmised, but my own opinion is that it is merely inflammation of the chest to a greater and more difficult excess than the attacks he has so often experienced, and the necessary bleedings of course debilitate, at his age, a corpulent and inactive man, who in early life lived in such excesses; inflammation may be fatal. How shall we manage under Clarence, whom they certainly were constrained to dismiss from the Admiralty on suspicion of craziness?

Yet Lady Jersey posted down to Bushey on the King's first attack to serve either the Whigs or the Duke of Wellington, and Holland, from his legitimate relationship, has also visited the rising sun.

Parliament sits like a hen,—never quits the nest

till long after midnight. God knows what chickens they may hatch, or any worth rearing.

Thursday we dined with Rogers. He said Luttrell [1] loved a newspaper so intensely that he read from the Calais steamer at the top of the first page to high water at the bottom of the last.

It was reported the King had ordered a superb dress from Paris for Lady Conyngham at the intended Drawing-room, and that the Londonderrys flew there immediately to get a finer.

Lord Lansdowne is returned after the agreeable exploit of three weeks' gout in a hotel at Paris. All sense of shame is lost, and people are exposing themselves in private theatricals daily. As none but geese would attend as an audience I marvel they escaped hissing.

When the poor Duke of York was so intent on his new palace, I looked at it always as his mausoleum. Another palace [2] now rising reminds me of that reflection.

Our loves to you all, and our regrets also, for under the present state of things I fear you cannot contemplate a visit to London.

SPRING GARDENS, *Monday, June 14th*, 1830.

I SHALL now break silence, as your two spies have left London. The poor King holds out miraculously, but the case remains hopeless, and we are daily misled by false reports of appetite. We are told of dissolution

[1] Mr. H. Luttrell, author of " Advice to Julia."
[2] Buckingham Palace.

of Parliament, but I should think there must be a Regency Bill previously enacted. I met the Duke of Wellington last week at Lord Camden's. He looked stout, but complained to me of perpetual work, and indeed he is ill seconded in the Lords by the bungling of Aberdeen.

I dined t'other day at Holland House. They speculate on a short trip to the Rhine. Newton[1] has painted a sweet portrait of Mary Fox, small whole length, and has preserved that pretty look of *espiéglerie*, and her hereditary dimples.

Tatham's son has really executed a clever bust of Lord Eldon, for a statue which some vulgar citizen is going to erect over a Charity School. Tatham was angry with me for saying if Eldon was still Chancellor he would prevent such a lunatic from spending his children's fortunes in foolery and ultra-Toryism.

Edward is committed to the Tower with other wild beasts for a few days. I asked him if the public were admitted to see the Guards fed. He said no, as Hume would complain of second courses and champagne. He has been again at Kew, and to complete the morality he has imbibed from the Duke of Carabas is become a crony of the Lord Marquess Wellesley, who lives at Marble Hall, and details more effusions of good fun and nonsense than I have been supplied with for a

---

[1] Francis Milner Newton, an American, whose early manner was formed on that of Watteau. "Yorick and the Grisette" is a specimen of his work in the National Gallery. He died insane in 1835.

very long time, and I only wish they were pure enough to be repeated. The Lady Marchioness of Carabas sojourns at his villa in the Regent's Park.

I also wish I could tell you to read six volumes of the "Memoirs of Madame du Barry,"[1] which are more amusing than can be imagined. The style is charming and graceful, but the topics are too often indelicate. Mrs. Norton's new poems seem overrated. Edward's new friend[2] sends me some comical verses of too gay description, and Edward adds that he abuses the Duke of Wellington by the hour.

Two days ago I was met by Peel in Hyde Park, and when he left me a companion observed how pale he looked. "So would you," I replied, " if you had been exHumed only this morning at three o'clock."[3] *A propos* of Hyde Park, last week I performed a Samaritan act there. I saw a gentleman lying on the grass just thrown from a starting horse. I offered my services, which were thankfully accepted, and the people with difficulty conveyed into my carriage Sir Frederic Lamb.[4] A surgeon in the crowd pronounced a fracture of both bones of the leg just above the ankle. We placed him on the floor of the carriage, with his back

---

[1] By the Baron de la Motte Langon and M. Paul La Croix. They are not authentic.

[2] The Marquess Wellesley.

[3] An allusion to the activity in Opposition of Joseph Hume. He kept several clerks to check the accounts of public expenditure, and was always a keen critic of the financial proposals of Government.

[4] Afterwards Lord Beauvale.

against the door and the limb extended; he was very faint from pain. I conveyed him down Constitution Hill to Melbourne House, so avoided the stones. Unluckily Sir A. Cooper was not found for three hours, so the swelling and inflammation postponed the setting of the fracture till the next day, when it was found that only the smaller bone was broken, and he is of course doing well, as Lord Melbourne told me this morning. I rejoice I was passing, as in twenty minutes after this fall he was at home.

I was told yesterday that my friend Allen, Lady Cawdor's neighbour, once had as a servant, Sellis, the Duke of Cumberland's assassin.[1] Allen had received a large sum of money, and was awakened in the night by a light and a movement of his curtain. He found Sellis at his bedside, who pretended the bell had rung for him. It is needless to say he contrived to dismiss him soon after, but without disclosing a suspicion which might have roused Italian revenge and excited the bump of murder in his craniology.

P.S.—Marquess Wellesley told Edward three or four stories of myself as having passed in a Court of Justice. The stories were excellent, but totally invented.

[1] Sellis entered the Duke's bedroom at St. James's Palace in 1810, with the intention of killing him, but the Duke awoke and beat off his assailant, who went to his own room and cut his throat. Owing to the general unpopularity of the Duke, an absurd rumour that he was the murderer of his valet was credited by the ignorant classes for some years.

He always quizzed the late Lord Liverpool, and he sent me this:—

Hink }
Jenk } inson.
Stink }

Hawks }
Jawks } bury.
Talks }

While he was Lord-Lieutenant there was presented to him at a *levée* Sir Lynch Blos, Bart. Show Willy what his Excellency wrote on the presentation, and how grammatically he framed a declension of the Baronet's name.

" Ut rosa flos florum, sic es Blos, tu quoque Blorum."

*Declension.*
*Singulariter.*

Nom. Hic Sir Linchpin Blos.
Gen. hujus Sir Linchpin Bloris.
Dat. huic Sir Linchpin Blori.
Acc. hunc Sir Linchpin Blos.
Voc. O Sir Linchpin Blos.
Abl. hoc Sir Linchpin Blore.

*Pluraliter.*

Nom. Hi Sir Linchpin Blores.
Gen. Horum Sir Linchpin Blorum.
Dat. His Sir Linchpin Bloribus.
Acc. Hos Sir Linchpin Blores.
Voc. O Sir Linchpin Blores.
Abl. His Sir Linchpin Bloribus.

I know no greater privilege than the right a man of great talents enjoys of talking or writing nonsense with impunity.

SPRING GARDENS, *Saturday*, 10 *o'clock*, *June* 26*th*, 1830.

MY poor King seems drooping daily. I fear the word " languor " which these stupid doctors adopt means the total sinking of the powers of life. When I think of the friendship and familiarity of forty-six years I remember what Dr. Johnson said of his dying bene-,factor : " Those eyes are closing for ever which during a long life were never turned upon me but with benevolence." I hear what I do not believe, that he said to the Duke of Clarence, " Do not let the fall of the Conynghams be without gentleness. I desire that you will act kindly towards them for my sake." They say they will dissolve Parliament immediately on his death, prematurely, I think, if they do not previously pass a Regency Bill.

On Thursday I dined with a host of Canningites at Sturges Bourne's—Harrowby, Goderich, Dudley, Huskisson, etc. Mrs. Huskisson a clever, ugly little body, with the air of a French woman. Mrs. Bourne is cheerful, but looks altered. Lord Harrowby grown very old suddenly, and wrinkled.

Joseph met Mrs. Leigh somewhere at dinner, and to-day she writes to him for our votes at the Athenæum, where the canvas is no sinecure as there are sixteen hundred candidates.

Yesterday at the Temple I called to the bar a

younger son of the Archbishop of York.[1] I hear his father gets an immense property by the death of Lord Harcourt.

Bishop Heber's life is amusing, but his widow has unnecessarily made two large volumes of it. Joseph and I dined yesterday at five o'clock with Rogers to accommodate old Lord St. Helens[2] and Brougham; the latter was detained in the House of Commons. Rogers told us St. Helens always sleeps with his face to the east, on some principle I do not understand, because the world turns half round in the night. Yet the old fellow does not want brains. Christians and Mohammedans bow to the East on account of Jerusalem and Mecca, but as the Saint of Helens is of neither religion I do not comprehend it.

As your prudery relents about Madame du Barry you will be much amused by her good stories.

I have bribed the Attorney-General for this frank by promising to convey his best remembrances to Lady Cawdor, who I hope is still with you. Joseph met all the world t'other night at Lady Stafford's, and the people would not quit the fine hall[3] in their perambulations, they were so impressed by it.

[1] Archbishop Vernon. He assumed the surname of Harcourt on Lord Harcourt's death.

[2] Sir Alleyne Fitzherbert, the eminent diplomatist, created Lord St. Helens in 1791. He died unmarried in 1839.

[3] Stafford House, the residence of the Dukes of Sutherland. It was built in 1825 by the Duke of York, it is said from his own designs, and after his death was acquired by the Marquess of Stafford. The Marquess and his family have since spent vast sums on this famous house.

*Saturday, 2 o'clock, June 26th,* 1830.

ALL is over. The King was released from a state of suffering about three o'clock this morning.

Edward came to me early this morning and said that he and other officers on leave were suddenly ordered on duty at the Tower.

I conjectured that the sad event had taken place, but I did not know it authentically till this moment. Shops shut, bells tolling, and very universal feeling.

*June* 1830.

I DO not pretend to be more sentimental than most people, but the minute guns of Thursday night brought many sad recollections of the weeks and days and hours with him "who now lies festering in his shroud." I agree with you that it was unfeeling and disrespectful to open theatres, but the cruel and scandalous abuse of many newspapers is absolutely disgusting. The "gentlemen of the press," as they call themselves, resemble those fabled vampires who issue from the grave and torment the living. The corpse was scarcely cold when the attack commenced, and on the very day it was consigned to its last abode the *Times* published a tirade of the most savage and atrocious character. Edward went to Windsor with the Grenadier Guards for the funeral. London will be in a singular and novel state for some time. There are to be *levées* and reviews, so many will linger here who are not to be occupied in carousing, and elections, and a Parliament assembling in the autumn will also be a very unusual event.

If Mrs. Timpson has the least wish to be Mistress of the Robes, let her come up to Berkeley Square by the very next Southampton coach, for Lady Jersey will dispose of all the Household. *Elle est rayonnante*, and looks in much better humour than Lady Holland.

Lord Clifden came yesterday, and mentioned a Dr. St. John Long,[1] a physician of Harley Street, who says he has been celebrated for cures of a complaint similar to Willy's. I told him I believed you were satisfied with the treatment of your present advisers, but that I would name him to you.

Edward is returned. Between Wednesday and yesterday the Guards marched sixty miles, as from want of room they were marched back on the first day from Windsor to Slough. He says the lying in state was mean, though exaggerated by the newspapers. The procession well arranged, and the solemnity of the silence, the *March in Saul* by the late King's band and those of the Guards, and the minute firing of the guns most impressive.

*July 8th*, 1830.

MY old friend, Lord Ashburnham, has published a vindication of his ancestor, who was at Carisbrook with Charles I., when among other foolish things of his reign

---

[1] A celebrated quack doctor, whose treatment seems to have consisted of rubbing and applications of cabbage leaves. He was convicted of the manslaughter of a Miss Cashin in 1830, and fined £250. He was acquitted on a similar charge in the following year.

he tried to get out of a window too narrow for him. It is but a dull book.

The King's will is dated 1824, and in the handwriting of Lord Eldon. He bequeathed his property to his successor, but without naming him.

Take it for granted certain favourites were adequately gifted in his lifetime, that their name might not appear in a will. It is kind in William IV. to pension poor Mrs. Tierney. That little spendthrift Wellesley has not £4,000 per annum, having sold all his pensions and resources, and keeps two establishments for wife and self. We are to meet him at Lord Sidmouth's, and Edward says he is delightful. There is no regular separation, but the Lady Marchioness lives at a villa in Regent's Park, and is going to Harrogate for an eruption which threatens her beauty.

This day the Duc de Montebello, Pair de France, son of Marshal Lannes, is to marry the daughter[1] of William's virtuous friend Jenkinson at Paris. Joseph's friend, young Flint, is fool enough to want to marry the said Duchess' sister, who has not so much fortune as would buy a joint stool, though the Duchess has *Le droit du tabouret*.[2]

A *Gens d'arme* at Paris stopped a passenger to look at his passport, and asked him from whence he came. "Gens d'arme," replied the passenger, "je suis né a

---

[1] Lady Eleanora Jenkinson, daughter of the 3rd Earl of Liverpool.
[2] *Le droit du tabouret* was the privilege enjoyed by Duchesses of remaining seated (on a folding stool) during the King's supper and the Queen's reception.

Paris." "Ah, menteur," said the *Gens d'arme*, "je lis dans votre passeport, 'nez aquilin.'"

*July 8th*, 1830.

A FEW days ago I dined at Holland House, which is, as you may guess, the very focus of political gabble. Lord Holland at the Lords till ten, and then returned to us with the Duke of Sussex.

Lord Farnborough tells me to-day that the poor King, whom he saw perpetually, suffered but little pain at intervals, and that he often mentioned me with kindness. I did not hear it from Lord Farnborough, but I know that the King mentioned Sturges Bourne's name as a fit person to be associated with him for affixing the stamp. It was observed that as Sturges Bourne loved retirement it might embarrass him, and it was given up; but as the King was but little acquainted with him, it marked his opinion of Bourne's integrity and character.

London is in a singular state, and will remain so till it exhibits the unusual spectacle of a Parliament reassembling in the autumn, and a court of a Queen full of ladies. You can send us three Maids of Honour, if you please. The squires are setting off to their constituents, and I am glad Dickinson has no opponent. Even the lawyers are departing for their assizes, and Lord Manners and I had a farewell dinner of our friend Lord Tenterden yesterday.

"The Americans," by Macfarlane, worth reading for its information as to Eastern manners. Mrs. Norton has published poems. Lord Holland was enthusiastic about her "Rosalie," but her "Undying One" in this new volume is a very inferior performance.

The doctors and the newspapers abuse the poor King's physicians, though yesterday at dinner we had Halford smirking under his Star of the Guelph, which somebody named "the Order of Refuge for the Destitute."

Brougham came to Holland House, and put under the protection of *Miladi* Miss Spalding, a handsome, clever woman, the daughter of Madame Brougham by her former husband.[1]

P.S.—I send an epitaph written by my poor friend Archdeacon Nares, on himself, but not on his tomb :—

> "'Time has not thinned my flowing hair,'[2]
> Nor laid my agèd temples bare,
> But he has played the barber's part,
> And powdered them with wondrous art ;
> Meaning, no doubt, to let me see
> He thinks to make mere dust of me.
> But let him know that on a day
> God will reanimate this clay,
> And life unchangeable will give
> When Time himself shall cease to live."

*Saturday, July* 17*th*, 1830.

EDWARD, I am sorry to say, gave a sad account of the King at the funeral, who, instead of silence and gravity during the procession of a good hour and a half, talked incessantly and loudly to all about him, so that

---

[1] Mr. John Spalding, of Holme. Lady Brougham's maiden name was Eden.

[2] A line in a popular song set to music by Jackson of Exeter.

most frivolous things were overheard. He looked ill, jaded, and most undignified; and it is unpleasant to add that there was a general impression made to the disadvantage of his understanding. Unless he can be controlled, which is difficult at sixty-five, I fear some awkward pranks will be acted. What minister can control him we are yet to learn; and without control where will the country be?

I knew him very much less than his brother, but I think him good-natured. The late King quizzed him, but loved him.

Edward said there was much bad taste in the decoration. The crown on the canopy in the chapel was twice as big as a coach. Women fainting from pressure, which they deserved for being there.

All Windsor drunk. Suppers and champagne for parties who remained there, and everything but grief or regret.

Between three and four thousand troops under arms, much exceeding the Duke of York's funeral.

The troops held flambeaux in the chapel, the smoke of which eclipsed the spectacle.

The Duke of Cumberland seemed much affected, and descended alone into the vault after the body was lowered to the place where it will remain till placed in the tomb-house at some distance through a subterranean passage. He has much to lose.

I asked Edward how the King looked. He said very like Mrs. D'Oyly. The Princes and some others slept at the Castle.

Theodore Hook, a clever fellow who writes in *John Bull*, got drunk with others last week at a Countess'. Somebody alluded to a secret, and said, "Hook knows." Hook, with the decanter in his hand, replied, "Bottle nose."

We are inundated by daily *on dits* of adhesions and negotiations—but last night's speeches of Lansdowne and Holland look hostile to the Duke. A novel called "The English at Home"[1] is read, as it alludes to Canning and other political characters, but I do not admire it.

Some of the mourners at Windsor despoiled my foolish neighbour, old Penn, of his watch. Edward says Mrs. Manners Sutton's ball was made up of scarecrows. Joseph would not go. I see Lady Stafford trotting about Pall Mall with the elasticity of eighteen.

SPRING GARDENS, *August 8th*, 1830.

UNLESS a revolution intervenes, I think we shall kiss four fair hands at Paultons on Thursday next.

Paris has read a potent lesson to Kings and ministers. Charles X. enthroned on Tuesday, and Philip on Friday, and a disciplined army defeated by a mob.

They talk of Lulworth Castle for Charles—a sequestered spot with a beautiful Catholic chapel, and the ruins of Weld's monastery of La Trappe. No neighbours for the ex-King but the ex-Chancellor Eldon. How naturally a youth of profligacy ends in an old age of bigotry and folly.

[1] By Colburn.

Lord John Russell lost Bedford by the single vote of the mayor. The great M. A. Taylor's vote was too late by seven miles when the poll closed. Lord William Russell [1] absented himself during the last session, and poor Lord John had abused the Methodists in his late "History of Europe," who compose half the town of Bedford. So Rogers tells me. A rebellion against Lord Lansdowne in my old pure borough of Calne, and a petition.

The spirit of reform, like that of the schoolmaster, is abroad, and, like that of the Catholic Question, will finally force its way, especially with a temporising Government. Lord Grosvenor is fortunate to buy two boroughs, and have two contests thrown into the bargain.

Plenty of men still in London society, but the weather is like November. Coals in requisition by dinner-time everywhere; and if I don't find a bonfire in my chamber on arrival at Paultons I will burn all Lord Mendip's old chairs and tables in the room.

I wish I could tell you to read Richelieu's "Memoirs," but they are too gay even for matrons and chaperons. Till yesterday I never saw "A Dream," Lord Holland wrote and printed in 1813; and a more foolish thing I never read.

Young Flint, who saw the whole scene at Paris, told me to-day that, notwithstanding the present tranquillity, many English had broken up their establishments and

[1] Lord William Russell, murdered in his bed in May 1840, by his valet Courvoisier, whom he had detected in a theft.

were returning home when he left Paris last Thursday. The greatest conflict was on the Wednesday, when the firing was incessant from five to eleven in the evening.

And so adieu for a few days.

SPRING GARDENS, *August* 10*th*, 1830.

THANKS for your delightful letter. I really was in debt, but I postponed payment till the immaculate electors of Stockbridge had agreed to save ninepence out of your pin-money.[1] My friend Leycester writes me word that his nephew Penrhyn and his colleague have had their success at Shaftesbury mixed up with as plentiful a shower of stones and brickbats as Charles X. had at Paris. The candidates at dinner with all their windows broken. The houses of the agents attacked till they decamped *incognito*, and the two members advised to take flight in an hour after the close of the poll. It seems the poor agent was unpopular because he was near-sighted, and consequently sometimes passed a voter without recognition, which was imputed to pride and insolence. Penrhyn reports to his Uncle Leycester, in speaking of the hard run at Stockbridge, that "William canvassed and kissed the voters' wives with a bottle of wine in his pocket, which, being poured plentifully into the female stomach, had a great effect in winning the female heart."

Morpeth and Brougham glorious![2] A few such

[1] By returning Lady Gertrude's husband to Parliament, and so extending to her the privilege of franked letters.

[2] Their speeches at the York election, when both were returned.

examples will alleviate my enthusiasm for Reform. The Duke has given one exemplary instance of the necessity of obedience to public opinion. The example of France and the tone of the General Election, I think, will hardly induce him to hazard any other course.

Joseph surprises me by disclaiming any intention of a visit to foreign parts this summer, though as a political scene Paris will be interesting. The letters from thence of a young friend of his are curious. In one I saw to-day, mention is made of an opinion delivered by a distinguished officer of ours, who says he never saw the most disciplined army remain so unshaken under a most murderous fire as the Parisian mob in the late conflict.[1] So kings must not rely on soldiers.

Some poet of Deptford kindly sends me to-day a packet of ballads to abuse my poor departed King, but I balance his doggerel with some good verses of Canning for you.

Lines to Canning's aunt, Mrs. Leigh, on the anniversary of her wedding, on her having sent him a pair of plush shooting breeches :—

> "While all on this auspicious day
> Well pleased their grateful homage pay,
> And sweetly smile and softly say
> A thousand civil speeches,
> My Muse shall strike the tuneful strings
> Nor scorn the grateful gift she brings,
> Though humble be the lay she sings—
> A pair of shooting breeches.

---

[1] The Revolution of 1830.

"Soon shall the tailor's nimble art
Have made them tight, and spruce, and smart,
And fastened well in every part
With twenty thousand stitches.
Mark, then, the moral of my song—
Oh may your loves but last as long,
And wear as well, and prove as strong,
As these, my shooting breeches.

"And when, to ease the load of life
Of private care and public strife,
My lot shall give to me a wife,
I ask not rank or riches.
For worth like thine alone I pray,
Temper like thine, serene and gay;
And formed like thee, to give away,
Not wear herself, the breeches!"

## PARODY.

*On Whitbread's Speech in Lord Melville's Trial.*

**BY CANNING.**

"I am like Archimedes for science and skill,
I am like a young prince who went straight up a hill,
And, to interest the hearts of the fair, be it said,
I am like a young lady just bringing to bed.
Would you know why the eleventh of June I remember
So much better than April or March or November?
'Tis because on that day, as with pride I assure ye,
My sainted progenitor took to his brewery.
That day in the morn he began brewing beer,
That evening commenced his connubial career.
On that day he died, having finished his summing,
And the angels sung out, 'Here's old Whitbread a-coming!'
So that day I hail with a smile and a sigh,
For his beer with an E and his bier with an I.
And on that day each year in the hottest of weather
The whole Whitbread family feast altogether.
My Lords, while the beams of this hall shall support
The roof that o'ershades this respectable court,

Where Hastings was tried for oppressing the Hindoos,
While the beams of the sun enter in at the windows,
My name shall shine bright, as my father's now shines,
Emblazoned on Journals as his is on Signs."

SPRING GARDENS, *August 18th*, 1830.

AT Holland House yesterday I had an uncomfortable bulletin. No danger, I believe, but he still keeps his chamber, and a second physician attends with Dr. Holland. Lady Lilford's health quite restored.

I am visited for the sins of my youth by the *Literary Gazette* of last Saturday, which revives an ancient epigram of Mr. Jekyll on Pitt's Taxation of Tea and Hair Powder.

"With his tax upon powder and tax upon tea,
Not a beau will be left, not so much as bo-hea."

The general expectation is that Parliament will sit five weeks at least on its meeting in October. A shorter period could hardly be allotted for two such pressing discussions as the Civil List and the Regency, independent of the arrear of important matters so abruptly abandoned last session. And I should guess the Christmas adjournment would only extend to February.

Forty years ago I little hoped my votes on the Catholic Question, the Slave Trade, and Reform of Parliament would be ultimately successful. The triumph of more enlightened times has accomplished the two first, and the recent elections are practically forwarding the last.

The French business is too wide a field for discussion. No man can yet predict how it will affect the general state of Europe. The first Revolution developed principles which have never since been silenced, and I tell my sons they must be prepared to witness extraordinary changes in their times.

William IV. has read Smollett's novels most profitably, and plays Tom Pipes the Boatswain to the admiration of the newspapers, who are ready to swear he even makes his tea with tar-water. All this panegyric will turn sour when the Civil List is to carry double by putting Adelaide on her pillion, with expensive donkeys for six Maids of Honour.

I must mention a trait of royal honesty. His Majesty to-day directed a payment to me of forty guineas, as the executor of Sir C. Bunbury, to whom he owed it many years ago, and which Sir C. despaired of.

So God bless you all, and I could say no more if I were a bishop.

Spring Gardens, *November* 13*th*, 1830.

By desire of the nobility, gentry, and others, the revolution is put off till further notice, or till Alderman Key,[1] the new Lord Mayor, who they merrily call Don-key, and Sir Claudius Stephen Hunter, choose again to frighten the Duke of Wellington with an army of pickpockets. There were twelve regiments in London— an army of 10,000 men, Edward and his Guards in the thick of it. Three nights did they bivouac under

---

[1] Key, Lord Mayor Elect, wrote to the Duke, warning him that there was danger in his coming to the city on November 9th with the King and Queen. Upon this the Cabinet advised the abandonment of the royal visit.

arms in the new Palace.[1] How my poor George IV would have stared to see Lancers and Guards eating oysters and drinking punch among his *scagliola* columns! On the second night Edward sent home for a mattress to rest his bones upon. Some slept on the inlaid floors, which had been newly oiled, and arose with the patterns inflicted on their new embroidered regimentals. He made out to me a sketch of the distribution of the apartments, which I enclose, as I think it is intelligible.

During his fortnight's duty at Kew the Duke of Cambridge told him to dine with them every day, but said he grew so fat that he had better not come to luncheon. The Cumberland boy is not so handsome as his cousin of Cambridge, but a finer fellow. The Duke sent them every day coursing with Edward.

As the new Civil List is not settled, the Duke said he had not sixpence, and must borrow of his banker, and I believe he never is in debt. He seems so ill that Edward read the newspaper every night to the Duchess.

The boys, in whose ages there are only two months of difference, have two singular horses—an Arabian sent as a present to Napoleon at St. Helena, and on his death sent to the late King; another taken in the Burmese War, and sent from India to England.

Joseph went to Lord Burghersh's opera,[2] performed

---

[1] Buckingham Palace, built 1825-30, at the cost of nearly a million. Nash was the architect employed by George IV., but large alterations were made after Queen Victoria's accession by Blore.

[2] *Catherine; or, the Austrian Captive*, by John Lord Burghersh, afterwards Earl of Westmorland.

before their Majesties by the pupils of the Royal Academy of Music. He says nothing could be worse than the opera, except the performers.

The Duke will not budge unless there should be some awkward division against him in the House of Commons, and some formidable questions approach which may leave him with majorities too slender for a minister's reliance. If St. John Long plays at whist as well as he does at manslaughter, his odd tricks and rubbers may succeed; but the dog ought now to be transported.

The Whigs two years ago elected O'Connell at Brooks's during the Catholic crisis. He never goes there now, as no one speaks to him.

Lord Holland is suffering at this gouty season. Lady Morgan's "France" is amusing, in spite of her ludicrous vanity and republicanism. Constant's[1] Memoirs excellent.

The town seems crammed with people. Dinners and *soirées* by wholesale. His Majesty feeds forty guests a day of all sorts and conditions.

Talleyrand is the great lion of the circles. Croker has published a caustic pamphlet, which was attributed to Brougham.

The squires look doleful, as their tenants are throwing up their farms in Devonshire, Oxfordshire, and Bucks.

As for our neighbours abroad, I think we shall have

---

[1] "Memoirs de Constant," 6 vols., Paris, 1830. Louis Constant Wairy was *valet de chambre* to Napoleon I.

no difficulty about Belgium, and no trouble from France.

It is said to-day that St. John Long after this second exploit has wisely run away. Think of so general an infatuation that Lord Clifden in the summer recommended the rascal for William's case.

I asked Edward generally the striking things of the new Palace. He said the staircase and the polish of the marble floors, which he represented to be so brilliant that they reflected like a mirror not only the person, but the dress of the individual who trod them; next, the effect of the pink, real marble which lined the staircase, and the capitals of the columns in the drawing-room, which, formed of the new mosaic gold, had the effect of transparency. He added that the staircase surpassed Windsor.

But we are too poor to complete this bijou. The garden is beautiful, the windows towards it of one entire glass, a piece of water with the effect of a river. As the walls were bare the soldiers could commit no injury, and great care was taken to prevent any. Furniture, of course, there was none. The officers ate their cold meat on a carpenter's bench, and Edward spread his mattress on the table of a joiner. Such are the horrors of war the Guards encounter, after all their perilous campaigns in Pall Mall and St. James's.

Your senator visited me on my safe arrival. I suppose he is now at Cheveley. But Tuesday he must be in town on Brougham's motion for Reform, as the Duke has declared open war on that subject.

It is incredible with what spirit and firmness the new police[1] has defeated the *canaille*, and we sleep safely under their protection without the aid of soldiers.

SPRING GARDENS, *Saturday, November 27th*, 1830.

I HAVE been most anxious to hear from you, though I knew that your excellent understanding would supply all the calmness and fortitude necessary in so unpleasant a state of things.

There is no longer any alternative—force and the law to put down the insurrection;[2] and this will be accomplished, but probably not without serious events. It is a singular opinion for a lawyer to pronounce, but a few volleys would be more effective than numerous trials and transportations.

When tranquillity is restored a most important matter still remains to be settled by the State—a system of employment and competent remuneration for those employed, or else desperation must lead to disorder. Such a system of cure must ultimately and necessarily reduce the value of every species of our property, and reduction of expenditure by economy affects trade and manufacture. Through such a labyrinth of conflicting evils no ministers ever had a more difficult course to steer.

The Right Honourable George Agar Ellis has just

[1] Peel's police were a little more than a year old. They began their duties on September 29th, 1829.

[2] The agricultural troubles of the autumn of 1830, chiefly in the south of England, which took the form of incendiary fires and destruction of machinery.

left me, highly pleased with his new office, which, he says, is the only one he would have accepted, and, to say the truth, it suits him exactly. It is in no way laborious to a man of slight health, and he has good taste and judgment for his different duties. He must visit all your forests.

I have been surprised to find that my friend, Sir H. Bunbury, married at Spa, last October, Miss Napier, the daughter of his *ci-devant* divorced aunt, the late Lady Sarah Bunbury,[1] by her second husband.[2] I knew her as a pretty girl, brought up by old Lady Louisa Conolly, and saw her four years ago at Bowood. She was always one of the most agreeable and interesting persons possible, and the widower with four sons could not have found a more delightful companion. She is now forty-six years of age, and, I understand, has been long so disabled by some defect in the ankles as to move about with difficulty.

It rejoices me to hear that poor Charles Wynne is to be Secretary for War, and I suppose a Yorkshire election has been in the way of Lord Morpeth's appointment to office. What a pantomime are politics! Who would have predicted at the Queen's trial that a slap of Harlequin's sword would have turned Brougham and Denman into a Lord High Chancellor and an Attorney-General?

Talleyrand is still the lion of the day. T'other night, at Lady Lansdowne's, he was even talkative. He has

[1] Lady Sarah Lennox.
[2] The Honourable G. Napier.

an avalanche of curls or wig, and a thin little *queue* of the *ancien régime*.

The French still believe the poor old Prince of Condé[1] was strangled by his English mistress,[2] and then hung up to give it the air of suicide. She had lived with him twenty years; and knowing that by his will he had left her great riches, she thought his property might be confiscated by the new Revolution, so rather than lose her legacy she hung him on to the window bar—a machine that I never could find in France would either open or shut, so its only utility now appears to be the hanging of a prince of the blood.

Ellis moves to Melbourne House in July, and will not inhabit the official residence. Lord Lansdowne's indolence was alarmed at the Home Office, and retreated into the armchair of President. The papers make Grey put sixteen relations into office, and Palmerston must speechify in the House for Althorp. The new Bishop Philpotts pleads his right to keep the great living also, as he tells Parliament he has fourteen young Philypotties to provide for. Sidney Smith must leave off joking, and get a mitre by Lady Holland's Duchy of Lancaster.

They persist in the story of Lord Lyndhurst's debts, nay, that he has sold his pension. He was long a bachelor with considerable gains at the Bar. On marriage I saw no expenses by him or her that were

---

[1] Louis Henry Josephe de Bourbon, Prince de Condé, found hung in his bedroom at St. Leu on August 27th.
[2] Madame de Feuchères (Sophia Dawes). See *post*.

unusual. On being Chancellor with £15,000 a year some great dinners, etc., of course, but still nothing of show or profusion.

I have no books to recommend. Galt's "Byron"[1] is not unworthy of perusal. I long to see Theodore Hook's "Maxwell."

Last week a member got leave of absence from the House of Commons to go and be married—the first time a special licence was held insufficient.

Drummond says Lady E. came to London alone, but luckily did not know the mob were stopping travellers to pillage them. Reform of Parliament goes on merrily, and will puzzle the lords and their boroughs. Wiseacres charge the Jews with the fires, to lower the Stocks.

In a *Gazette* or two I think you will see Lieutenant Edward Jekyll promoted to the rank of Captain in the Grenadier Guards, where he will stick till he becomes a Lieutenant-Colonel.

*December 1st,* 1830.

YOUR letters are always interesting to me, but doubly so at this distressing period. We entertain hopes that by the promptitude of law and force mischief will now be arrested. To-day I saw a Wiltshire letter from the sister of Mr. Penrhyn, Lord Grosvenor's member for Shaftesbury, with a sad account of the injuries to the skull of Mr. Pyle, a neighbouring farmer. The

[1] "Life of Lord Byron," by J. Galt, 1830.

newspapers have worked much evil by falsehood and exaggeration, and the punishment of seven years' transportation for breaking machinery, as a Bow Street officer said yesterday, only makes villains more adroit on their return or escape. A most extraordinary story, and believed to be authentic, circulated yesterday, that two or three days after a gentleman's property had been burned, he received a letter saying it had been destroyed by mistake, and enclosing £300 to indemnify the proprietor for his loss. This is systematic organisation with a vengeance. They talk nonsense of foreigners.

I dined yesterday with my old friend, the widow of General Gwyn, a positive Ninon de l'Enclos. She is a beauty near eighty, and does not look fifty.

We hear Lord Shaftesbury's daughter is to marry the rich nephew of the late Rundell the Jeweller, so both ends of the town will unite on an income of forty thousand a year.

Poor Lord Anglesey is under an attack of his sad complaint. Viceroyalty, alas! is no equivalent for pain.

It is said Agar Ellis is tinctured with Methodism, and a constant attendant at the Lock Hospital sermons. He was always of a religious cast, which is thus frequently misinterpreted.

I expected a better thing than "Maxwell" from the talent and humour of Theodore Hook. The plot hinges on an impossible event. The body of a murderer executed in London is uniformly by the sentence publicly dissected at Surgeons' Hall, and never could reach alive the hands of a private practitioner.

I am sorry for Dr. Jones' pistol, though fired in self-defence, as the rascals may mark him for it.

My engagements are diversified among Whigs, Tories, and ultras of both sorts. To-day I dine with Lord Farnborough, on Friday with Gordon's Duke, who plays battledore and shuttlecock about office with the Duke of Argyll.

The Reformers say that Holland in taking Lancaster has got a sinecure place, and that it was included virtually in the King's surrender by that blundering speech of the Duke of Wellington's crammed into his mouth. There really are a great many people who believe in a dissolution, but I should think that Grey will first feel the pulse of the new Parliament. What a task he has before him, difficulties enough to hazard a dozen Administrations!

Read Northcote the painter's "Conversations" by that clever coxcomb Hazlitt. Mrs. Gwyn sent it to me, and I found a page of compliments to her Ninon preservation of complexion.

*Saturday, December 11th, 1830.*

I TRUST that you are now in a state of tranquillity, and lament only that a wiser and more vigilant resistance to disorder had not been adopted at its commencement. The times, however, are still most feverish, and the new Ministry has a task formidable enough to overthrow a dozen Administrations.

The papers assert that your mummies have been frightened out of a heavy diminution of rent. At this crisis there should at least be some concert among neighbours on so important a subject, as dissentients might become marked men; and if ever there was a period when the country gentleman stood most in need of prudence and calmness it is the present, for their property as well as that of the whole country seems put to the hazard.

The mass of the people within the last ten years has been enlightened, and abuses no longer will be tolerated because they are ancient; but it will require time to reform them, and for the first time the minister of the Reform has the support of the throne.

Joseph conversed yesterday with Madame de Montalembert,[1] an English lady married to a peer of France, and who comes here on a visit during his detention on the trial of the ex-ministers. She says there is still much murmuring at Paris. The Cabinet is continually shifting its members. The populace clamorous at the Chamber, and calling for its dissolution A fear that on a fresh insurrection pillage might become the motive, and an idea that the present armament is political, to divert the people to a new object.

My *Captain* went last Friday to begin three months' duty at Windsor, and the very next day was detached,

---

[1] Wife of Comte de Montalembert, author of "Histoire de Sainte Elizabeth de Hongrie," and editor of *L'Avenir* newspaper, in which latter capacity he endeavoured to excite the sympathy of French Catholics for their Irish co-religionists during the agitation of Daniel O'Connell.

with eighty Grenadiers and *an officer under his command*, to High Wycombe, where burnings and machine breakings abound. Their arrival was hailed by the trembling mayor and justices and corporation; dinners offered to the warriors.

In the year 1745, a soldier returning after the victory at Culloden is said to have thus upbraided the keeper of an alehouse, on his march back—

"You now ungratefully refuse me good ale and quarters which you promised if we beat the rebels; nay, you then said we soldiers were the pillars of the state."

"You rascal!" replied Boniface, "I said caterpillars."

Boaden's "Memoirs of Mrs. Jordan" amusing.

*December 18th, 1830.*

EDWARD is still on duty at High Wycombe, and reports tranquillity, which I trust prevails also in your neighbourhood; but on conversing with the lower people he finds a very bad spirit prevails, and that the miscreant Cobbett is read in every cottage where the march of intellect has enabled them so to do. They admit that they have seen formerly much worse times, and that the poor rates in that county are diminished one half, but their language is "the landlords and the parsons eat our bread." Disaffection which does not arise from distress is formidable.

The Hollands went to Brighton yesterday, but I think *Miladi* will not succeed in her laborious efforts to be presented at St. James's. The Queen,[1] I take it, is all morality, and will probably adhere to old Charlotte's exclusion of divorced ladies. This is severe on the mother-in-law of His Majesty's daughter; but it is said that the FitzClarences have so teased and tormented the King by applications, that he has sent them all to the rightabout.

Joseph and I dine to-day with Rogers. The poor poet is just convalescent from a bilious fever, which does not improve a *tête morte* in complexion.

The town is still full, and the playhouses crammed by Byron's tragedy,[2] but we have had fogs and candle light at breakfast.

Going down to dinner at the Duke of Gordon's my ears (though not too susceptible) were assailed by the most dreadful din imaginable; fifty screech-owls could not have equalled it. At the bottom of the stairs I found in plaid and philibeg the hereditary piper of the illustrious clan of Gordon blasting out a pibroch to the full extent of bag and breath, and I declared that I had rather endure the extraneous melody of Scotland than its instrumental music.

[1] Queen Adelaide.
[2] *Werner*, at Drury Lane. It ran for seventeen nights.

# CHAPTER IX.

*MR. JEKYLL TO LADY G. SLOANE STANLEY*
(*Continued*).

*January 8th*, 1831.

BAD accounts to-day of Flintshire colliers; a battle and a rescue. We have a gentlemanly parson at the Temple, our Reader and Librarian, who maintains a sick wife and eight children. Brougham heard him once at our church two years ago. The poor man told me yesterday the new Chancellor sent him word last week he meant to give him a living. The parson's wife is a sister of the young person to whom Birdy left her money—a good-natured trait; and here is another. Erskine came to us in Cornwall on a great cause, and swore his lodgings smelt of paint, and he would not enter them. I got a poor old curate and his wife to lodge him, who refused payment for the two days he stayed. A week after he became Chancellor he said to me, "Jekyll, I have this morning given your poor Cornish parson a living."

*Morning Herald* uses me scurvily to-day.[1]

[1] By attributing the following to Mr. Jekyll: "Her Majesty has expressed her intention of appointing the Scots Greys to be her escort during their Majesties' projected visit to Scotland in the ensuing year. 'Why not?' said Jekyll. 'When the English

*On dit* O'Connell called on Anglesey, and said, " I will oppose you to the utmost." Anglesey replied, " Thanks for your candour ; and to be candid, on my part I advise you to keep within the law, otherwise I will hang you." Bad advice of Anglesey, and I fear O'Connell will follow it.

Dowager of Cork and Orrery bivouacs somewhere in Gloucestershire, gets the lady of the house to supply paper, and makes her write crazy letters to me, and the poor young Lord Redesdale frank them. But the beldame gets no answers.

*Saturday, January* 18*th*, 1831.

As, except a few specimens to be hung up for show at Winchester, my lords the judges [1] have been sending half the country gentlemen of Hampshire to Botany Bay, it is natural that I should inquire about the health and happiness of those who are left.

The landlords have been accused of hard hearts and the farmers and parsons also. Providence has been very kind in hardening their skulls at the same time, or they never could have resisted the sledge hammers of their neighbours and friends. Would to God the *Poles* on the other side of the water were equally impenetrable to the Czar and his Cossacks, and I would advise the schoolmaster to be no longer abroad, as he is a species of thrashing machine, and may be roughly treated !

Greys have got hold of the King, why should not the Scots Greys have the Queen ? ' "

[1] Two special Commissions were appointed to try the incendiaries and rioters in the agricultural districts. They convicted some hundreds of persons, and checked the outrages. Two executions took place at Winchester.

## SOME EFFECTS OF THE AGITATION.

The town is empty, but morning visitors abound. They are the cholera morbus of a great city. I wish they were taxed, or, like the new police, marked on the collar with "M. V." that decent servants might know to shut them out.

What with revolution abroad and disaffection at home, ministers have not a merry Christmas to get their lessons by the opening of Parliament. The footmen read Cobbett in the servants' hall, and complain of rents, tithes, and taxes. The oranges look as pale as if Miguel had frightened them out of Portugal, and mince pies are melancholy and out of spirits till you set fire to them with brandy.

Tom Moore's second volume of "Byron" tired me. Joseph says Byron's play of *Werner* has been fitted to the stage by Macready, who plays capitally in it.

SPRING GARDENS, *Thursday, January 27th*, 1831.

My Captain and his comrade, to their regret, marched back to Windsor the Grenadiers last week, with thanks from the county for their services and protection. Not a dry eye left in High Wycombe, the Mayor and Corporation in tears, and all their pretty daughters in hysterics at the desertion of the gay deceivers!

George Cholmondeley, whose father[1] was a poor parson, and whose mother was a sister of Peg Woffington, the celebrated actress of ancient days, has left to his only son ten thousand a year, and one hundred and twenty thousand pounds to the two Archbishops, to be distributed in charity. How such a fortune has been

[1] Robert, the second son of the third Earl of Cholmondeley.

accumulated it is difficult to calculate, for he had only an office.[1] Old parson Cholmondeley, then in the Guards, ran away at the battle of Dettingen, and was found snug and safe in a ditch with a cold fowl in his pocket. He then went into holy orders, which were less troublesome than those of the War Office, and the militancy of the Church preferable to that of a German campaign. John Wilkes told me it was beautiful to hear with what emphasis and fervour the old parson read that part of the Litany which deprecates "battle and murder, and sudden death."

Dining with the two members at Marlow, one of whom has the Hussar yacht, Edward met that right Reverend Father in God, Kent, Lord Bishop of Cowes, and chaplain of the Yacht Club, with the members of which the said prelate forages during the winter at their respective *châteaux*, and quaffs the champagne of those distinguished commanders gratis.

Lady Stafford showed Rogers a French epigram of two lines which I forget, but the turn of it was this: the sovereign mob makes a riot daily under the windows of Philippe's apartment in the Palais Royale; a stranger inquires the cause of the tumult, and is answered,—

"Le Souverain va visiter le Roi."

The Prince of Orange[2] has much popularity in the society of London, however little he may possess in the

[1] He was Receiver-General of Excise.
[2] William I., King of the Low Countries. Belgium declared its independence, and its separation was acknowledged by the powers on December 26th, 1830.

*beau monde* of Belgium. Lately at a supper he hobnobbed with Lady Dudley Stuart, Napoleon's niece, and as he filled her glass said, "*A nos grandeurs passées!*"

It is believed that the Duke of Northumberland is to purchase the Pimlico Palace,[1] and surrender his house to Government for the Strand improvements as part of payment. Of course he will not be expected to pay in any proportion to the enormous expense the Palace has cost. George the Third bought it for £26,000. The Duke, it is supposed, will pull down the wings, but two vast triumphal arches seem an inappropriate access to a private peer's residence.

Magnificent structures now fall from kings and princes to their subjects, and if the splendid new Bedlam [2] were sold, I do not see why Sir Claudius Stephen Hunter should not buy it.

Lord Holland is still tormented with gout, and unable to attend Councils or Cabinet dinners. He made an effort last week to go after dinner to Lord Grey's, and was the worse for it.

On the subject of health I must send you an anecdote of the late Dr. Baillie. He attended a very fine and very fanciful lady who bored him an hour with questions on her numerous symptoms and maladies, and ended by saying she was going to the opera. At last the doctor escaped from her, but as he was shutting the door she screamed after him, "My dear Dr. Baillie, I forgot

[1] Buckingham Palace.
[2] Bethlehem Hospital, St. George's Fields, built in 1812 from designs by James Lewis.

another question. May I eat a few oysters when I come home from the opera?"

"Yes, ma'am," he said, "shells and all."

They say Colonel Fox refuses to be called Sir Charles, and does not wear the Guelphic Order, which is called "The Refuge for the Destitute."

The malignants report that with the five difficulties they have to encounter, the Ministry will not last two months; if so, all parties have been tried in vain, and we have no resource but Mr. Hunt.

A bitter pamphlet to Scarlett[1] on the imprudent publication of his speech at the Malton Election. He is sadly fallen, and feels it deeply.

The Queen lectures ladies on want of drapery, and Lady —— has been told to adopt warmer clothing in the winter.

It is said the judges on the late Commissions are dissatisfied at the reprieves Government has accorded to some capital convicts whom they thought fit subjects for execution, and after the deepest consideration.

Lord Clifden thinks a Dublin jury may be easily found to convict O'Connell, and I think the legal net, provided the jury are not intimidated, will be sufficient, though some of the Irish lawyers are of a different opinion. I wish it may be so, as an acquittal would be a most serious triumph.

I wish Anglesey would not ride about Dublin. It is useless and foolish, as it tends to excitement and personal danger from an Irish rabble.

[1] Sir James Scarlett, afterwards Lord Abinger.

*Monday, June 20th,* 1831.

MY old friend Hippesley had played in early life, and when he and a learned foreigner named Paradise were presented for doctors' degrees at Oxford, Vansittart, a man of wit, proposed this address—

> "Insignis Vice-Cancellarie
> Et vos Egregii Procuratores
> Præsento Vobis Dominum Hippisley cum
> Pair-o-dice."

Let your Oxonian translate this for country gentlewomen, but not in the way Paradise did by the help of his dictionary.

> " Most remarkable Vice-Chancellor,
> And you very singular Proctors " !

Dictionaries are fallacious guides. An English lady at Paris wanted a chest of drawers, and unluckily resorted to her Boyer, where she found *poitrine*, "chest," *caleçons*, "drawers," which sorely puzzled her cabinet-maker.

I sat an hour on Friday with your charming sister, pleasant and blooming as ever; and what none of us could ever do at three months, she is almost able to go alone.

Within this fortnight I have also dined with no less than three immaculate Countesses—she of Cork and Orrery, she of Blessington, and she of Harrington. At Harrington House a superb banquet and a jollification of twenty merry folk—Alvanley,[1] George Colman, and

[1] William, second Lord Alvanley, the famous sayer of good things, died 1845.

James Smith of the "Rejected Addresses," and more than this, Lord and Lady Tavistock! The bride pretty and interesting, but she looks thin and worn, and all the freshness of youth has vanished. They called here next day. He left a card and she a bouquet. On my card of return I wrote most gallantly—

"When Beauty pays visits her card is divine,
For roses, carnations, and kindness combine."

*Nostra senora*, of Blessington, has a house of *bijoux* in Seymour Place. Le Comte d'Orsay, an Antinous of beauty and an exquisite of Paris, married the rich daughter of Lord Blessington, and they live here with *la belle mère*.

This Dandy D'Orsay, says a friend, asked another to whom he was writing. "To my father," was the answer, "to condole with him on the loss of my mother-in-law." The writer then called for a glass of water, and sprinkled the letter with his fingers. "What are you about?" said the friend. "Only giving an appearance of tears to my paper," said the writer.

The crazy Londonderry gave a dinner yesterday to the leader Mansfield and eighty Anti-Reformers, Lords and Commons, but still disdains to mend his windows or his manners.

The Duchess of Coutts,[1] Edward says, had an ambulatory cow at her breakfast to administer syllabubs.

Theodore Hook is celebrated as an *improvisatore*. He was charged t'other day with preparing his impro-

[1] The Duchess of St. Albans.

visations beforehand, and that they were merely *les impromptus faits à loisir*. "Put me to the test," he said, "and tell me who was that man that called just now and received your money so immediately?" "Why," they said, "it was Mr. Winter, the tax-gatherer." Hook replied instantly—

" Mr. Winter, I find, is collector of taxes,
And seems to get money whenever he axes,
And he gets it without either menace or flummery,
For though his name's Winter his process is summary."

So adieu till the 30th, when the Queen brings all dancing damsels to town.

*Monday, July* 18*th*, 1831.

EDWARD commanded the King's Guard on the night of the Opera House benefit for the Irish. He says the Duke of Braganza[1] is not an Adonis, short and sallow. They have put Lady Holland's son, Major Webster, about him as a bear-leader, as they did Poodle Byng to gallant the unfortunate King and Queen of Otaheitee. Poodle gave them the measles, of which they died, and, I believe, as Poodle is poor, Government gave him leave to take what he could find in their royal pockets. So far the Poodle was better off than the Major.

Yesterday I dined with Colonel Fox and Lady Mary. They have one of the new small villas near Holland House. I had pleasanter *fitzes* than the gout gives. Lady Frederick Fitzclarence, the divine's wife, and Lady Sophia Sidney, who is herself divine, so good-

[1] Pedro IV. of Portugal.

looking, so clever, and so lively that my "withered nut" was in danger. The passion was mutual, and she invited me to the Arcadian shades of Penhurst. I sent her to-day a curious and scarce print of the great Sir Philip Sidney, one hundred years old. The modern Sir Philip will not write an Arcadia, but she manages him, and Shakespeare agrees that "when two ride on a horse one must ride behind," which is fortunately Sir Philip. They say, too, she manages the whole family with royalty at the head of it.

Lord Holland has built a new entrance lodge at Kensington, and I congratulated a lame man who could thus improve his gait. The Countess of Blessington gave a dinner to us on Friday. Lord Wilton, General Phipps, Le Comte d'Orsay, and myself—*Cuisine de Paris exquise.* The pretty melancholy Comtesse[1] glided in for a few minutes, and then left us to nurse her influenza. The Misses Berry tell me they have dined with the Speaker and wife, who have thrown my Blessington overboard. The English at Naples called my friend the Countess of Cursington. If Mr. Speaker outlives the Reform Debate he may defy *la grippe* and the cholera. I can recommend no books, for the booksellers declare nobody reads or buys in the present fever. The newspapers furious, the Sunday papers talking treason by wholesale, and the *Age* for his sins has got hold of his lordship the Lord Dover, and

---

[1] The Comtesse D'Orsay, Lord Blessington's daughter by a first wife. After D'Orsay's death she married the Hon. C. Spencer Cowper, and lived until 1869.

quizzes him unmercifully for puffing himself in newspapers, and toad-eating Princes and Ministers. Peel does all he can to make his friends behave like gentlemen. But the nightly vulgarities of the House of Commons furnish new reasons for Reform, and not a ray of talent glimmers among them all. Double-distilled stupidity.

The town remains crowded and crazy, and we are to have a Coronation at half price. Leopold is off to his Belgians, and we hope soon to hear "he is as well as can be expected." He has done the right and handsome thing towards England by letter to Lord Grey, signifying that after some annual payments to servants and others he desires his pension may be paid in to the public as long as he remains on the throne of Belgium. This will quiet the Republicans abroad who abused the new King as a British pensionary, and please John Bull. The influenza still lingers here. Lady Lyndhurst was in danger, and her husband sent for from his circuit. Lady Morley, too, was very ill.

The King continues to wear himself, and his health is doubtful. It is believed the whole army in Portugal is ripe to receive Don Pedro, and to kick out Don Miguel.[1] The Tory M.P.'s abuse Peel and Wellington for lukewarmness, and the Tory Peers begin to hold the language of expediency and prudence; perhaps, too, they have just brains enough to keep out of the fire.

The *Court Journal* to-day had a squib of infinite wit and humour in a mock trial of Londonderry and

[1] Miguel did not capitulate until the early part of 1834.

Croker. They say Calcraft has fallen into a state of such nervous hypochondriasis that he cannot be persuaded to enter the House of Commons.[1] To be sure he is no ordinary *girouette*, so ratting cannot have depressed his spirits.

A breakfast under an umbrella every day at a villa. Dull dinners of twenty people every day in town, with the sempiternal saddle of mutton, and the doleful master of the house on a pillion behind it, making clumsy efforts at conviviality till the dumb Shees grow merciful and draw their gloves on. Yet such are the pleasures you abandon for ponds and *pinasters*. The Ladies Morley and Holland have made peace after the war, about Henry Fox and Miss Villiers, as she has got a preferable husband. Colonel Trench proposes to-night in Parliament to convert the Pimlico Palace into a laundry for half-pay officers to wash their own linen.

*July 18th*, 1831.

THE Coronation expense is limited to £20,000, so perhaps Gunter will contract for the whole of it. There must be galleries for Peeresses, and a new organ, which the Dean and Chapter pouch as a perquisite.

It is said that for economy Hume suggests a hand

[1] John Calcraft, who held office in the Granville Administration. He temporarily abandoned his Whig convictions 1828–30, when he took office under Wellington, but he returned to his old faith, and voted for Reform in 1831, when the Bill was carried by a single vote. He was so reproached by the Tories with whom he had acted that his mind gave way, and he committed suicide in September 1831.

organ. No Coronation robes for Peers, but the parliamentary robes only. To accompany the anthem it was thought a single fiddler on a single string would be the cheapest way, but Paganini asked £30,000.

The Treasury would not hear of this.

SPRING GARDENS, *Monday, August 1st,* 1831.

THE fever of politics and dissipation runs as high as ever, and the thermometer increases it,—dinners, breakfasts, and Billingsgate in Parliament. Edward was to have marched away with his battalion for Bristol and Dublin this day, but it is postponed till to-morrow, as they are suddenly ordered to remain under arms, for a most multitudinous mass of Radicals is to meet at Copenhagen House, near Islington, the scene of Mr. Hunt's former triumphs, and a tumult may arise while the world is gazing at Royalty in the city. I hear there was rioting yesterday at Oxford, and the Life Guards sent for.

Mrs. Gore's pin-money novel pretty, and her new comedy very successful. She has desired old Corky to invite Rogers and me to meet her on Wednesday to dinner at Corky's house. They say she is handsome. She married a captain who spent her money, and they now live by circulating libraries and managers of playhouses.

My lively little Dowager, Lady Morton, is taking a very young husband.[1]

But I must be serious, for I have just heard distressing

[1] Mr. Edward Godfrey, of Old Hall, Suffolk.

news. Poor Manning [1] is ruined; his house has stopped payment; the debts enormous. West India distresses have produced the catastrophe, but his honour is unsullied. A meeting of his creditors on Friday next, and perhaps his bankruptcy in the next day's *Gazette*. I feared some misfortune, as I saw his Kentish Coombe Bank advertised for sale last week.

They are a family of excellent people reduced to poverty. Duke of Wellington has wisely declined the stupid Mayor's invitation to-day, as he thinks his presence might excite the mob, who would delight to reform anything but themselves, and might duck the man who saved the country. Such is popularity.

Little Master of the Rolls gone off for Rome and the malaria to-day. Lady Glengall in tears, of course.

We have hired sixty ragamuffins to-day to keep the peace of our garden, and to beat the new police if they threaten to protect us; and we have given our gardener a sumptuous present to prevent bribery for admission.

As Falstaff says, "would it were bedtime and all were well"; but I expect all the miseries which generally befall intended felicity.

Pearse says Claud Hunter is to propose the Queen's health at the Bridge, and has been hammering out his speech these three days.

To return to poor Manning's case—" From gay to grave, from lively to severe." I hear his house owes

[1] Mr. William Manning, of Coombe Bank, Brasted, Kent, the father of Cardinal Manning.

£100,000 to their bankers Smith. Lord Carrington's brother, John Pearse, is also a creditor of some thousands, but does not speak in despair of ultimate payments, though Manning's partner and son-in-law, Anderson, seems to think ill of the result.

Thus it is while the world is fiddling, dancing, feasting, and flirting all round us.

Poor Edward sends his best love to you all. I am very, very sorry to lose him for nine months. I gave him a line to the Lord-Lieutenant, who I know will be kind to him.

Rose Bank, where Londonderry affected to give a *fête*, is a cottage and garden at Fulham not fifty yards square. I once visited friends there.

SPRING GARDENS, *Monday, August 15th*, 1831.

POOR Isted has taught Willie what certainly does not abound in the House of Commons, eloquence at his finger ends. How fortunate it had been for the stammering idiotism of Londonderry if he had been visited by Isted's fatality, and how fortunate will it be for the Radicals if the Tory Lords reject the bill,[1] for then *Vive la République! A bas la Patrie.*

But we have been fiddling here while Rome is burning. *Fêtes* upon *fêtes*. We feasted five hundred belles and beaux in our Temple Hall and Garden on the London Bridge Day. Lord Hertford's, too, was gay as royalties, beauties, turtle, and venison could make it, and the weather on both days was propitious.

[1] Reform Bill.

To keep the grim antiquity of St. Dunstan's clock and figures in countenance, there sate the three weird sisters of Rutland, Richmond, and Hertford. The horrible spectacle the first exhibits is indescribable. Yet it was once super-eminent beauty. I rejoice that I never was pretty.

The Duke of Cumberland presented me to his Duchess, who said a thousand kind things about Edward, and is a very agreeable person; of course *le bon papa* thought so.

Dowager Corky gave us a *dilettante* dinner last week—Rogers, Luttrell, Mrs. Gore, who writes pretty novels, and Mr. Bulwer,[1] who cannot.

The King is at times unwell; his advisers cannot dissuade him from eternal bustle and publicity. He says he is never so well as in a state of excitement, which he will find is not a very salutary opinion.

Lady Jersey scolds me for neglecting her Calcutta *soirées.*

Tom Moore's "Life of Lord E. Fitzgerald" worth reading. Lord George Seymour told me they were willing to lend Norris Castle to the Duchess of Kent, as it would have given an *éclat* to the place, and secured a better sale of it. But she insisted on paying for the summer residence, I think £500.

Windsor is a zoological menagerie of German Princes and Princesses at present, and a merrier, pleasanter little fellow than Braganza never lost an Empire. I am quite enamoured of him.

---

[1] Lytton Bulwer.

I sate an hour t'other day with poor Armstrong, who has at last resorted to the medical conjurer of Bromley, but gains no ground. Armstrong has produced an illegitimate son and daughter, who are a comfort to his confinement. The girl is womanly, and Dowager Cork protects her, for the filthy lucre of stealing her father's wax and writing paper. Minerva, I think, except Eve, was the only lady who never had a mother, but proceeded at once from the skull of Jupiter, and as a warlike goddess was probably of the Armstrong family.

They say that crazy Dudley has put two years' income into the American Fund. Some add that Hertford has sent £200,000, but he is too wise to follow such lunacy. Dudley has adopted a boy relation, and sent him to Eton as his successor. Marriage is out of the question, as it would force him to buy a new coat and hat, but then it would give him pin-money to supply the place of buttons to his waistcoat.

Poor Leopold! I wonder how many times he has already wished himself parish clerk of Claremont?

Mrs. Ashton I remember, a comely, plump flirt with a dull squire *sposo*. The sister, a romp, married a sort of *friseur*, the son of the old Viscount Fitzwilliam. When we were at Paris last she pressed Joseph, but in vain, to her *soirées* in the Rue de Rivoli. I marvel how the French pronounce *la femme de Fitch Villiame*.

I flirt with Lady Dudley Stuart, Napoleon's niece—pretty French eyes and· clever—and yesterday passed three hours with some new foreigners at the Zoological, which is the best lounge of London. The young elephant is so sensible and agreeable, that next to Napoleon's niece and yourself, I prefer him to half my acquaintance. I wish to God he was in Parliament. I brought him a white paper full of buns, which I had placed on the seat beside me of a wheeling chair. Turning my head to hear Sir H. Hardinge detail a new defeat of the Belgians, I felt two cold pats on my head. It was the trunk of my friend. I told him the last bun was gone. He looked grave, patted me again, and devoured the paper.

*August 15th*, 1831.

A GALLOWS with two halters was erected on Lord Hertford's lawn, on which a fellow performed various antics, and suspended himself by the ropes. Drapery he had hardly any, but the ladies said he was meant to represent Hercules, and that it was proper.

Duke of Sussex said the execution of the Russian band was perfect, which I denied, as their hanging was omitted.

Mrs. Siddons left Mrs. Fitzhugh only a ring—for her nose, probably—as the common legacy to bores.

Leopold was very nearly made a prisoner in this last defeat of his cowards.[1] I reminded Sir H. Hardinge of the Duke of Wellington's contempt of the Dutch troops at the outset of this quarrel. Hardinge said that

---

[1] At Louvain on August 12th. The conduct of the Belgian troops in the short campaign against Holland was so bad as to excite the derision of Europe.

the Dutch had now Swiss regiments and other foreign officers and engineers.

> SPRING GARDENS, *October 27th*, 1831.

"CONFOUND ye all! I hope you will all be mutton chops in a week."

This was the fulmination of the celebrated Earl of Chesterfield, when he found his post-horses impeded by innumerable flocks of sheep on the road, and in which we religiously agreed when the Winchester fair on Monday poured forth more *moutons* than Ajax slew, or Don Quixote attacked in the Sierra Morena.

Yesterday at three o'clock we reached our household gods; the roads in good order, and not a shower while we were on our wheels. The turtle at Popham Lane well dressed, and Mrs. Martin's *fricandeau* exquisite. Her hock inferior to her *côte-rôtie*, as the former had some flavour of the Bagshot chalybeate.

At Hyde Park Corner we found Wellington[1] and Gloucester had not missed deal, for their windows were boarded up—" Boarding without Lodging," the reverse of the Bath invitations. Missing deal would be an awkward blunder at the present game of political whist, where the odd trick is played by the bishops and the Lords are almost at nine, when honours go for nothing.

The morning papers redouble in fury, and the *Morning Chronicle* modestly suggests a National Guard.

[1] The new Parliament met this day. The Duke was very unpopular, and less than a month later his Ministry was defeated, and resigned.

The Countess of Harrington (*née* Foote) is about to give a young Lord Petersham to the peerage.

I have a note to-day from my clever friend James Smith, one of the two brothers who wrote " The Rejected Addresses." George Eyre's late partner, old Andrew Strahan, the King's printer, was a great friend of his. The old man was very clever, but had lost the use of his legs. Smith sent him an epigram last year, and he left him by his will £250. This was Smith's epigram :—

> " Your lower limbs seemed far from stout
> When late I saw you walk;
> The cause I instantly found out
> Soon as I heard you talk.
> The power that props the body's length
> In due proportion spread,
> In yours concentred, all the strength
> Is got into the head."

Stanley goes to Dublin in a fortnight, so there will be no early meeting of Parliament. They think little of the cholera at Hamburgh, and Dr. Chalmers, the physician there, laughs at our panic.

*Saturday, November* 12*th*, 1831.

As game is now saleable by Act of Parliament, I expect a bill will also pass to permit apothecaries to hang up dead patients at their doors for anatomical purchasers, and as cheap as pheasants and partridges. I don't think old ladies and gentlemen will sell for more than nine shillings apiece, and a brace of young ladies who are not yet out for a crown, and a leash of dandies for a couple of shillings. The law would be most prolific. Graves would be undisturbed, science promoted, and as apothecaries are duly qualified to kill they have a right to sell.

If I have not a new peerage I have had a new title conferred upon me. The newspapers, on puffing the poets and poetesses of the *Keepsake*, add, that Mr. Jekyll, "the Nestor of *beaux esprits* of the day," has contributed a lively trifle.

Poor Armstrong is much better, and can walk about his room without crutches. After a year's confinement to his couch his illegitimate son, a clever young man in a public office, whom Willie knew at Harrow, is sent in a decline to Gibraltar and Malta.

The rector of my parish, who was Lord Dover's tutor in the Medlar School, threatens me with a printed paper that a Committee will call next week to see if I keep my house and myself in cleanliness.

I dined *tête-à-tête* yesterday at our Temple banquet with Sir E. Wetherell,[1] who also lives in my parish, but did not mention the doctor's menace, as it might have put the Recorder of Bristol to the expense of washing a change of linen, which I believe is only an annual practice with him.

I saw Lady Stafford yesterday on foot in Pall Mall, brushing with hasty steps the mud away, and was sorry to observe she stoops very much. But I was soothed in Jermyn Street by "nods, and becks, and wreathed

[1] Sir E. Wetherell, Solicitor-General and Attorney-General in the Liverpool and Wellington Administrations. He first came into prominence by his able defence of the Cato Street conspirators. In politics he was a violent anti-Catholic.

smiles" from a beauty in a cabriolet, driven by a much-mustachioed cavalier. Need I mention the Earl and Countess of Harrington?

*November* 24*th*, 1831.

YOU ordered me to write soon, so here goes to fill a letter if I can. The *Herald* gives you news of the day past, and the stupid *Albion* of the last week. The Antis are ill off with *Albion*, *Standard*, and *Morning Post*, and are now reinforced by the *Age*. They have long renounced arguments, and content themselves with calling names.

The active William IV. is all alacrity for Grey. They were going to Brighton for a council to settle about the meeting of Parliament, and William came to town to save trouble.

A letter from Dickinson very desponding, and overgrown with moss like a country Squire's; going to the Pinneys at Lyme Regis, where the hope of that family is a candidate for the Reformed election. Dickinson's son is gone to Cambridge by his father's apostacy from Oxford and Christ Church, but he has been bit by a Cambridge private tutor and mathematician.

I did not recollect Vernon at the Staffords with a new name and extraordinary head of hair. Poor Lord Stafford seems nearly annihilated. I thought of the mummy of the Cheops the Egyptian King found in the most splendid of the Pyramids.

I have seen nothing of the Viscount Clifden nor the Peer of Dover for ages, so conclude they are Burked.

Old Lady Glyn immortalised in the Duke of Rutland's tour through England said, "One's acquaintance wears out like one's clothes, but one gets new ones."

Old Dowager Cork has been passed back to London by sundry country parishes, and to-day, at her earnest request, I saw her an hour in her nightcap attended by a toady to write her notes. A womanuensis is necessary for her spelling. She abused me for leaving her to visit Lady Blessington, whom she called the worst of women. I told her my virtue was impregnable, and I never troubled myself about the morality of countesses if they were agreeable, and did not try to borrow my carriage.

If we are to have a new batch of peers to counteract the lunatics who are committing suicide I wish we may find as good materials as the French have.[1] A selection of better judgment or more free from party could not have been imagined. Yet peers for life are mere puppets, and, in France, when hereditary were beggars, and never analogous to ours. So it is a mere court of aldermen, and leaves France what the last Revolution meant, a King with a Republic.

Lady Ellenborough is going to marry her youngest daughter of nineteen to the eldest son of Sir Charles Desvoeux, an Irish baronet. Her eldest sisters yet unmarried. By a long minority she will be richer than they ; but the honeymoon will not be opulent, as Lady Ellenborough tells me.

[1] Thirty-six new peers created in 1831, in order to carry the motion for the abolition of the hereditary peerage in France.

Such are the dangers of the portentous year of 1832, that with the exception of a few whom you can easily think of, it is believed that under some arrangements in the bill the way through the Lords will be smoothed. Foreigners, nevertheless, are daily investing their property in our funds as the best depôt in Europe. Poor Manning's affairs wind up deplorably, and I fear the inferior creditors will suffer sadly. Out of the wreck this unfortunate couple will not have £1,000 per annum to exist upon. His first wife was Lord Carrington's sister, who with the rich Smiths it is hoped may assist them. Lady Sidmouth is in so debilitated a state from long illness that her life is very precarious. The *Keepsake* contains my squib of eight years old, and sundry withered nuts of Dover Pier, Lord Holland, Morpeth, and rhyming ladies. The outside of the book as usual the most attractive. Williams, M.P., became the Captain's acquaintance by dining with him at Marlow, when he commanded the Guards at High Wycombe on the riots there, and at whose house he met Parson Kent, who blesses the yacht commanders in the winter. The papers have been killing Winchester and Ely, and the mob roasting the rest of the Bishops. The cigar-smokers of Dublin use spitting vases in the shape of mitres.

SPRING GARDENS, *Wednesday, December* 23*rd*, 1831.

THE Antis threaten to repeat their antics in the Lords. So William IV. must make his noble bundle of faggots, and swear them in as special constables to prevent lunatics from cutting their own throats. The cholera is fading away, and Burking is suspended as well as its professors, or they are both excellent receipts for pulling down a majority.

Lord Dover is just gone, and has given me a vote for Thomas Garrett. Lady Garrett is in town for her confinement. I have just got his "King of Prussia." This fascinating Madame de Feuchères[1] lived formerly with Nugent, the brother of Luttrell. The share that would come to the Duc d'Aumale would be £50,000 per annum. It is believed the will is to be confirmed, as French judges are always well disposed to royalty.

Rogers gives Joseph and me dinner to-day, and to meet all the wits and wags that can be recruited in London.

*Tuesday, December 27th, 1831.*

JOSEPH dines all over the town, and protects Madame Vestris.[2] God forbid! it should be in the bad sense of that unhappy verb. My friend Lady Harrington[3] has produced a young Petersham, to the great dismay of a whiskerandos, second brother of my lord, who flattered himself the noble earl would only philander with dramatic heroines, and not marry one.

The Altar of *High-men* has been auspicious to pretty actresses; and when Peers have brains enough to buy

[1] Sophia Dawes.
[2] The popular actress, wife of Armand Vestris, ballet master of the King's Theatre. She afterwards married Charles James Matthews, the comedian.
[3] Miss Maria Foote.

beauty and talents with their coronets, one has great hopes of their lucid interval on the Reform Bill.

Joseph knew Madame de Feuchères at Paris. She is handsome, and has shown much talent in theatricals at Chantilly, and the daughter of old Dawes, the fruiterer, in Oxford Street, and had already forced the poor old Duke[1] to give an estate to young Master Dawes, her worshipful nephew, and to get him made a peer of France.

Somebody wrote to Grosvenor and addressed him, "Expensive Wig," "Dear Bob."

I felicitated R. E. N. Lee on the nuptials of his dandy, who hath espoused a tall thin widow with a thinner jointure.

Watson Taylor sends me two volumes of his verses privately printed, but has not eclipsed Byron as yet. Lord Nugent's "John Hampden" not ill done. I wish I could name something better worth the skimming.

LONDON, *January 9th*, 1832.

JOSEPH and I dined on Tuesday at Dover House. We had only Lord Clifden and Sir Robert Wilson.[2]

[1] The Prince de Condé. Madame de Feuchères was the wife of the Baron de Feuchères, whom she married in 1818 Originally an actress at Covent Garden Theatre, she later became the acknowledged mistress of the Prince. She died in 1841 in England.

[2] Sir Robert T. Wilson, a distinguished soldier, who was dismissed the service by George IV. for his known sympathy with Queen Caroline. The occasion was the part taken by Wilson at the Queen's funeral, where he endeavoured to prevent the collision between the people and the military.

The former looked ill and out of spirits. The latter became a violent Tory, because Ministers do not give him a regiment, though he might have been contented with the restoration of his rank, and the subscription at Brooks' of £14,000 to indemnify him for the forfeiture of his commissions, and which was double their value. Lady Dover and I chatted on the sofa all the evening, and the next day she produced a daughter. So the Barony of Dover has presumed to increase the Cinque Ports by the addition of a sixth. He wanted a boy.

Lord Romsey marries the widow of George Cholmondeley, by which she forfeits half his churlish will bequeathed her. He left £100,000 to the two archbishops to distribute in charity, and left his eldest son scantily provided for. A vain, heartless man.

Hayter, who painted the "Queen's Trial," is employed, I hear, by His Majesty on a family picture of himself, the Fitzclarences' and the late Mrs. Jordan in the male attire of Little Pickle in the farce of the *Spoiled Child*.

The King borrowed Mrs. Jordan's portrait of Sir H. Bunbury, who begged him to accept of it. This was to enable Hayter to transfer the likeness to his group on the canvas. Rogers does not look well. Dudley says he never did.

The Northamptonshire squires subscribed for a statue to Lord Althorp; but the sculptor was puzzled about a dignified posture, as *Milord* usually speaks with his hands in his pockets. Luttrell said, "The attitude is obvious. A Chancellor of the Exchequer should be represented with his hands in other people's pockets."

George Colman, James Smith of the "Rejected Addresses," Rogers of the "Pleasures of Memory," and Campbell of the "Pleasures of Hope," dined with me yesterday at a Parisian repast of much refinement given us by the Countess of Blessington. There was wit, fun, epigram, and raillery enough to supply fifty county members for a twelvemonth. *Miladi* has doffed her widow's weeds, and was almost in pristine beauty. Her house is a *bijou*, or, as Sir W. Curtis' lady said, "a perfect bougie."

A pretty girl showed me this morning a small lump of lead which the fire had melted into a sort of foliage. She said it was a present from H.R.H. the Duke of Cumberland.

It seems there is a custom in Germany on New Year's Day for the lord and lady of the house to chuck into the fire various lumps of this precious metal. They come out melted into fantastic forms, and are gravely presented as souvenirs to affectionate friends. This solemnity is religiously observed at Kew. My pretty friend added that as his new house had beds in plenty, H.R.H. told her he must have *me* to pass a week there!!! What would my Whigs say?

Lord Dover's "King of Prussia"[1] is extremely well done, and with great industry. He has got together and condensed the scattered memoirs of Voltaire,

[1] "Life of Frederic II., King of Prussia," 2 vols., by George James Wallace Agar Ellis, Baron Dover.

Thibadeau, and the Royal *vaurien* himself. People are reading " Eugene Aram," a mean schoolmaster and a sordid assassin, whom Bulwer, M.P., has exalted into a romantic lover and a paragon of sensibility. When I was a very young boy I saw this prodigy of learning and virtue hanging in chains for murder at Knaresborough. Last week I condoled with Sir James Mackintosh that his borough of Knaresborough had been poked into Schedule A, after having immortalised itself as the *Alma Mater* of three such historical and oratorical characters as himself, Tierney, and Eugene Aram.

Lord Tavistock has got Lord Dover's late house in Spring Gardens. Campbell the poet is going to write the life of Mrs. Siddons, and sends to me for anecdotes. Sir C. Flint, who visited Chantilly often, says that Madame de Feuchères is very amiable, and that her care and kindness preserved the Duke's life and happiness for eighteen years, and that a great rogue instigated the Rohans [1] to the law-suit, and tried to support it by subornation. However, the will has not been shaken, as we lawyers think.

The King has given the Bishops leave to abandon wigs except in the House of Lords or the pulpit. Bishop of London dined at General Phipps' on Sunday without one. Upon my word, the poor Right Reverends are in a sad way. The Crown plucks off their wigs, the

---

[1] The heirs-at-law of the Prince de Condé. There was great diversity of opinion as to Madame de Feuchères' conduct. M. Louis Blanc said: " Madame de Feuchères gagna sa procès devant les tribunaux, et le perdit devant l'opinion publique."

Radicals will make cravats of lawn sleeves. The boys burn prelates with Guy Vaux, and the judges hung an unfortunate Mr. Bishop for Burking under an unpopular name.

Cobbett's last number on Saturday is high treason, and his address to the Yeomanry Cavalry more atrocious than all his atrocities. The law seems asleep. George Colman grows old and gouty, and has wisely sold his Lieutenancy of the Yeomen of the Guards for £6,000. I addressed him on Saturday from Sheridan's *Critic*—

"Am I a beefeater now?"

P.S.—How I rejoice the "Squires are become poulterers." I was ruined by shillings for porterage of game, and had rather eat magpies, or any pies but those you make for the unfortunate Taty.

Whole battues are hung up at the corner of every street, and so cheap that servants on board wages had rather be poachers of eggs.

*Monday, January 9th.*

Postscript the second, for I scorn to write across.

It is whimsical that Lord Romney's first wife was Moreton Pitt's daughter, and that George Cholmondeley's first wife was Moreton Pitt's sister.

This moment a letter from Edward dated from some unpronounceable château in the Wicklow Mountains. Troops have been sent from Dublin to Kilkenny, but still he reports general tranquillity.

He saw Kean play Richard so drunk that he fell in

the Battle of Bosworth Field before Richmond had condescended to kill him, and while lying on the ground blew his nose. He arose at last and stammered the following apology—

"Ladies and gentlemen, you see—you see—*argumentum ad hominem!*" He then reeled off nobody knew whither, or comprehended the *argumentum*.

*Friday, January 27th,* 1832.

I HAVE been sending you the *Town*,[1] sent to me on Sundays by the editors, Captain Stanhope of the Navy, and young Reynolds, the son of the comedy writer. It does not as yet seem to surpass its rivals.

*On dit*, Lord Cawdor to be Chamberlain to the Queen; little bandy-legged Arthur Stanhope, the favourite of George III. and George IV., is to lose his place of £1,500 a year in Post Office by the new economy.

Joseph and I had a visit and a dinner of a singular sort three weeks ago. For the first time in his life rolled in Jack Fuller. He roared out, "Name your day, and I will get wits and choice spirits, whom you live with, to meet you at dinner. I will give your son a skinful of Burgundy such as England never tasted." Naming a day could not be carried. We went expecting an Abyssinian feast. We were disappointed. Jack had read Lord Chesterfield of course all the morning. He was quiet and well bred, and all the *beaux esprits* had agreed

[1] A weekly society paper, price 7*d*. The first number appeared on January 1st, 1832, and it ran for ten years.

to meet me. A dinner of taste and magnificence, a superb service of plate, a pack of lacqueys in rich liveries, a French cook of £150 wages, a splendid dessert, pictures of the Sussex Domains by Turner, some, as Joseph said, Turner must have been paid £500 for. At night we had four musical artistes, the nephews and nieces and Miss Stevens, to whom Jack had given a magnificent pianoforte. Jack rang a silver bell for silence when a piece began. We found above stairs the Dowager Lady Ashburnham and daughters and a few ladies. She told me the good Jack did in Sussex to the tenants and the poor was exemplary. He took Joseph aside, and said, "You are like your mother. I loved her when a girl; she was the best of the bunch. I never liked old Sloane nor the rest of them nor the *chap* his son, who has always his eyes in his pocket." I never had such a day in my life. Ask William whether he was not his mother's first cousin? His £15,000 a year will go to his sister's son, Sir T. Acland, a young baronet in Somerset. What relation was he to the fiddling divine at Paultons?

In spite of the lady protocols I am glad to see our Dummy Taffy was elected. One day last week I met at dinner Lord Cavendish, the prodigy of Cambridge, who, like other prodigies, disappointed the House of Commons. He was dead silent, and reminded me of what Congreve says in one of his comedies: "At the bottom of the table sate my Lady's eldest son, who, not having learned from nature to breathe through his nose, sate with his mouth open."

Did not William go to the Duke of Rutland's birthday? I have always thought he who keeps his birthday desires his friends to congratulate him on what must have happened to every one of themselves.

I am reading a pretty French book by Blacas, "Les Scenes de la Vie privée." Lord Dover's "King of Prussia" is liked.

Jack Fuller said he never dined out. I should think inviters were scarce. Joseph and I could not make out whether he meant to impute to the *chap* William stinginess or great caution against those who meant to pick his pocket. Joseph says the Bonassus or the Polar Bear will soon ask us to dinner.

*January* 27*th*, 1832.

YOU see a newspaper admirer of mine congratulates me on deafness, and instead of considering it a defect or a misfortune, tells me it is an advantage, and even an accomplishment, inasmuch as it relieves me from hearing the dull absurdities uttered at fashionable dinners.

It reminds me of a retort I heard Mrs. Pitt make to the late Duchess of Gordon. "Well, Pitt," she said, "we have not met for a long time; have you been talking as much nonsense as usual?" "Perhaps," replied Pitt, "but I have not heard so much."

Poor old Greenwood,[1] a good-natured friendly man,

[1] Charles Greenwood, the Army Agent. He had dined with the King at the Pavilion, Brighton, on January 25th, 1832, and died while playing a game of whist after dinner. He was eighty-four.

a good deal of vanity, which would have been gratified had he known he was to die at the table of a king. I knew him much in the Duke of York's time, who showered upon him two-thirds of the regimental agencies. I believe Greenwood occasionally assisted him under his embarrassments, but have heard lost a very few thousands only by his insolvency, and which former benefits and patronage had amply balanced.

My friend the Countess of Blessington sends me a beautiful print of herself from Lawrence's portrait.

I pity Peel, who must feel mortified in leading such a wretched fry of Opposition. The House is sick to death of such worthless repetitions, and members are *rongés d'ennui*, and don't attend as they ought to do, for the divisions are all that is necessary for newspapers.

SPRING GARDENS, *August 1st*, 1832.

THE Captain has been playing Adjutant at the Tower for a sick comrade, and is now released from the garrison and the cholera there. It has pleased his most gracious Majesty to form a camp in Windsor Park of the flank companies of the Guards and some artillery, so in a few days the gallant Captain and his light infantry are to pitch their tents for some weeks, which they suppose will supersede his balls and breakfasts.

The Duchess of Coutts,[1] he reports, had a cow with gilt horns at her *déjeuner*, to supply her noble milkmaids with syllabubs, and went about laying the dust at her

[1] The Duchess of St. Albans.

ball with a silver watering-pot, the contents of which were so glutinous from aromatic gums, that it glued the misses' shoes to the floor, and many danced barefoot. His Grace took no part in the shower, but walked about very like Miss Bagster in male costume.

Joseph is in a blue-striped shirt on the Thames, and has hitherto escaped the coroner's inquest, and continues a very regular spectator of Mademoiselle Mars. Dr. Quin, a disciple of Joseph's idol, Dr. Hahnemann, is fixed in London, and every old lady has a bottle of his cholera drops in her reticule. Dr. Wolff, of Dresden, has sent Joseph a most curious present, a box not larger than an octavo volume, containing two hundred phials. Each phial contains one thousand globules of the smallest size from every known drug in use. So the sum total is two hundred thousand doses, and eclipses all the apothecaries' shops I ever heard of. Joseph dined t'other day with his godpapa Lansdowne, who mentioned a singular observation of medical people—that when cholera renewed its visit to any country it attacked persons of a superior class to those it first demolished.

Of all the horrible attacks on Lady Holland, Lady Blessington's "Memoirs of Byron" in the last *New Monthly Magazine*[1] are the most *sanglans*. He does not spare her son Henry, and deplores Lord Holland's slavery to his rib. These "Memoirs" will be continued monthly, and Byron's former associates are frightened to death; some, too, who deluded themselves into a

[1] Vol. xxxv., p. 8.

belief they were beloved. As Lady Blessington is stout I hope she will be merciful. She recited to me most dreadful verses by Byron against his friend Rogers, but will not publish them, or the poet must inevitably plunge into the Serpentine. The conversations of a dead man cannot be contradicted, so if *Miladi* is not scrupulous on the score of veracity she may report Byron as she pleases. I was alarmed enough to ask if I was safe. She said, to my comfort, that she spoke of me as a favourite.

Emboldened by the success of her Italian translations, Elizabeth Law is about to print privately some English verses I never saw,[1] and declares she will dedicate them to me.

As you have now room for "meditation even to madness," I wish I could recommend to you some food for the mind; but I think I am only disporting myself with a deluge of new French novels in the highest style of Paris nonsense and trash. But I am turning author, and composing an account of the antiquities of the Temple Church.[2]

How you country folks have contrived to ripen your harvest without hothouses I know not; but I sate by

---

[1] "Miscellaneous Poems," by E. S. L. Miss Law, afterwards Lady Colchester, was the author of several volumes. She translated Goldsmith's "Traveller" into Italian, wrote "Views in London," etc. A tale of hers, "Algernon Graham," was published so late as 1872.

[2] "Facts and Observations Relating to the Temple Church and its Monuments." It was published in pamphlet form in 1811. Mr. Jekyll was also responsible for "The Letters of Sancho, with a Memoir," 1803.

my fireside some evenings last week and sharpened a pair of skates for immediate use. Lord Hertford gave us *fêtes* with lighted tar barrels for warmth and perfume, and has left town I hear with a cold and a doctor, and the hailstones broke half my skylights.

Almacks and marriages are all over for the season, and the Board of Health permits us at last to eat anything but cucumbers, so we hope to be alive till the winter.

The two Houses of Parliament have ended in calling one another very bad names; and if you can send us as romantic a title as Lyndhurst for the Speaker's peerage,[1] we shall be obliged to Hampshire for it.

P.S.—The Dovers gone to give him some sea air at Ramsgate. I am going to dine with Burdett to-day; bumpers to Reform. There never was a doubt as to the result, and the whole botheration has now passed over us "like a summer cloud."

SPRING GARDENS, *Monday, August 27th*, 1832.

EVEN His Majesty's ministers have fled to landscapes, and Lord Lansdowne has made a fruitless effort to seduce us to Bowood with Rogers. We dined yesterday with the poet, who says poor Crabbe left some finished tales in verse, which I think Rogers will give to the public. I am reading very interesting "Memoirs of Louis XVIII.," said to be written by himself. Of their authenticity of course I doubted, but I am told Talleyrand believes them to be genuine.

[1] Viscount Canterbury.

The Hollands are disposed to let Ampthill, which Lord Ossory left him. *Miladi* cannot get people down there, and £500 a year for it may probably be convenient in other respects. The King makes speeches from morning to night; a good-natured creature, and means well, when he has any meaning at all. The Queen is of use; and whenever his tirades grow foolish beyond the usual mark she either interrupts him or talks across so as to stifle the nonsense and turn the conversation. The Castle is gorged with Tories, and the poor Ministers seem only occasional guests by solemn invitation. If Wellington could muster a ragged regiment able to form a Cabinet, my love Lady Sophia and the Duke of Cumberland would try hard to throw Grey and Brougham overboard with the help of that comical club called the House of Lords and the Bishops. There is a clamour in London for a short session of Parliament in autumn, to tinker the Reform Bill, but it will not take place.

There is another fable, that Leopold's bride[1] has a prior attachment in France; but Palmerston must settle that by a hundred and twentieth protocol. Nobody cares about Pedro and Miguel except the amateurs of dog-fights. So much for the chapter of politics.

My friend's, Lady Blessington's, " Memoirs of Byron " in the last *New Monthly Magazine* fall desperately foul of the Jerseys, insinuating that *Miladi* has more talk than brains, and that her lord lives upon horseflesh at

---

[1] The Queen of the Belgians, Princess Louise of Orleans, eldest daughter of Louis Philippe.

Newmarket, with a clever allusion to Pegasus. But I suppose you have seen it, as nothing is so relishing as a libel on friends.

Lord Lansdowne is just as safe at Calne with his two hundred and ten 10-pounders as he was with my score of burgesses, and has sent Lord Kerry on a summer tour to Germany.

Leopold has lost all his teeth, and they say that Prince Otho of Bavaria, whom they have now made King of Greece,[1] is uglier than Sharpe or Quintin Dick. It is hard upon a country which sculptured the Apollo Belvidere.

I cannot touch upon the fine Arts without mentioning that young Eddis has made two very good portraits of my beauties Joseph and Edward, and I hope all the inhabitants of the Zoological Garden will sit to him.

Sad work with the Church! They pelt Archbishops at Canterbury. I am glad I did not buy a living for Edward, though he would have made an exemplary parish priest.

> "Our parson called, and took French leave,
>   But took his Tithe Pig too.
>   The ungodly call for a farewell,
>   The godly for a due."

This avalanche of nonsense I trust will reach you if the Post Office can decipher my friend Wetherell's hieroglyphical frank; but Tories always make a bad hand of it.

[1] Otho I., son of King Louis of Bavaria. He was deposed in 1862.

SPRING GARDENS, *October* 31*st*, 1832.

THE Captain having fulfilled his duty at the Tower, which lasted only three days, dined with us on arrival. Joseph is in his altitudes, for a homœopathic hospital and college have been founded at Leipsic, another at Lyons, and His Majesty of Prussia patronises the doctrine, as one of its disciples has cured a princess of his royal house of the epilepsy.

Mr. Reynolds, the editor of the *Keepsake*, sends me the new volume most undeservedly. The engravings of these annuals induce the world to endure their prose. Mirabeau once told me that Diderot was so jealous of his fame that he hid himself daily at his bookseller's to watch who came to purchase his volumes, and was mortified by a *Milor Anglais*, who said to the bookseller, "Cut out the printed parts, for I only want the pictures."

The Memoirs of the late John Taylor[1] are amusing. I knew the good-natured old gossip, who cantered his pony about Parnassus in bad prologues and epilogues, and used to puff me in his newspaper, for which I was thankful, of course, as scandal is now the only attraction of readers. Mrs. Ramsbottom, in *John Bull*, calls the unfortunate Foreign Secretary Lord Pumicestone; and Cobbett, in his last register, mobs poor Lady Stafford plentifully for forcing her bag-piper shepherds of Sutherland to become fishermen.

James Smith, of the "Rejected Addresses," was here

[1] "Records of My Life," two vols, 1832. John Taylor, the author of "Monsieur Tonson."

just now, and wrote this epigram on the two great rival Gunsmiths, Manton and Egg:—

> "Two of a trade can ne'er agree,
>   Each worries each, if able.
> In Manton and in Egg we see
>   The proverb proved a fable.
>
> "Both deal in guns, whose loud report
>   Confirms the fact I'm broaching—
> Manton's are made for lawful sport,
>   And Egg's are best for poaching."

Sheridan said he preferred *Lear* to all Shakespeare's tragedies. John Taylor replied, "That's because you married an Ogle."

SPRING GARDENS, *November 15th,* 1832.

LONDON is full enough—of men, at least. Discussing the other day the absurdity of ever leaving it, Alvanley said that he had always suggested a plan to make a London house full as interesting as a house in the country. "You have only," says he, "to invite a parson of the parish to dine with you on Sunday, and to order your servants to bring you no newspapers nor letters on Monday."

Lady W. Williams gives her two daughters twenty thousand pounds apiece, and if they die unmarried she gives the forty thousand to poor Charles Wynne and his children. She gives her house in Upper Brook Street (which *par parenthèse* was built by my aunt, Lady Anne Jekyll) to her son-in-law, Lord Delamere.

Mrs. Gwyn has just sent me an unpublished curiosity, a folio volume of most horrible sketches, drawn and etched by the Princess Elizabeth, now Homburgh. It is entitled "The Progress of Genius," and inscribed, by a most ungrammatical dedication, to her talented mother, the antiquated Charlotte. Such hideous drawings no eye ever saw; and as Mrs. Gwyn was favoured with the gift of them, she begs, out of pure gratitude to the unhappy artist, that I will not show them. Thank God Freddy and Carry were not born Princesses.

The pretty poetess, Mrs. Norton, discovered that her maid was corresponding with a private soldier of the 3rd Regiment of Guards, recently named the Scotch Fusiliers. She made the poor girl give up his letters, one of which concluded in the following romantic manner:—

"Dearest and loveliest of beings, farewell; but let me beg of you not to direct your next charming letter 'to the Fuzzyleers.'"

My friend Denman, Chief Justice, the triumph of consistency. Poor Scarlett must for ever lament the course of *Girouettes*.

*Thursday, November 29th,* 1832.

*Mille graces* for a newsy letter, and the list of an avalanche of visitors. I like Lady Pollen, and, God knows, it is not the lust of the flesh; Sir John is like Shakespeare's Gratiano,

"And speaks an infinite world of nothing."

Edward writes in high glee from his sports at Herefordshire, and says Lady Ellenborough angled last year there with her daughter Anne for his friend Colonel Clive, but the line broke. The Colonel is the eldest son of my old friend, M.P. for Hereford, at whose mansion the Captain now bivouacs, and returns about the end of the month, when he has slaughtered their pheasants; and as the Cootes, though called *Eyre*, are waterfowl, I suppose by this time his uncle has shot his landlord near Ringwood. Cootes, I believe, are not game, so he cannot be tried for poaching, but has the pleasing alternative of being hanged for murder.

I knew old Jerningham[1] well—a good-natured goose, who dreamed he was a poet till Gifford (Lord Grosvenor's tutor) undeceived him by two lines in his clear satire the " Baviad " :—

"See snivelling Jerningham at fifty weep
O'er love-lorn oxen and deserted sheep."

Jerny was the laughing-stock of a circle of women I lived with, at whose *soirées* he used to shell off, I am sorry to say, almost all his buttons. He was then the platonic *cavalier serviente* of the late old Lady Harcourt, who had a head like the bust of Homer on a bookcase. After her loss of the Prince the late Lady Jersey said to me, " I loved the Prince's fame as I did his person. I wished to make him as splendid a monarch as Louis XIV. I made suppers for him of men of talent. I wished to detach him from his idle companions. I used to invite Jerningham, and tell him to bring the small harp he placed on the table."

[1] Edward Jerningham, author of "the Siege of Berwick," "Stonehenge," and many other volumes of plays and poems.

I burst into immoderate laughter, and she ordered me out of the room. You will admit I did not banish the poor poet, like John Taylor's anecdotes.

"Memoirs of Banditti," two volumes, a pretty book by Macfarlane, who wrote the clever "Tour from Constantinople."

This is a sad loss to the poor Archbishop of York[1] at his time of life, and I am very sorry for him.

I have condoled with my pretty friend Lady Blessington on the probability of *burking* her beauty, as she and le Comte D'Orsay were menaced in the papers with a pamphlet signed "Dissector." She suspects a cast-off friend of Lord Byron. Politics keep men enough in London. Ladies scarce except those who frequent bazaars, and mistake other people's property for their own. It was the blunder of my client Mrs. Leigh Perrot, in former days, and I am told is still frequently committed. The mother of these unlucky misses had a handsome sister who married Sir T. Plumer, Master of the Rolls.

I thought the Game Laws were abolished in France. But as they now *make game* of kings they begin to shoot them.

Sotheby will not let poor Sir Walter lie quietly in his grave, but *vampires* him with verses that would disgrace even the annuals; gives us "Syren Bay" twice over, and makes "to trance" an English verb,

---

[1] Archbishop Vernon Harcourt. This refers to the loss of his wife, Lady Anne Leveson-Gower.

unheard of before by Dr. Johnson or any other lexicographer.

Their Majesties invite such mobs to dinner at Brighton that I really read the arrivals at Margate t'other day by mistake for the list of their guests.

Joseph's friend, Newton, the American painter, has imported a pretty little wife from New York, and brought her to see me. Her peculiar phraseology amused me, but by no means was it burlesque, as given by Mrs. Trollope in her new novel, "The Refugee"; and, by the way, Mrs. Trollope seems never to give us the manners of any but the inferior towns of America. Lady Wellesley has visited her compatriot, the little Newton, and Joseph says the Republican bride was not the least dazzled by the presence of a live marchioness, but chattered away with all the simplicity of liberty and equality.

Edward says they have a house full of Whigs at Clive's, and daughters of the late Lady Oxford, and eternal rain. Willie produced a bad caricature of Talleyrand and Palmerston as an old spider catching a fly, and John Bull calls P.[1] "the Romsey Dandy."

My neighbour Scarlett affects high spirits to conceal his disappointment, and has given a grand dinner last week to his highness of Gloucester, and a batch of other Conservative conjurors, which we entitled "Le Festin des Girouettes." According to the Tory papers, the Reformed Parliament will be the best that ever was, as all their candidates are to succeed; and certainly

[1] Palmerston.

it will be the most numerous, as half a dozen of their friends are sure of coming in for the same place. This expression of delight reminds me of the plough-boy who whistles in a churchyard at midnight to show he is not afraid.

The active are all busy at their elections. The loungers crawling to Brighton, as London has no attraction. A good many idle people here seem to amuse themselves by dying; but except a few occasional twinges of gout or rheumatics I have weathered November very auspiciously, and don't intend to partake of their divertisement.

# CHAPTER X.

*MR. JEKYLL TO LADY G. SLOANE STANLEY*
*(Continued).*

SPRING GARDENS, *January 9th,* 1833.

ROGERS has lost a favourite brother, and in the midst of his sorrows was assailed by the dreadful verses of Byron[1] against him, a copy of which has appeared in *Fraser's Magazine*, and of which I have always heard only three were known to exist.

The cleverness of the libel almost equals its bitterness and cruelty, especially as the public believed they were linked in friendship. Rogers may perhaps have been caressed into vanity, but I know he is possessed of a thousand good qualities, and will feel this deeply.

Dickinson writes me word that his sister has bivouacked half the summer at Lyme, to secure her son's election. She must be an admirable canvasser, for she has routed the ancient family interest of the *leather-headed* Earl of Westmorland, who, the late Lord Ellenborough said, had

---

[1] The following is not an unfair specimen of these lines:—

> "He's the cancer of his species,
> And will tear himself to pieces,
> Plague personified, and famine,
> Devil, whose sole delight is damning.
> For his merits, would you know 'em?
> Once he wrote a pretty poem."

never been educated at all, inasmuch as he was born before Sunday Schools were invented.

Your Hampshire confoundatives came to a dismal end. To be ridiculous is worse than to be kicked out in every quarter. I condole with William on the oaths and guineas he squandered to save his property from revolution, by supporting the talent of Fleming, and unfortunately giving a victory to such villains, rascals, scoundrels, burkers, vampires, cheats, and swindlers as neighbours Palmerston and his gang. As he has had a long experience of managing lunacy, Brougham thinks the Hampshire Tories might be confided to his care in Chancery.

It is pleasing to find that distress does not always depress the spirits of philosophical persons. I read that the Castellan of Belvoir does not only keep a fifty-fifth birthday, but dances upon it, and that Wellington dances before him. Two Graces instead of three is not classical, especially as the slender addition of his Grace of Bucks might have corrected the number. When the old Duke de Brissac danced at Versailles some wag slyly pinned on his back a paper with these words—

"A cinquante ans on ne danse plus."

The Duke overheard everybody behind him reading it aloud, and, as it therefore appeared to be the expression of a general opinion, he sate down. My father had an old Irish lieutenant who always kept his birthday when he received his half pay, which occurred *three* times a year.

I sent you young Reynolds'[1] extravaganza of "Miserrimus; or, the History of a Devil Incarnate." Old Lady Milbanke used to swear that Byron declared an hour after the ceremony, that he only married her daughter to acquire the right of tormenting her. When old Fuseli designed to paint a horrible group he supped on toasted cheese, and the dreadful faces his indigestion produced in dreams he sketched when he awoke in the morning. Reynolds must have followed him. There is less talent than I expected in Lady Dacre's three volumes of "A Chaperone." There seems only the common quantity of ragamuffins in the new Senate. In one of Pitt's Parliaments I remember sitting with two waiters of a Tavern,[2] two M.P.'s who had been found lunatics on a commission, and one honourable member who had stood in the pillory. We have exchanged Hunt for Cobbett; and though Newmarket was not elevated into a borough, I suppose Gully may fairly be considered as its virtual representative. James Smith wrote to me the following :—

"EPIGRAM ON GULLY, BOXER, AND M.P. FOR PONTEFRACT.

" You ask me the cause that made Pontefract sully
Her fame by returning to Parliament Gully.
The etymological cause I suppose is
His breaking the bridges of so many noses."

I was sorry to lose my old friend, Lord Conyngham,

[1] Frederick Mansel Reynolds, author of "Coquette" and "Parricide."
[2] Sir Robert Mackreth and Sir Thomas Rumbold, both in early life connected with White's Chocolate House.

by a rapid liver attack, in his pretty daughter's honeymoon—a rich widow, fair, fat, and fifty; but I have no thoughts of her, though at present free from the gout. I suppose Gully and Cobbett are at Brighton dining with their Majesties, or I would have got a frank to you. So you must take eightpennyworth of our loves in the most expensive way.

SPRING GARDENS, *Tuesday, February* 12*th*, 1833.

YOUR tidings of this morning have afforded me such real delight that I will not hunt for a frank to express it.

Pretty, dear girl,[1] she deserves all the good that can happen to her, and so do you; for never did a woman, by example as well as precept, more effectually than yourself prepare her girls to be excellent wives and mothers, and it seems a talent inherent in your family.

They say it is natural to fall in love with the sister of a friend, and I think it will make Willie happy to have Mott allied to him. Edward has often said to me, " Mott is an excellent fellow"; and he became intimate with him at Paultons.

As happiness is of more importance than money, I trust that the fathers will easily make such arrangements on a quiet scale, for the present, as may enable "the course of true love to run smooth." And with these anticipated satisfactions, I wish you joy sincerely, for next to my own brats I love yours.

Parliament amusing with the *pas de trois* of O'Connell,

[1] Lady Gertrude's daughter Caroline, who married Mr. J. T. Mott, of Barmingham, Norfolk.

Hume, and Cobbett. A Manchester schoolmaster in jail for threatening letters to our sovereign; so even Brougham begins to think "the schoolmaster ought not to be abroad."

Alvanley dined with some grandee, whose mansion had been recently fitted up in great splendour, but the dinner was scanty. Alvanley said more carving and less gilding would have been preferable.

A friend said to Claud Hunter at Paris, "My dear Alderman, you speak French execrably. You for ever confound the articles. Why cannot you remember that *le* is the masculine and *la* the feminine article?"

"It is no such thing," replied the worthy baronet. "Is La Fayette a lady?"

My friend Mrs. Gore has published "The Sketch Book of Fashion," three volumes of six pretty novels.

P.S.—I used to congratulate Carry on the fortunate moles of her hand, and now the ring finger will be *mottled*.

I send you another squib of James Smith on Sunday newspapers, received this morning from Twickenham, so he signs himself Alexander Pope, and the verses are no bad imitation of Pope's. Old Sir J. Jekyll was a friend of Pope's, so Smith quotes from him.

"TWICKENHAM, *April* 22*nd*, 1833.

" DEAR SIR,—Having had the pleasure of being well acquainted with your great uncle, Sir Joseph Jekyll, 'who never changed his principles or wig,' I think it right to send you some lines which I have written with a pen dipped in Styx, and plucked from Mercury's left heel as he was ferrying the Rev. Reuben Hill down that inky stream. The stanzas relate to your Sunday newspaper, a Sabbath recreation unknown during the lifetime of

"Dear sir,
"Yours very truly,
"ALEXANDER POPE.
"JOSEPH JEKYLL, ESQ."

"Hard is his task who edits—thankless job!—
A Sunday journal for the factious mob;
With bitter paragraph and caustic jest
He gives to turbulence the day of rest.
Condemned, this week, fresh rancour to instil,
Or thrown aside, the next, for one who will.
Alike undone, or if he praise or rail—
For this affects his safety, that his sale,
He sinks at last in luckless limbo set,
If loud, for libel, and, if dumb, for debt."

P.S.—Dowager Lansdowne's £4,000 per annum a godsend to Berkeley Square. We think Duke of Norfolk should have the blue ribbon.

*August* 31*st*, 1833.

PARIS is electrified with Victor Hugo's last novel of "Notre Dame," which is unintelligible nonsense.

The Countess of Blessington's house broken open, and robbed of trinkets, buhl, clocks, odes, pastorals, and charades. She has a volume of poems on the anvil; contributory, I find, but she will not catch me for a couplet; but Lord Morpeth has sent her verses on the jasmine growing out of Naworth Castle, full of all the sentiment and prettiness of the annuals.

Lady Holland going to drag *sposo* to meet the bridal son and daughter[1] at Paris. All the old men in London are marrying themselves, so it is prudent for me to quit it. Ailesbury began, but it is not true that Somerset's Duke marries my poetess Lizzie Law. I told her, if she could not be one of the Muses, she should be one of the Graces. When the Duchess of St. Albans denied her love affair with the romantic Duke, " and let concealment feed on her damask (damaged) cheek," she said, " There are plenty of duchesses, but only one Mr. Coutts."

" Village Belles," three volumes, rather a pretty novel. I read yesterday " Mémoires de l'Impératrice Josephine," par Mademoiselle d'Avrillion, Dame de sa Chambre; it is amusing.

On Brougham's parliamentary assertion, that the King could advance a negro to the peerage, D'Orsay has made a wonderful caricature, and even uglier than the learned original. He is represented as a naked negro, with a full-bottomed wig and coronet.

The Whigs have wound up the session famously; and in spite of too much talking have accomplished most important things, and laid the basis for many more. Public opinion must now govern, and Toryism can never revive. They had a hard struggle, though their enemies, after a silly experiment, confessed they were too weak to form a Government. For thirty-three long years

[1] Lady Mary Coventry, daughter of the eighth Earl.

I gave hopeless votes for Reform, Catholics, Dissenters, and black men, but all has been accomplished, and I may now sing the song of Simeon, and be let depart in peace.

P.S.—We have got rain at last as a godsend, though it may not be relished at Aberdeen and Ramsgate, and I delighted in a damp, wet day as an excuse for a fire. The measures of Government have produced much tranquillity in Ireland,[1] and Cobbett refuses to attend political unions. The home politics look peaceably, and the good harvest will give a quiet winter. If the foolish lords had not sneaked off in time it might have provoked the people to a revolution. As for foreign politics, Spain and Portugal are too priest-ridden for a free constitution, and as for those gemini of baboons, Pedro and Miguel, nobody cares if they were at the bottom of the Douro. The foolery of your Yacht Club, with its commodores, vice-commodores, and salutes is really sickening. I am sorry it is to make us ridiculous at Cherbourg.

Spring Gardens, *September 7th*, 1833.

Joseph and his friend steamed to Ramsgate on that dreadful Friday, though they arrived there before the storm was violent. They had the rashness to attempt their return the next day, but the tornado still continued and forced them back, after six hours of a tremendous

---

[1] Measures reducing the incomes of the bishops of the Irish Church, and throwing the payment of tithe on the landlord, and Acts for the reform of grand and petty juries.

sea, during which they saw vessels founder. However, he reached home on Monday last.

If I had a numerous family, my sons obligingly supply me with every chance of its diminution which wind and weather can afford. Foote said to a man with twelve children, " When do you begin to drown ? "

The Windsor treasurer grumbles terribly at snug dinners to one hundred and twenty tags and rags every week. Yet poor William has no other expenses, for he buys no pictures, statues, racehorses, nor diamonds for pretty ladies. His babies, they say, pillage him, as the parish does not feed illegitimates ; and he was literally removed from the Admiralty for his expensive tours to the seaports, to make speeches of four hours' length to unhappy tars who would have been flogged if they did not listen.

In the present *New Monthly Magazine*, the tenth continuation of Lady Blessington's " Conversations with Lord Byron " is given. In it he paints, in a most eloquent and enchanting manner, the character of his sister, your friend Mrs. Leigh, and which we know she well deserves. He delighted in mystification, and I believe he humbugged Lady Byron a good deal. " Lights and Shadows of German Life " is a bundle of pretty stories.

I am in high feather for a gentleman who on the 23rd of next January will complete the age of eighty years, and has survived almost all his contemporaries, after a happier life than most men have experienced, if he could blot from memory one deprivation as premature as irreparable.

SPRING GARDENS, *October* 23*rd*, 1833.

LONDON, of course, is a desert. Nobody left but beggars and Cabinet Ministers. The Radicals gone to Brighton to swamp the pierage, and I suppose that of Southampton, being only illustrious by courtesy, will follow its predecessor. Captain Ross[1] is the lion of the day, has dined and grogged with messmate William at Windsor. I long for the publication of his log book, and his account of those amiable Esquimaux, who must have read penny magazines or got Brougham's schoolmaster to polish them.

I find the fame of my erudition and talent is established all over Europe. King Philippe has founded in France "La Société Statistique." All the crowned heads are directors. A hundred English members are nominated, and associated with the other *savants* of the universe. To-day I have received a diploma as an honorary brother, splendidly engraved and signed. The Duc de Montmorency is President, who requests my assent through the Viscount Palmerston, as that minister is instructed by his royal master to forward gratuitously all such important communications to him.

As I expect you will now treat me with more respect, I have thought it right to mention so new and so unexpected an honour. To compare great things with small, I will now transcribe for you a letter from the proprietor of the Learned Pig, to a Cheshire friend of mine.

[1] Sir John Ross, the famous Arctic explorer. He had just returned from his second expedition of 1829.

"SIR,—Having had the honour to exhibit my sapient pig at Sir Thomas Stanley's, Baronet, at Alderley Park, at Honourable T. Erskine's at Adlington Hall, in the drawing-room, to the greatest admiration, at the Duke of Devonshire's at Chatsworth, and at Sir P. Egerton's, and nearly at all the nobilities and halls in Europe, I will call to know if I am to bring it up clean before company.

"The quadruped is clean in his exploits, and I hope to have the honour to attend. "J. BERMET."

Pray inform William that I will leave Harry Bunbury's clever drawing of the old jockeys in Curzon Street. They are rather portraits than caricatures. I make out of the whole group of fifteen or twenty very few—Duke of Grafton, Lord Clermont, Lord J. Hamilton, old Mr. Vernon, Mr. Wastell, Sir C. Bunbury in the margin, and Colonel O'Kelly, the owner of the famous Eclipse. The late King made them all out. The drawing is in perfect preservation, but very dirty. It must be varnished and cleaned by means not to injure water-colours.

Henry Fox's Coventry wife is little, and not to be called pretty, but she will be very rich, so the Hollands will not vote her to Coventry again.

*November 21st,* 1833.

THANKS for your letter and Lord Surrey's account of his eccentric neighbour Stanhope. An old friend of mine was his contemporary at Eton and Cambridge, and found him at Paris in 1816, where he had lived through all the storms of the Revolution, and had escaped the guillotine.

He had a wife and children with him. Went to bed in the afternoon, and got up for his wife's *soirées* and musical parties. My friend added that the Lord Chesterfield could not hammer the graces into him. Stanhope is a man of parts and reading.

Farebrother, the Lord Mayor, is an auctioneer. Somebody asked which way his politics inclined, and was answered by "always to the best bidder."

Emigration goes on. On Tuesday Lady Jersey sent me a note about a charity vote, and added that they were going abroad only for a few months.

Lord Palmerston is to be congratulated, for he has got Lady Holland for his neighbour in Stanhope Street. With her usual spirit of domination and restlessness she has seized and possessed herself of her poor, quiet son-in-law's[1] mansion for cabinet dinners; and most likely will attempt to enthrone herself at the head of the table, and suggest secret measures for the conduct of ministers in Spain, Portugal, and Belgium. I saw Mrs. Bowles yesterday near Palmerston's, but did not stop her to announce this new volunteer in the Cabinet.

Joseph and I dined last week with Rogers, who is going to publish the "Pleasures of Memory" with engravings like his "Italy." We had Tom Moore in high glee, and that oddity little Kenney, the successful author of *Raising the Wind*, and other clever farces. A merry day.

[1] Lord Lilford.

Read "Trevelyan," a very clever novel, by the widow of Admiral Scott, a relation of Sir Walter. I hear she also wrote another of merit called "The Inheritance." They say our unwashed bencher, Sir E. Wetherell, wanted to marry some plebeian miss,[1] who preferred the most noble the Marquis of Ailesbury, because he was thirty years older than herself.

And they say also that Doctor Halford is not to marry one of the princesses of the House of Brunswick, to the great vexation of the College of Physicians.

But I must finish—for I had rather be put on Cobbett's gridiron than write across—so I send my benediction to Benedict and Co.

### LINES BY LADY BLESSINGTON.

*To a Friend[2] who, in her presence, had received a very rude answer on account of his deafness.*

  Giuseppe's head's so stored with wit,
   That, fearing in a lapse of years
  It might be sullied, time thought fit
   To keep it safe, so closed his ears.
  Thus he escapes each noisy bore,
   Whose dulness might his drums invade.
  And happy, heard not Bufo's roar,
   Nor the coarse joke the blockhead brayed.
  But when our modern Attic Bee,[3]
   With sparkling wit delights the ring,
  The hoarded honey all may see,
   Though few have ever felt the sting.

*July* 10*th*, 1833.          M. B.

[1] Lady Ailesbury's birth was scarcely plebeian. She was the daughter of the Hon. Charles Tollemache.
[2] The friend was probably Mr. Joseph Jekyll.
[3] A name given to Lady Blessington's friend by Lord Byron.

SPRING GARDENS, *January 2nd*, 1834.

NOTHING like glorious London for quiet and retirement, you shut out the pack of Cossacks called morning visitors, who, tired of themselves, claim a right to tire the rest of the world. Mr. Hood, the most disagreeable of men, next door to you, dares not knock as neighbour Hood ; but if Mr. Hood lives three miles off in the country from you he rides over as neighbour Hood, and perhaps forces you to dine with him and his merry family the first moonlight night. Nor have I been solitary, for my two little boys have remained in the nursery. There is another reason also for an epistle to you. We old gentlemen are disappearing so rapidly that it is necessary to afford some proof of being alive. Your neighbour of Cadlands I see has departed, and poor Sotheby is no more. Of what he died I am ignorant, as it is a long time since I saw him.

He was a man of considerable talents and many virtues, as a husband and parent exemplary, kind, friendly, generous, and charitable. Many of his original compositions were highly poetical, but his principal fame will rest on his translations. His "Virgil," his "Wieland," and I think, too, his "Homer," manifest a scholar's intimacy with the idiom of their respective languages, and extraordinary facility of versification.

Joseph has been really in distress at a late event. Newton, the American painter, with whom and Washington Irving he went abroad two years ago, and to whom he has been long attached, manifested symptoms of insanity last month, and is now in a private house of reception for lunatics. Independent of his high talents as an artist, his pleasing manners had been a passport into the best society. *Pour comble de malheur*, a pretty little wife he brought from America last summer, has just produced an infant, and is interdicted by the physician from seeing him. Washington Irving, his friend, has left England for ever, but Joseph's kind feelings have been exerted in every arrangement for him. There is no violence, but singular delusions, which, I believe, Joseph first discovered.[1]

The confusion of tongues at Broadlands I suppose has terminated, and Palmerston returned to Talleyrand and protocols.

The Tory châteaux have also assumed as much Christmas gaiety as they were able to pretend. The newspapers mentioned an untoward accident at the ball of Hatfield House, where the dancers unluckily threw down the Dowager Marchioness of Salisbury, and behold it is now written thus :—

> "Conservatives at Hatfield House
> Are really harum-scarum ;
> What worse could the Reformers do
> Than overset *Old Sarum*?"

*Friday, January 24th*, 1834.

ROGERS sends me his costly and splendid volume with proof prints,[2] price two guineas and a half. The engravings beautiful, after Turner and Stothard.

[1] This madness ended in the painter's death a twelvemonth later.
[2] The "Italy," now a rare and valuable book.

Sir Charles Flint died last week, at the age of fifty-four only; he was a pleasant, clever man. Lamartine the poet disappointed the Chamber of Deputies at Paris lately by a speech much inferior to what was expected from him; but every poet is not an Orator.

La Duchesse de Guiche (the relation, if not the mother, of Le Comte d'Orsay) is possessed of an authentic Memoir, if not a journal, of that madcap the Duchess of Berri[1] during all her Quixotic escapades in La Vendée. The Duchess de Guiche does not know Lady Blessington but as a good writer, and volunteers these curious papers to her for publication in English. It will be a most amusing book.

Among the delusions of Joseph's poor friend Newton, the painter, he believes he is Lord Dudley, and that the house of confinement he is consigned to is his own, and the gift of the Duke of Wellington.

Poor Lady Lyndhurst has followed her generous friend Lord Dudley most rapidly. From the strange legacies he left it is said his will is to be contested on the ground of insanity.

SPRING GARDENS, *Wednesday, January* 30*th*, 1834.

LADY HOLLAND sends affectionate notes to invite Joseph to dinner, and the *sage* never goes. Edward

[1] Caroline, daughter of Ferdinand I., King of the Two Sicilies, and wife of the Duc de Berri, second son of Charles X. She tried to raise a civil war in France against Louis Philippe in 1832, but was captured and imprisoned in November of the same year. This book of Memoirs does not seem to have been published.

has escorted the Bishop of London with a Guard of Honour, who came in lawn sleeves to consecrate part of the Tower Ditch as a *Père la Chaise* for their dead Grenadiers, and they erected a tent for the Right Reverend Prelate's prayer and luncheon on the model I suppose of that in the Isle of Paultons.

Rogers declared to-day here that he had never seen Byron's horrible verses. The assertion seems rather poetical. Poor Manning called, and from anxiety and misfortune looks ninety years old. Wolff has left his wife, Lord Orford's sister, these two years at Malta, and is preaching at Babylon.

Lady Dacre's "Chaperone" is no great performance. Godwin, the author of "Caleb Williams," is about to publish "Deloraine," a novel which raises expectations. "The Georgian Era" is come out in four stupid volumes, and contains, I am told, a life of myself with more lies than lines in it.

It was right to make Sutton Speaker. There was no one from experience so fit, and a Speaker's politics are immaterial, as he cannot display partiality, and never attempted it during the two years' war on the Reform Bill.

Besides in these times the Whigs should abstain from the example of rancour adopted by their opponents.

*Monday, March 10th,* 1834.

DULNESS itself. I have not read Miss Edgeworth[1] nor heard much in her praise. I was in hopes of some

[1] She had just published her last novel, "Helen."

Irish stories, of which I heard the following yesterday. When the Custom House was on fire some years ago, they dragged out of the cellars all casks of inflammable liquor, and threw so many pipes of port wine into the Thames as to discolour the water.

An Irish labourer said to his companion, "Why, Pat, I have heard tell of the river Tagus, but I never saw the river Nagus before."

Bulwer's "Pilgrims of the Rhine" is most fantastical, and bedizened with pretty pictures of the newly adopted fashion.

Yesterday came anonymously a present of a novel of three volumes called "The Hamiltons," from the author of "Mothers and Daughters," whom I do not know, but I suspect my friend Mrs. Gore.[1]

God knows where our poor new Attorney-General[2] is to get a seat in the House. If he had duly read the Scriptures, he would have learned that the borough of Dudley is like unto the eye of a needle, and difficult of access to a camel.

"Imaginative Biography," by Sir Egerton Brydges,[3] is not ill done.

Poor Macaulay was much alarmed just before he

---

[1] They are both by Mrs. Gore, and both published in 1831.

[2] Sir John, afterwards Lord Campbell. Three months after his rejection at Dudley he was returned for Edinburgh. Lord Campbell is now best remembered as the author of "Lives of the Chancellors" and "Lives of the Lord Chief Justices."

[3] Sir Samuel Egerton Brydges, the Early English editor and genealogist. His autobiography was published the same year. He died in 1837.

departed for India with an eruption on the lip, which he feared was cancerous; but it was dispelled entirely by a very slight excision, for £10,000 annual salary would not have balanced it.

A lady asked this of an Irish physician, "Doctor, how do you treat a cold?" "Why, madam," said the doctor, " I treat a cold as I do a lumbago, with sovereign contempt."

So my blessing on you all, though I am no bishop, nor desire it, as it seems they are likely to be put on half pay.

*Friday, July* 18*th*, 1834.

THANKS for a satisfactory bulletin. So you are really a grandmama! What a venerable personage in your bloom. Don't despair of your small descendant. George III. came into the world as long before he was invited, and lived long enough to survive everybody else, as well as the interests of England.

We have had a famous political pantomime, and our theatre was in danger from a flare-up of the actors;[1] but we have patched up the scenery, got a new harlequin, and trust a generous public will permit us to play through the season.

Yesterday I had a letter signed "Richmond, Sutherland, and Holland," desiring a subscription to present Lady Grey with a statue of her husband at the cost

[1] Lord Melbourne's Administration. Earl Grey had resigned on July 9th, on the rejection of the Irish Coercion Bill in the Commons.

of 2,000 guineas. Now the statue of a great statesman should be in public, and not consigned to a boudoir; but I believe it is a rule in that case that the great statesman should die first, which probably a great statesman and his wife might object to.

This bustle and the eternity of parliamentary sittings keep London in a state of interest and *soiréety*; but the Captain describes Almacks last Wednesday as manifesting a desertion of beauties. Lord Hertford invites me to dance at a ball in the Regent's Park next week, but I decline passing so near the Zoological Garden, as I might be caught and shut up for life as a singular specimen of a dancing animal.

All extraordinaries are dying, so I wonder at my existence. Michael Angelo [Taylor] is gone, and so is St. John Long, whose epitaph I proposed from Hamlet's soliloquy—
"Ay, there's the rub."

Of love affairs I have nothing to report except an epigram on elopement:—

> "If Margaret Watson ran away,
> I'll bet a golden guinea
> 'Twas only to convince papa
> She was both *Peg and Ninny*."

If one's lady friends will write novels one is bound in conscience to read them. Lady Morley calls herself only the editor of "Dacre," but it is suspected to be a joint performance by herself, and her niece and nephew Mr. and Mrs. Lister. It turns on a fact equally improbable and impossible. Lady C. Bury gives us two stories, the "Disinherited" and the "Ensnared"—the latter the best, but both feeble in the catastrophe. But read Poet Campbell's life of Mrs. Siddons, which is much better than the miserable book by Boaden.

To show the contrast in character of Mrs. Siddons' correspondents, he gives a letter from Hannah More, and another from Joseph Jekyll. Rogers tells me that Lady Morley's father, a Norwich apothecary, of the name of Talbot, left her £2,000, with which she went abroad to accomplish herself, in company with Lady Cholmondeley. At Rome a rich citizen of London desired to marry her, as he said it had been clear to him that she was descended from Sir John Talbot, who is represented as a man of rank in Shakespeare's tragedy of Henry VI. But she preferred Morley, who found her one morning copying a Raffaelle in the Vatican.

Samuel Prout, the artist, quarrelled with Stanfield, the scene painter, for putting over the door of a greengrocer's shop in a pantomime,

## S. PROUT.

Now you are to come fairly to an anchor. I have ordered the *Herald* to you, which is grown almost Tory, and will not indemnify you for William's *Standard*. In revenge, I wish him sour ale and the worst toasting cheese Taffyland can supply. I envy my native soil nothing but the possession of your sister.[1]

The heat yesterday was uncommon, but I am very

[1] Lady Cawdor.

well, and all the better for it, for I am such a chilly crater that I should not object to take a summer lodging on the ground floor in Vesuvius. I had always more gaiety than Sturges Bourne's under jaw; and even in the gout I never think with despondency of the end of the world, though I am getting personally so very near it.

I am glad, however, I am not William IV.'s "old woman," as he calls her, for I should have been sick seventeen hours on my voyage to Rotterdam, with all my maids of honour and maids without honour sick round me, and nobody but Lady Errol to bring me a basin.

*Saturday, August 20th,* 1834.

A LETTER to-day from Lord Clifden. Thanks to the Coercion Bill, he reports Kilkenny the riotous as quiet as Hampshire, says the rejection of the Tithe Bill is starving the parsons, that the wheat harvest has been saved, but that as corn is as cheap as it was seventy years ago rents will be problematic. He adds that the Lord-Lieutenant[1] is clear and strong in head and mind.

Read "Truth and Anecdotes of the 19th Century," three volumes. Amusing, and has not been puffed like the stuff called fashionable novels; and Crabbe's[2] son has added to his father's works a volume of unpublished verses.

[1] Marquess Wellesley.
[2] In the complete edition of Crabbe's works, published by Murray in eight volumes, 1834.

*September 10th*, 1834.

THE Captain arrived this morning at daylight, and in an hour set off to Windsor on military duty, so I hardly saw him. On his return he must be contented to beat the covers of St. James's Street, get a shot at some of Crockford's [1] pigeons, or bag a few old Boodlers.

William, I conclude, like Nebuchadnezzar, is walking on all fours to recover his footing with the quadrupeds of Newmarket, and your youthful quartette of emigrants are preparing to cheat Beddome of emetics by steaming up the Rhine with *beau Monde* of Fleet Street and Whitechapel. Joseph says travelling in foreign parts is an infantine disease, like measles and whooping cough, which he is satisfied to have had so favourably, and which, like those calamities, are not likely to recur.

Four or five cronies of mine have places about Richmond, Sheen, and Roehampton, so I sometimes take a villa-nous day with them. Mrs. Gwyn lately showed me (as she knew I loved conservatories) the exotic gardens of Kew, and told her neighbour H.R.H. the Duke of Cumberland of it when he called to take leave of her. "You did well," said the illustrious Duke, "for I know that among his other acquirements Jekyll is admitted to be one of the best botanists in Europe." Now this is a new feather in my cap, for you well know that so little of King Solomon's wisdom do I possess, that I cannot distinguish between "the cedar of Lebanon and the hyssop on the wall."

[1] The noted gaming house in St. James's Street kept by William Crockford, now the Devonshire Club.

Let no royalty visit Hampshire, for it is a most regicide county. You began by murdering William Rufus for no other reason I could ever learn, except your dislike to red hair. You nearly murdered King Charles in the dungeons of Hurst and Carisbrooke, and now you have murdered the poor Queen of Spain at Gosport.

*Tuesday, December 9th,* 1834.

OUR crisis[1] here has been entertaining, and Peel is expected to-day. I wish he could have remained long enough at Rome to have learnt Mosaic, of which party-coloured materials our Cabinets have been constructed for twenty years, and for want of cement have fallen to pieces. The Whigs squall out, "Let us depart, for the Reformers grow too impatient." The Tories squall out, "Let us come in, and we will be very good boys, and become Reformers ourselves." However, the country is safe by the Reform Bill; for as no minister can remain in office now by corrupt Parliaments, he must act with the approbation of the country, or lose his cabinet in a couple of months.

Pinney *père* called yesterday, and said his son has a contest at Lyme; for old Westmorland has repaired his breaches with the corporation, and to revive an

[1] William IV. dismissed the Melbourne Administration quite suddenly on November 15th, and sent for the Duke of Wellington. The Duke advised the King to place Sir R. Peel at the head of the new Administration. Peel was in Italy, and the Duke held the seals until he reached London on December 9th, when the Duke took office under him as Foreign Secretary.

interest as obsolete as the leather article of his costume, starts Lord Burghersh. I do not envy you the braying of your county politics.

*January 19th,* 1835.

SOMEBODY complimented Sydney Smith on a charity sermon he had preached, to which the divine wag replied, " I believe it was effective, for old Lady Cork borrowed a sovereign of a stranger in the pew to put in the plate, and scuttled out of sight before he could catch her again."

Charity should not begin at home. The King has given £1,000 a year to Lady Mary Fox, as her husband[1] has lost his place, which was their only income. I congratulate you most cordially that the foolery and violence of your county is over.

The hospitality of Windsor is very little afforded to His Majesty's ministers, who are kept on board wages while the family visits Sion House, Kenwood, Hertford's Villas, and other conservatories. I congratulate you on Morpeth's success in a very complicated business, though I cared but little for the speeches, as the only real question in the debate was, whether on a polling match Peel or Melbourne should be churchwarden of our parish for the next three months, and the victory has still to meet the fury of the Lords.

Of course I read all the trash daily vomited by publication. " Tales of the Peerage and the Peasantry," edited, if not written, by Lady Dacre, are two pretty

[1] Henry, fourth Lord Holland.

stories; and Mrs. Shelley[1] has written a clever novel called "Lodore," in which there is such a pretty, loving couple that the reader feels as if he had dined upon sweetmeats. Don't read Captain Ross, for it is more tiresome than going to the North Pole in person. I hope if there is to be a double crop of Yeomanry Cavalry in Hampshire half your squires who get no rents, and half your farmers who can't pay any, will divide into two armies, and send half the warriors to fight for the young Queen of Spain.

*March* 10*th*, 1835.

YOUR solicitude about me is not thrown away, and I feel all the kindness of it. I pronounce myself perfectly well, as the old Lord Liverpool concluded all his sentences, "in every respect whatsoever."

Poor Manning, whom I had not seen for a long time, called last week, broken down, altered, and shattered all to pieces. He has had losses "enough to weigh a royal merchant down," when everything was shipwrecked but his honour, as Francis I. said after his defeat at Pavia.

Lord Albert Conyngham's translation of the "Natural Son," from the German, is well done, and worth reading. So is Washington Irving's little volume of "A Tour to the Prairies."

No truth in Wellington's resignation, but the lies on all sides are intolerable. The present Ministry[2] is a

---

[1] Mary Woolstonecroft Shelley, wife of the poet, and author of "Frankenstein," etc.

[2] Sir R. Peel's Government. They were defeated on April 4th,

mere experiment, and its existence depends on the chapter of accidents; though, thanks to the Reform Bill, no worthless Cabinet can ever again maintain its post long. But unfortunately, such is the splitting of parties, that whatever Cabinet succeeds them will be sure to encounter a very formidable opposition, so that I think our national prosperity is postponed for a serious period.

The merry Doctor of Swatling visited me last week, and I saw by his cheerfulness that the Southampton railway was now sure to be accomplished. Edward is recruiting in the north of Devon, and I expect every day to hear he is on the King's duty at Windsor, a quarter, strange to say, all the officers dislike. He expects to be sent to Brighton, so will be an alien to the paternal roof for some months.

Fine ladies are beginning to muster, operas are announced, and I see Lady Cawdor at the Drawing-room, so expect you will not linger much longer in the politics of Belvoir.

*August 27th, 1835.*

A LETTER from you always delights me, but you send me an unpleasant story of dear Caroline, and the loss of her poor little Neapolitan. It seems decided by the Fates that you do not look sufficiently solemn and respectable for a grandmama.

on Lord J. Russell's resolution in Committee of the Irish Church Bill, and resigned the following day, when Lord Melbourne again took office.

As to public affairs, Windsor is full of foreign princes, and luckily our Sovereign's French is not so fluent as his English. The Lords are delighting the Radicals with the hopes of confusion and a Republic, and they are gratifying the Pope and O'Connell by starving the poor Protestant parsons of Ireland. I am very well, very lame, a double-distilled bookworm, and a worse joker than ever. I can recommend nothing for your studies. Mrs. Norton's "Coquette" is dull. In a life of Sir J. Mackintosh she writes thus after a visit at Dunrobin :—

"The most remarkable feature of the place was its mistress, a woman of great understanding, spirit, and dignity, with more of the character and talents of a queen than any other female whom I have seen."

Lord Canterbury is so totally ruined that he sells all he has, and becomes a fugitive in foreign parts. Three generations of extravagance—himself, his father, and his son. I will now send you some squibs, showered upon me by my neighbour, James Smith, of the "Rejected Addresses."

> "Where'er a hatchment we discern
> It hath before ne'er started,
> The motto makes us surely learn
> The sex of the departed.
> If 'tis the husband sleeps, he deems
> Death's day a *felix dies*
> Of unaccustomed quiet dreams,
> And cries *in cœlo quies*.
> But if the wife, she from the tomb,
> Wounds Parthian, like, *post tergum*,
> Hints to her spouse his future doom,
> And threatening cries '*Resurgam.*'"

EPIGRAM ON A NOSE.
"A truth erst unnoticed now drops from my pen,
The nose and its actions all start with S N;
The fact, as I state it, is placed beyond doubt,
Snort, snivel, sneeze, snigger, sniff, snarl, sneer, and snout."

I asked James Smith "why he never married." He replied :—

"Should I seek Hymen's tie?
As a poet I die,
Ye Benedicts mourn my distresses.
For what little fame
Is annexed to my name
Is derived from 'Rejected Addresses.'"

ON THE CITY OF LIMERICK PROPOSING TO ELECT TOM MOORE THE POET.

"When Limerick in idle whim
Moore as her member lately courted,
The boys, for fun's sake, asked of him
To state what party he supported.
When thus the answer glibly ran,
'My friends, I scorn to tell a story,
I am a Whig, sirs, as a *man*,
But as a *poet am—a—Tory*.'"

*Morning Herald* is a twaddling, lying paper, professing reform and abusing the Whigs, but I like to read the enemy to counteract my daily perusal of the *Morning Chronicle*. *Herald* said yesterday, "The Duke of Rutland was dead from the bite of a mad dog inflicted five years ago!"

SPRING GARDENS, *December 7th*, 1835.

I AM in the Park daily with my coterie of dowagers, and have *levées* of gossips to murder my books and my time. To chronicle and contradict the falsehoods they and the hostile garreteers of the newspapers supply would fill a folio; and faction is grown so virulent and vulgar that Whig and Tory aldermen cannot be brought together by turtle. The wisdom at the pavilion I think, if it had materials, would not be disinclined to *da capo* the successful farce of last year. The Mayor of Oxford apologised to Charles II. for omitting a royal salute when the King entered that city. He said he had three excuses, and the first was that he had no cannon. The King graciously dispensed with the other two.

The two-year-old person on the throne of Spain is a long time scratching and biting her uncle, and the French House of Peers, though reformed, is a long time puzzled how to hang a gentleman,[1] who admits he has murdered a whole covey of marshals.

We are going on as merrily as usual here, steamers killing parties of pleasure, suicides at each of the six bridges, railroads burying labourers alive, Poor Laws fattening paupers in St. George's parish, and creating gluttons and epicures at thirteenpence per week, a tragedy at Hatfield House,[2] and Mr. Braham opening a new Opera House.[3]

[1] Fieschi, who in attempting the assassination of Louis Philippe on July 28th, killed many of the suite and some bystanders. He was condemned to death, and guillotined, after long debates in the House of Peers.

[2] The death of the Dowager Marchioness of Salisbury. She was burnt in her boudoir in a fire which destroyed a part of the palace, and which it is supposed was caused by Lady Salisbury's head-dress catching fire at a candle.

[3] The St. James's Theatre.

Joseph maintains his hereditary love of a metropolis, and thinks rustication has no vitality, and could not be revived by the Humane Society. Old George III. condoled with the Austrian minister because ambassadors could not leave London. "Sir," replied his Excellency, "I am not fond of duck-hunting and other usual country sports."

My little poetess, Elizabeth Law, writes for my consent to marry Lord Colchester after Christmas, to which I have agreed. He is a very excellent man, has property in Sussex and his father's pension as Speaker, and the mother has a good jointure to fall in. Elizabeth has her £15,000, is, I think, thirty-six years old, and a year older than the bridegroom. Lord Colchester was a famous good scholar at Westminster, and his father tried hard to prevent his entering the Navy; but he is now a captain and distinguished officer.

A friend of mine tells me to-day he saw the *ci-devant* Lady Ellenborough last summer at Munich; she has married a Bavarian Baron, whose name I can neither spell nor pronounce. She is received at Court and everywhere. The ladies of the Bavarian Almack's know all her pranks, and say the poor child was sacrificed in marriage in London to an old, rich, ugly Lord. Her *liaison* with the King is never denied. The King is a man of talents. My friend saw in one of his palaces a fine painted ceiling of the "Triumph of Neptune," and among the sea-nymphs discovered the portrait of Lady Ellenborough, which the King had given orders to introduce, and which the guide reported readily.

Old Lord Stowell, aged ninety, and now unconscious of events, has lost his only son, a dissipated man, so the new peerage is extinct. His brother, Lord Eldon, lost all his sons, and his earldom descends to his grandson, Lord Encombe, to whom will probably pass the principal amount of his great riches. Lord Stowell, I know, has £22,000 a year. I trust he will not fail towards his daughter, Lady Sidmouth; but she has no descendants, and is a valuable woman, though in very precarious health.

Lord Eldon was reconciled to his eldest daughter, who married Repton,[1] an architect. Her sister married a son of my old friend and schoolfellow Bankes.[2] I should not be surprised if the great mass of property these two old Crœsuses possess ultimately centred in Lord Encombe.

King of Bavaria and a "Triumph of Neptune" remind me of Corporal Trim's long story of the Seven Castles, when he was puzzled by my Uncle Toby's asking him why he called the King of Bohemia unfortunate? "Because," said Trim, "he has no seaport in his dominions." "How could he," replied my Uncle, "seeing that Bohemia is an inland country, and if near the sea would cease to be Bohemia?" "It might have been near the sea, your honour," quoth Trim, "if it had pleased God." Uncle Toby could not deny this.

The city has rejected an Alderman because he is a Jew, and a candidate literally of the name of Tagg has

---

[1] George Stanley Repton.
[2] Henry Bankes, M.P. He died in 1834.

been proposed. It is very pleasing to mark the delicacy of Mr. Rag, and Mr. Bobtail, who decline coming forward.

Lady Blessington tells me she thinks of writing a book called "The Old Gentleman." I offered to sit to her as a specimen of an old gentleman preserved in spirits, and who laughs nearly as often as he did twenty years ago.

It seems like a dream to reflect how imperceptibly two years have elapsed since I saw Paultons, in all gouty probability, for the last time, and I shall never visit any other château. Don't forget the innumerable and pleasant summers I have spent with you there, for I never can.

*January 5th, 1836.*

HEAVEN and earth are grown political, and we live in a confusion of Tory frosts and Liberal thaws. But my dowagering is of the *juste milieu*, so was only two days suspended, during which a select party of sensible anti-Reformers conserved themselves under water in the Serpentine and canal. Except putting the New Palace into the latter, it could hardly have been more tastefully and beneficially applied.

As to knotting and splicing to make a new Ministry I do not expect it, because I think it is impracticable, and if practicable of no value; and unless the good-humoured fellow who keeps a *table d'hôte* at Brighton could play over again the celebrated comedy of *November*, which ran so few nights, I think he will remain contented with no other variation than a drive to Shoreham on Monday and to Rottingdean on Tuesday.

Volume the second of the *ci-devant* Lady Ellenborough. "My dear Queen," said His Majesty of Bavaria, "I wish you would permit her to be presented."

"My dear King," said the Queen, "it is impossible. Consider her position with respect to yourself. Why don't you get her married, and then she would be presented, of course?"

"That may be difficult," quoth the King.

"Not the least," rejoined Her Majesty. "Order one of your marshals or barons, and the man will be flattered by the mark of your favour."

The thing was done. A baron was instantly found; old loves preserved; and three people made happy.

Joanna Baillie's new "Dramas"[1] are curious but unequal. Mrs. Trollope's "Paris" very amusing; but if you want humour read "Gilbert Gurney," by Theodore Hook. Last week Alaric Watts, the poet, asked his publisher, Murray, to dinner, and made him very drunk. Hook said, "Watts turns his wine cellar into his bookseller."[2]

James Smith said here, just now, that Incledon, the singer, once complained to him in the Green Room that his headache was so intense that he should never be able to sing "Mackheath" that evening. "The first song

---

[1] "Dramas," three volumes, 1836.

[2] The joke was made by Mr. Murray himself on refusing to take more wine.

will relieve you," said Smith. "How happy could I be with ether!"

James Smith's fame stands conspicuously on his "Rejected Addresses," so I did not reject his address to me yesterday, as followeth :—

"DEAR G KILL,—1 congratulate U on the new Year and on the Thaw. F U C A B settle on your window U need not be surprised. There is a tame J at my neighbour's on Northumberland K with wings L wide. M N ent for Beauty of Plumage. You remember the O P War. What a Q for passion it was. I wrote X L ent song called 'Heigho! says Kemble.' Not that I mean to W in wit. Are U an F.R.S.? They meet after T, but not to drink XX. My Y Y Z is now exhausted."

In case the Hampshire brains remain as foggy as formerly, I think it right to subjoin some glossary for the use of country gentlewomen :—

| | |
|---|---|
| F U C A B | = If you see a bee. |
| A tame J | = A tame jay. |
| Northumberland K | = Quay. |
| M N ent | = Eminent. |
| Q | = Cue for passion. |
| To W in wit | = To double you in wit. |
| XX | = A new sort of ale. |
| My Y Y Z | = My wise head. |

Death has been busy here. Poor Billy Churchill, who died rich, and made a liberal will. I, too, lost Leycester on Saturday last. His infirmities and very advanced age had taught me to expect the event at any moment. He died without suffering, and maintained to the last his fine temper and powerful intellect. A more exemplary and beloved man never existed, and a blow which has severed the uniform friendship of more than half a century is severe.

SPRING GARDENS, *March 7th*, 1836.

POLITICS in a drowsy state. As yet the Lords have not even yawned and stretched themselves, nor, even as last year, talked in their sleep. The Commons as yet gabble parish affairs, but next month may produce some symptoms of animation, though the Ministry has never stood in so safe a position as this session.

Lady Sidmouth derives for her life an enormous income of many thousands, and her Lord resigns his pension, an example which poor Lord Eldon will think insanity. Old Stowell had an income of £23,000, and began the world a college tutor.

Londonderry threatens to go abroad. I remember a bad actor who was hissed at Paris turning round indignantly on the pit and exclaiming,—

" Publique ingrat ! Je te quitte."

Charles Hatchett,[1] the gentleman chemist, sent me his

[1] A writer on scientific subjects, of some note in his day. He was a member of the famous literary club founded by Johnson and Reynolds in 1764, and he succeeded Dr. Burney as secretary in 1814. He furnished Croker with a complete list of its members, which appears in his "Boswell." The print mentioned is by J. C. Lewis, after T. Phillips. Hatchett died in 1847.

mezzotinto head on the 30th of January, and I thanked him for selecting a day so appropriate to heads, hatchets, and Charleses.

Smith, of the "Rejected Addresses," versified my note to Hatchett, and put it into this number of the *New Monthly Magazine*.

MARTIAL IN LONDON.

MR. JEKYLL TO MR. HATCHETT, ON RECEIVING HIS PORTRAIT.

"An answer, Charles Hatchett, thou claimest,
 I'll make it both pithy and short;
And surely so able a chemist
 Can never refuse a retort.
Thy portrait, no painter can match it;
 I laugh at their critical snarls;
Like Cromwell, I owe to a hatchet
 My gaining the head of a Charles."

*Monday, June 4th,* 1836

I HAVE seen since the trial several of Mrs. Norton's letters to her most intimate female friends, and one to the clergyman of the parish. They breathe the air of innocence—and indeed no human being gave credit to the evidence. For the sake of the unfortunate children she would even return to this luminous police justice. The ass[1] thought antlers would be ornamental to an animal of that species, but could not accomplish them, so will now have to pay the expenses of Melbourne and his own. His father, the old Lord Grantley,

[1] The Hon. G. Norton, a police magistrate. He brought an unsuccessful action against Lord Melbourne for *crim. con.*

Speaker of the House of Commons, was the greatest liar of his time, and on retiring the usual pension was granted. John Wilkes said his title was composed of his two favourite objects—a grant and a lie.

I am very well, dowager daily; and the town remains full of loungers to infest me with morning visits.

My friend Mrs. Gore, who still resides at Paris, sends me to-day her new novel of three volumes, "Mrs. Armytage; or, Female Domination."

I grow fastidious perhaps, but I have been considerably bored by many new publications which are liked. Wraxall's second series of Memoirs,[1] Cooper's "Switzerland,"[2] Lawyer Talfourd's Tragedy,[3] Coleridge's[4] two volumes, clever, but too abstruse and metaphysical for ladies.

I grieve for the Duke of Gordon,[5] of whom I saw a great deal for many years; but I begin to outlive everybody, and for no use.

When Monsieur de Tartines was Minister of the Police Department at Paris, a vagabond was brought before him for a hundred rogueries. The Minister asked him what he had to say for himself. "Monseigneur," said the culprit, "I must *live*." "Upon my word," said the Minister, "I see no necessity for it."

So now for Hyde Park, after giving special orders

---

[1] "Posthumous Memoirs of Sir Nathaniel Wraxall, Baronet."
[2] "Excursions in Switzerland," by J. Fenimore Cooper.
[3] *I'on*, a tragedy in five Acts, by Sir James Noon Talfourd.
[4] "Letters, Conversations, and Recollections of Samuel Taylor Coleridge," two volumes, edited by T. Allsop.
[5] George, fifth and last Duke.

to my coachman not to run over any foreign prince, potentate, margrave, vizier, stadtholder, or bashaw of three tails, as the town really swarms with vermin of the highest rank on the Continent; and if we possessed Whittington's cat, it would puzzle her which she should destroy first.

Did I ever tell you the following story of that pompous ass, the late Lord ——?

Blazing in his star and ribbon he met a country gentleman wandering alone above stairs at the Opera, in the passage to the private boxes.

"Are you the box-keeper?" said the Marquis of Carabas.

"No," said the Squire. "Are you?"

SPRING GARDENS, *October 4th*, 1836.

As no one can form a better judgment on such a point, I am glad to hear your approval of Edward's choice of a wife, whom, with Mrs. Hammersley, he brought to me for an hour a day or two before their marriage. They express great pleasure on their kind reception at Paultons, and have just concluded a visit in Cornwall to its county member, from whence they were to return to Devonshire, like Dr. Syntax, in search of a residence, though I think they are to visit Colonel Clive, near Hereford, at the close of the autumn.

Adversity taught Louis Philippe how to be a good ruler, but prosperity has made him an ass. We must repair three cells in Bedlam for him and the brace of sensible ladies, who have got straw crowns on their empty noddles in Spain[1] and Portugal.[2]

Thank God James Smith is not a crowned head, for I should lose all the fun he sends me as follows, and within one short week :—

1. A stupid witness would not speak out. The counsel exclaimed, "The man is an ass!" "Let him be Balaam's," muttered the judge, "and he will speak out."

2. A mass of raspberries found in the stomach of a mummy three thousand years old. Smith said they must be elder berries. No offence to the ladies of that name.

Southey, the Poet Laureate, writes that the ancestors of the Duke of Wellington and of old John Wesley, the Methodist preacher, were the same. If so, said James Smith,—

> "Each takes his seat on glory's bench,
> And finds in Fame his level;
> Arthur as boldly fought the French
> As John engaged the devil."

Dowager Countess of Cork and Orrery, at ninety, goes to six o'clock prayers. I hope it will succeed.

Don't you admire His Serene Highness the Duke of Brunswick[3] paying the poor woman merely her

---

[1] Queen Christina, Regent during the minority of her daughter Isabella.

[2] Maria II.

[3] Charles, ex-Duke of Brunswick, deposed in 1830. He ascended, with Mrs. Graham, a professional aeronaut, from Bayswater, on August 22nd, and in preparing to descend near Brentwood, the

fare in the balloon, after he had nearly broke her neck? No highness could manifest more serenity. Highness was bad luck to the unfortunate lady.

Yours affectionately,

JOSEPH JEKYLL.

car was turned on one side, and both fell out, Mrs. Graham from a height of thirty feet, the Duke just as the car touched the ground. Mrs. Graham was seriously hurt, the Duke hardly at all.

FINIS.

# INDEX.

### A.

ABERCROMBY, J., Lord Dunfermline, 178.
Adelaide, Queen, 262, 268, 300.
Agricultural troubles in 1830, 259, 260.
—— —— 1831, 264, 268.
Aigues-vives Convent, 1775, 41.
Aiguillon, Duc d', 1775, 34.
Albans, St., Duchess of, 188, 228, 270, 296, 315. *See* Coutts.
Ali Pacha, 116, 117, 136.
Almack's, last'of, 145.
Althorp, Lord, 289.
Alvanley, Lord, 209, 269, 303, 313.
Amboise in 1775, 33.
—— and Charles VIII., 33.
Angerstein, J. J., 92.
Anglesey, Marquis of, 193, 258, 264, 268.
Ashburton, Lady, 182.
"Auld Robin Grey," 92.

### B.

Baillie, Dr. M., 110, 267.
Ballantyne & Co., 158.
Bankes, Rev. E., 90.
Barry, Madame du, 34.
—— and her brother, 34.

Baxter's "Last Words,' 172.
Bedlam, 267.
Belzoni, 91.
Bergami, Queen Caroline's courier, 103.
Berri, Duchess of, 324.
—— in 1775, Province of, 43.
Berry, the Misses, 145, 272.
Béthune, Countess of, 21.
Betty, Master, 213.
Birdy, 202.
Blessington, Countess of, 102, 270, 272, 290, 296, 297, 300, 306, 314, 317, 321, 341.
—— lines by, 321.
Blois in 1775, 21.
—— and Windsor, 29.
—— and the Kings, 29.
—— the Bishop of, 63.
Blos, Sir Lynch, *declined*, 235.
Boar hunt in 1775, 25.
Boehms, the, 106, 154.
Bolingbroke, Lord, 19.
Boswell, Sir A., 218.
Bowood, 1824, 142.
Braham, 338.
Brandling, Miss, a reigning beauty, 230.
Brighthelmstone in 1775, 1, 2.
Brighton in 1828, 182.
—— in 1829, 212.

Brougham, Lord, 74, 91, 103, 225, 242, 247, 255, 263, 310, 315.
Brydges, Sir S. E., 326.
Buckingham Palace, 231, 251, 253, 267, 274.
Buffon's son, 33.
Bulwer, Lytton, 276, 291, 326.
Bunbury, H. W., caricaturist, 110, 319.
—— Sir H., 130, 255.
Burges, Sir J. B., and Pitt, 92.
Burghersh, Lord, opera by, 251.
Burvill, Mr., 23, 31, 33.
Byng, "Poodle," 144, 271.
Byron, Lord, 70, 75, 81, 82, 90, 120, 122, 126, 146, 175, 224, 297, 300, 308, 311, 317, 321.

C.

Calcraft, John, M.P., 274.
Cambridge, Duke of, 251.
—— Prince George of, 199.
Campbell, Lord, 326.
—— poet, 291.
Canning, 119, 139, 158, 165, 176, 226.
—— lines by, 247-249.
—— Lady, pamphlet by, 226.
Canterbury, Viscount, 299.
Cardière, Miss, 46.
Caroline, Princess and Queen, 76, 94, 96, 99, 101, 102-105, 107-109, 110, 111, 114, 117.
Casas, Marquis de las, 166.
Catholic disabilities, Roman, 169.
—— emancipation, Roman, 197.
Cato Street conspiracy, 98.
Cavendish, Lord, 294.
Celles in 1775, château, 42.
—— gallery at, 42.
Chambord, Marshal Saxe at, 43.

Chante-loup, Palace of, 34.
Chantrey, 78, 183, 211.
Charles X. of France, 209, 244.
Charlotte, Queen, 96.
Chartreux Monastery, a, 41.
Château in 1775, 15.
Chatham, Lord, 228.
Chaumont château, 37.
Chenonceau château, 41.
Cher, river, 41.
Choiseul, Duc de, 34, 61.
—— Duchesse de, 35.
Cholera, the, 282, 297.
Cholmondeleys, the, 152, 267, 289, 292.
Clarence, Duke of, 108, 230.
Cleopatra's Needle, 91. *See* William IV.
Cobbett, 150, 169, 261, 292, 302, 316.
Codrington, Admiral, 201.
Cognac in 1775, 38.
Colburn, Henry, publisher, 135.
Cold, an epidemic, 58.
Colliveau, life at, 1775, 51.
Colman, George, 208, 292.
Condé, Prince of, 256, 288.
Constable & Co., 158.
Constant's Memoirs, 252.
Constantine, Archduke, 186.
Conyngham, Lady, 95, 117, 157, 200, 202, 226, 231.
—— Lord, 311.
Cooke, T. P., 210.
Cooper, J. Fenimore, 198, 346.
Copley, Solicitor-General, 104, 107, 163.
Corbrand, 31.
Cork, Lady, 89, 183, 264, 276, 285, 333, 348.
Coronation, the, 1821, 114, 116.
—— —— 1831, 274.

## INDEX.

353

Coronation of Louis XVI., 1775, 28, 38, 39.
Coutts, Mr., 125.
—— Mrs., 79, 91, 125, 126, 130, 156. *See* Albans, St.
Cox and the diamonds, 17.
Crabbe, 75, 76, 330.
Crockford's, 331.
Croft. Sir R., 68.
Croker, pamphlet by, 252.
Cumberland, Duke of, 179, 200, 202, 219, 221, 226, 234, 243, 275, 290, 331.

### D.

Dacre, Lady, 325, 333.
—— Mary, 205-207.
Dawes, Sophia, Madame de Feuchères, 256, 287, 288, 291.
Denman, Lord, 103, 108, 255, 304.
D'Orsay, Comte, 270.
Dictionaries, using, 269.
Diderot, 302.
Dieppe, 3.
Diet in France, 1775, 4, 5, 11, 15, 22, 44, 53.
Dissenters, relief of the, 179.
"Don Juan," 185.
Dover, Lord, 272, 290, 295.
D'Oyly, Mrs., 66, 80, 91, 125.
Dress in France, 1775, 19-21, 28, 47, 57.
Dudley, Lord, 75, 277, 324.
Dumont, Mons. P. L., 204-209.

### E.

Eaton Hall, 200.
Edgeworth, Miss, 325.
Eldon, Lord, 340.

Ellenborough, Earl of, 146, 148, 176-213, 227.
—— Lady, 146, 148, 187, 339, 342.
—— Lord, 70, 74, 227.
Ellis Correspondence, the, 190
"English at Home, The," 244.
—— at Orleans, 1775, 38.
*Equivoque* on *solvo*, 165.
Etiquette in France, 1775, 16, 17, 28, 38.
"Eugene Aram," 291.

### F.

Farming, depression in, 252.
Farnborough, Lord, and George IV., 241.
Farren, actor, 74.
Fieschi, 338.
FitzHughs', dinner at the, 229.
Fonthill Abbey, 134.
Foote, Miss. *See* Harrington
Foscolo, Ugo, 67.
Fox, Colonel, 268, 271.
Francis I. and Franche Comté, 37.
*Freischütz, Der*, 147, 148.
French *équestriennes*, 1775, 47.
Fuller, Jack, 293, 295.
Furniture in France, 1775, 6, 35.

### G.

Gaillon, 5.
Galley slaves, 25.
Galt John, author, 141-143, 257.
Galway, Lord, 17.
Garth, Captain, 194.
Garveys, The, 4.
Genlis, Madame de, 159.
George III., 83, 91, 93, 110.
—— IV., 101, 115, 117, 118, 166,

23

354

INDEX.

172, 175, 179, 180, 184, 186, 189, 193, 195, 200, 202, 210, 224, 230, 231, 236; death, 238; lying in state, 239; will of, 240; funeral of, 242.
Gibbs, Sir Vicary, 96.
Goderich's ministry, Lord, 175.
Godwin, author, 325.
Goldsmith, 216.
Gore, Mrs., 276, 278, 313, 326, 346.
Gough, Sir Harry, 45, 48, 55.
Graham, Mrs., authoress, 192.
Graves, Lord, suicide of, 225.
Greenwood, army-agent, 295.
*Grippe*, the, 64.
Guilford's will, Lord, 172.
Gully, Mr., M.P., 311.
Gwyn, Mrs. General, 199, 258, 259, 303.

H.

Hahnemann, S., 162.
Halford, Sir H., 80, 200, 242, 321.
Hangman, the French, 1775, 53.
Harrington, Lady, 269, 287.
Hastings, Marquis of, 88.
Hatchett, Charles, 344.
Hatfield House, fire at, 338.
Hatsell, John, 66, 96, 101, 105.
Heber, life of Bishop, 237.
Helens, Lord St., 237.
Hennesy, Mr., 33-37.
Herem, Marquis de, 64.
Hertford, Lord, 77, 115, 136.
Hervey, Lady Mary Lepel, 120.
High Wycombe, riots at, 261.
Holland, Lady, 140, 160, 161, 176, 185, 209, 224, 297, 315, 320, 324.
—— Lord, 69, 78, 81, 84, 92, 148, 149, 209, 217, 222, 267, 272.

Homœopathy, 162, 297, 302.
Hone, W., 87.
Hook, Theodore, 244, 257, 258, 270.
Horses in France, 1775, 5.
Houses in France, 1775, 47.
Howley, Bishop, 113.
Hugo, Victor, 314.
Hume, Joseph, M.P., 233, 274.
Humour. *See* Wit.
Hunt, Leigh, 175.
Huskisson, Mr., 200.

I.

Ibrahim Pacha, 187.
Influenza, the, 272, 273.
Irving, Washington, 208, 322, 323, 334.

J.

Jacobite, English, 1775, 5.
Jekyll, Edward, 115, 138, 144, 159, 166, 167, 177, 183, 197, 198, 200, 201-208, 211, 217, 221-224, 225, 232, 234, 239, 242, 250, 253, 257, 260, 261, 266, 271, 280, 292, 296, 304, 324, 331, 347.
—— Joseph, 143, 145, 146, 151, 159, 176, 177, 183, 189, 191, 196, 200, 207, 211-218, 223, 224, 247, 251, 260, 262, 287, 288, 293, 297, 315, 322, 324, 339.
Jekyll's, Mr., works, 298.
Jelf, R. W., 179, 199.
Jerningham, Edward, 305.
Jerrold, Douglas, 211.
Jersey, Lady, 81, 209, 230, 239, 305.
*John Bull*, 93, 118, 191.

# INDEX. 355

Johnson, Dr., 71.
Jordan, Memoirs of Mrs., 261.

### K.

Kean, 74, 125, 292.
Keen, Mr., 48.
Kemble, Fanny, 201, 213.
Kenney, playwright, 320.
Kent, Duchess of, 276.
Kerr, Mr., 16.
Kew Gardens, 199.
Key, Lord Mayor, and Wellington, 250.
King, Lord, 222.

### L.

Ladies of Llangollen, the, 159.
Lamartine, 324.
Lamb, Lady Caroline, 154.
—— Sir F., 233.
Lambert, Sir J., 8, 9, 10.
Latham, Dr., 80.
Law, Miss E., authoress, 298, 339.
Lawrence, Sir Thomas, 180, 189, 220.
Leopold I., King of the Belgians, 273, 277, 300, 301.
Letter-writing, on, 52, 55.
Lewisham, Lord, 50.
Lieven, Madame de, 140.
Liverpool, Lord, 170, 334.
Lloyd's, 92.
Loire, the, 10, 14, 19.
—— from Amboise to Tours, 36.
London in 1819, 86.
Londonderry, Lord, 270, 275.
Long, St. John, quack doctor, 239, 252, 253, 328.
Louis XVI., coronation of, 28, 38, 39.

Louis XVIII., Memoirs of, 299.
—— vigil of St., 48.
Luttrell, 171, 193, 231.
Lyndhurst, Lord, 256.

### M.

Macartney, Lord, 229.
Macaulay, Lord, 224, 326.
Mackintosh, Sir James, 83, 209.
Macready, 265.
Mahmoud II., 208.
Majocchi, "Non mi ricordo," 103.
Manning, Mr. William, 278, 279, 286, 325.
Marigny, Marquis de, 58.
Martin, Mr., 13, 16.
Mathews, Charles, the elder, 119.
Melbourne, Lord, 327, 332, 335, 345.
Members, queer, 311.
Menârs, palace of, 58.
—— pictures and statues, 59.
"Methusalems, The," 66.
Miguel, Don, 174, 179, 189, 273.
Milman's *Fazio*, 69.
Molly Dacre, 205-207.
Montalembert, Comte de, 260.
Montebello, Duc de, 240.
Moore, Thomas, 81, 123, 142, 158, 184, 205, 208, 222, 265, 276, 320.
Morellet, L'Abbé, 203.
Morgan, Lady, 72, 115, 252.
*Morning Herald* and Mr. Jekyll, 263.
Morpeth, Lord, 190, 194, 209, 247, 255, 314, 333.
Morris, Captain, 205, 206.
—— Colonel, and the '45, 37.
Murray, publisher, 75, 122, 342.

## N.

Nares, Archdeacon, 242.
Newton, F. M., American painter, 232, 307, 322, 324.
Northcote's "Conversations," 259.
Norton, Mrs., 194, 233, 241, 336, 345.
Notre Dame, 1775, 6.

## O.

O'Connell and Brooks's, 252.
—— and Lord Anglesey, 264.
—— trial of, 268.
O'Donnell, Mr., 31.
Opie, Mrs., 151.
Orange, Prince of, 266.
Orleans in 1775, 10-21.
Osgood, Mr., 20, 37, 45-53.
Otho, King of Greece, 301.

## P.

Paganini, 275.
Palmerston, Lord, 196, 216, 229, 256, 302, 307, 310, 320, 323.
Paris in 1775, 6-10, 12.
—— 1776, 65.
—— 1830, 245, 247, 260, 266.
Peasants in 1775, French, 32, 37, 51.
Pedro I., of Brazil, 192.
—— IV., of Portugal, 271, 276.
Peel, Sir Robert, 111, 233, 273, 296, 332, 334.
Pensions, 1775, expenses at, 45.
Perreau, the forger, 14, 48
Persian ambassador, the, 83.
Petre, Miss, death of, 227.
Philepeaux, Comte de, 61.
Philpotts, Bishop, 256.
Piozzi, Mrs., 105.

Police, Peel's, 254.
Pompadour, Madame de, 34, 58.
Pont-le-voy convent fête, 39.
Pope on reading, 151.
Prout, S., 327.

## Q.

Quin, Dr., 297.

## R.

Reform, parliamentary, 245, 247, 257, 260, 273, 275, 278, 286, 299, 307.
Regent, the, 77, 79, 87. *See* George IV.
Regent's Park "Menagerie," 171, 277.
Relics, 4, 32, 34, 36.
Reynolds, F. M., author, 302, 311.
Richmond, Duke of, 84.
Rockliff, Mr., 50, 53, 55.
Rogers, 75, 161, 173, 185, 207, 213, 262, 287, 308, 320, 323, 325.
Roman remains in France, 32, 42.
Romilly, Sir S., 72, 74.
Ross, Sir John, 318.
Russell, Lord John, 245, 335.
—— Lord William, 335.

## S.

St. Germains in 1775, 5, 6.
—— Gervais, 23.
—— Paul, Mr., 8.
Sandwich Isles, King and Queen of the, 144-271.
Saumery family, the, 54, 60.
Scarlett, Sir James, 268, 304, 307.
Schools, the public, 133.
Scott, Mrs., authoress, 321.
—— Sir Walter, 70, 78, 158, 166, 189.

## INDEX.

357

Seal of the Athenæum Club, the, 184.
Sellis, the assassin, 234.
Session of 1833, the, 315.
Shaftesbury Election, 1830, 246, 257.
Shee, Sir Martin, 220, 223.
Shelburne, Earl of, 165.
Shelley, Mrs., 334.
Siddons, Mrs., 166, 171, 280, 329.
Sloane, Mr., 69, 83, 85, 93, 100, 101, 107, 121. *See* Stanley.
Smith, James, joint author of "Rejected Addresses," 282, 302, 311, 313, 336, 342, 345, 348.
—— Sir Sidney, 213-216.
Soin and its curate, 1775, 42.
Solas, Abbé, 35
Sotheby, poet, 127, 149, 209, 322.
Spring Rice, Lord Monteagle, 178.
Stafford House, 237.
Staircase, double screw, 1775, 43.
Stanfield, painter, 327.
Stanley, Mr. Sloane, 129, 130, 133, 134, 139.
Stapylton, "Life of Canning," 226.
Stowell, Lord, 206, 340, 344.
Stuart, Lady Dudley, 161, 267, 277.
Studies, 1775, 11, 18, 21, 44, 62, 63.
Sturges Bourne, 82, 196, 241.
Sutton, Manners, 187, 325.

### T.

Tabouret, Le droit du, 240.
Talleyrand, 252, 255, 299.

Tatham's *cimetière*, 227.
—— bust of Lord Eldon, 232.
Taylor, John, author, 302.
—— Watson, poet, 288.
Tea in 1775, 18, 48.
Test Act Repeal, 184.
Theatre, 1775, the French, 49.
Theatres, December 1823, the English, 131.
Thesée, Labienus at, 42.
Tierney, Mrs., pension of, 240.
—— Sir M., 78, 94, 178, 225.
Tilly's memoirs, Comte de, 181.
Tory M.P.'s and Peers, 278.
Tostes, 4.
*Town*, the, 293.
"Travellers, The," 82.
Tree, Miss Ellen, 122, 211.
Trollope, Mrs., 307.

### V.

Vallière, M. la, 46.
—— a curious bedding at, 46.
Vansittart, Lord Bexley, 149, 269.
Veil, taking the, 1775, 24, 33.
Vernon, 5.
Vernon-Harcourt, Archishop of York, 237, 306.
Verrât, Château, 1775, 34.
Vestris, Madame, 287.
*Voiture*, the, 1775, 3.

### W.

Weare, Mr., murder of, 131.
Wedding, a French, 1775, 25, 27.
Weippart, Bandmaster, 181.
Wellesley, Lord, 159, 170, 232, 233, 234, 330.
Wellington, Duke of, 73, 184, 185, 197, 200, 232, 250, 253, 259, 279, 281, 310, 332, 334.

"Werner," Byron's, 262, 265.
Westmacott, 211.
Wetherell, Sir E., 138, 283, 321.
Wheel, breaking on the, 1775, 12.
Wigs, bishops', 291.
Wilkes, John, 266.
William IV., 240, 242, 250, 273, 276, 284, 300, 317, 333. *See* Clarence.
Wilson, Sir Robert T., 109, 288.
Winchilsea, Lord, 197.
Wit and humour, 71, 75, 83, 95, 112, 117, 119, 150, 152, 156, 163, 165, 182, 185, 188, 205, 223, 224, 233, 235, 240, 244, 249, 261, 264, 266, 268, 269, 271, 282, 288, 295, 301, 303, 304, 310, 311, 313, 317, 323, 327, 328, 329, 336, 337, 342, 344, 345, 347, 348.
Wolff, D.D., Rev. J., 168, 325.
Wollstonecrafts, the, 149.
Woronzow, 74, 229.

Y.

Yarmouth, Lord, 105.
York, Duke of, 94, 99, 101, 154, 160, 161, 163-165, 167.

THE END.

Printed by Hazell, Watson, & Viney, Ld., London and Aylesbury

www.ingramcontent.com/pod-product-compliance
Lightning Source LLC
Chambersburg PA
CBHW030344230426
43664CB00007BB/524